Twice the Family

*A Memoir of Love, Loss,
and Sisterhood*

Julie Ryan McGue

SHE WRITES PRESS

Published 2025

Printed in the United States of America

Print ISBN: 978-1-64742-786-3
E-ISBN: 978-1-64742-787-0
Library of Congress Control Number: 2024916623

For information, address:
She Writes Press
1569 Solano Ave #546
Berkeley, CA 94707

Interior design by Katherine Lloyd, The DESK

She Writes Press is a division of SparkPoint Studio, LLC.

Names and identifying characteristics have been changed to protect the privacy of certain individuals.

"Julie Ryan McGue's recent memoir gives the reader a poignant view of a childhood mixed with love, laughter, sadness, life as an adoptee, and a peek into a life lived with an identical twin sister and their life-giving bond. As an adoptee myself, it gave me enormous comfort and relief to hear of Julie and her sister Jenny not having been separated at birth by adoption. However as the author reflects, the profound loss she and her sister experienced from mother/child separation and relinquishment will be something the sisters will contemplate for a lifetime. I applaud Julie for her courage to write about a more three-dimensional view of what it's like to live life as an adoptee. In addition, how to live with the biological children of your adoptive parents, as well as other adoptive siblings from a different biological family. Because of memoirs like hers, conversations can ensue so hopefully a more child-centered approach to adoption can be the norm instead of the rarity."

—EMMA STEVENS (aka Linda Pevac),
author of *The Gathering Place* and *A Fire Is Coming.*

"Julie Ryan McGue's brilliant storytelling ability takes us through the darkness and light of her coming-of-age years. Gripping, raw and profound moments hit emotional high notes in her life with the meaning of attachment, belonging and family."

—JENNIFER DYAN GHOSTON, author of *The Truth So Far:
A Detective's Journey to Reunite with Her Birth family,*
and podcaster, *Once Upon A Time . . . In Adopteeland*

"For Julie Ryan McGue, an adoptee and identical twin, devotion is intrinsic and mutual. But in *Twice the Family*, twin-ship is not self-portrait, as separately the sisters navigate adopted life—their mirrored appearances, notwithstanding. The author has enriched the context of her earlier memoir, *Twice a Daughter,* by featuring post-World War II, middle-class aspirations to upward mobility, social inclusion, and privilege. The Catholic couple adopts, hoping to fill a deep void of personal loss, as much as to fulfill a duty to their faith. Loving, yet flawed, they guide their brood to seek comfort and strength in the face of moral challenges from a higher power. The pursuit of adopted identity and belonging continues. Five Stars!"

—MARY ELLEN GAMBUTTI, author of *I Must Have Wandered:
An Adopted Air Force Daughter Recalls*

For Mom,
*Your love and devotion were the glue
holding our family together.*

For Steve,
*You made my life better.
Forever and always, my love.*

*I have found the paradox that if you love until it hurts,
there can be no more hurt, only love.*

—Saint Mother Teresa of Calcutta

*We do not choose to be born.
We do not choose our parents.
We do not choose our historical epoch,
the country of our birth,
or the immediate circumstances of our upbringing . . .
But within this realm of choicelessness,
we do choose how we live.*

—Joseph Epstein

Contents

Part Three: BECOMING

Author's Note

Twice the Family is a work of nonfiction written as a seamless narrative to engage readers in the story. The scenes recreated in this book are based on conversations I witnessed or heard from trusted family members, as well as my own memories, notes, records, correspondence, and journal entries. All the characters in this book are real people and have not been condensed. Some identifying and non-identifying information has been altered to protect the privacy of those involved.

Prologue

S trange voices, clamoring. White lights. Too bright. My eyes sting. My chest hurts. Out of my mouth comes a piercing howl that frightens me even more than the unwavering overhead glare. I'm cold. The white stuff coating my skin no longer warms me. What happened to the balmy water that surrounded the two of us?

Where is my sister?

Moments ago, we were cuddling breast to buttocks as we have for months, and then the god-awful squeezing began. It started off as a gentle press, but then it intensified into a violent wringing. The pulsing sent our warm pool of water thrashing about, which flipped me upside down and shoved my head into a dark, hard place. No matter how hard I paddled and kicked, I couldn't right myself.

What is this place, and why are these voices so loud? I used to feel my sister behind me, now I can't. I'm so scared.

"Wait. There's one more. Nurse! Clean this first one up, stat. The second one is crowning. Did anyone from the agency let us know that this woman was pregnant with twins?"

This loud, deep voice has rough hands that send my slick skin into spasms. Where is that other voice, the soft one whose gentle murmur the two of us heard as we stretched and cuddled in our cozy womb? I think I hear it, but it doesn't sound the same. It's no longer muffled. It hurts me to hear her whimper and moan now.

Where is my sister?

Every cell in my little body throbs with confusion and fear.

I want to return to the warm water, to cuddle with my sister, to hear the muted sweet noises of *her* voice, to feel the surge of food through the tube to my belly. I want what I had before.

"Nurse! Get the first baby girl warmed up. And get this woman to stop wailing. Okay, people! I've got a big tear here to fix and another little babe storming its way out. Move it, people! Let's get this last one out, sew this unfortunate soul back to what she was before she got herself pregnant, and get on with our afternoon. Somebody, call the folks at Catholic Charities. Tell the good sisters they have two more babies to find homes for."

Part One

IDENTITY

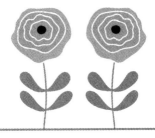

1

In Between

Winter 1959

On a cold and cloudy February night, my twenty-six-year-old birth mother, who called herself Ann Jensen at the time, left the downtown Chicago women's home where she'd moved with her trusted friend Mary. Three weeks shy of her due date, Ann was having pain she assumed was labor. As directed by Catholic Charities, she reported to Lewis Memorial Maternity Hospital, a facility on the city's South Side that had previously operated as a hotel.

As was the custom back then, the doctor on call put Ann into "twilight sleep," a type of sedation administered through an IV that makes a patient calm and groggy but alert enough to follow directions. When she was in recovery, my birth mother was surprised to learn that the pregnancy she'd hidden from family and friends had resulted in the birth of twin daughters. At a little over five pounds each, my sister and I were healthy newborns. The hospital authorities deemed us fraternal twins despite our looking exactly alike.

Out in the hospital waiting room, Ann did not have a nervous husband pacing, a man who might have fingered a pocketful of celebratory cigars to pass out when the doctor informed him he was now the proud father of two perfect little girls. Instead, my birth father was several states away, oblivious to Ann's whereabouts, her well-being, and her due date. After refusing to marry the girl he "got in trouble," my birth father went about living his life. By the time my sister and I were sitting up and crawling, he'd found a new love interest and was engaged to be married.

Also absent from the maternity waiting area were my biological grandparents, people who might have studied the clock and wrung their hands while their oldest daughter labored throughout the night. Like my birth father, my maternal grandparents lived several states away. Oblivious to Ann's situation, they were struggling through another snowy, bitterly cold Midwestern winter on the family farm where they worked with my many aunts and uncles. Had my grandparents learned about my birth mom's unplanned pregnancy, they might have disowned her.

So, the only soul lingering in the waiting area was Ann's long-time friend Mary. The two met in grammar school and became fast friends. Throughout their lives they shared many secrets between them, but this one—hiding Ann's unplanned and unwed pregnancy—was the truest test of their lasting friendship.

I assume that the labor and delivery nurse located Mary slumped against the wall in the corner of the waiting room, asleep. The nurse would have shaken Mary's shoulder gently and informed her that Ann's ordeal had reached a healthy conclusion. Mary might have wept. And then, I expect she did what she and Ann had done every morning and evening during their months of seclusion: Mary prayed. She sent urgent pleas heavenward that this shameful chapter in Ann's life would remain—as promised by the adoption gatekeepers at Catholic Charities—a secret for a lifetime.

While Mary prayed in the waiting room, Ann slipped out of the fog of her twilight sleep, and her hand went immediately to her belly. She explored its soft contours, scarcely believing that such a small space had held two babies. Twin girls! What a shock. She never expected that, even though multiples ran in her bloodline.

Ann squeezed her eyes shut, hoping this effort might stem the flow of tears, tears of relief and shame, and then she draped an arm across her face. She had a choice to make. Thinking about it made her head throb. Should she heed the advice from the Catholic Charities social worker or follow the longing in her heart? Would it be easier to surrender her parental rights if she did not view or hold her newborn daughters?

Once my sister and I had been cleaned up, weighed, and tightly swaddled, Ann requested that we not be brought to her, thus depriving us of precious skin-to-skin, mother-daughter bonding time. She named us Ann Marie and Mary Ann Jensen, and we remained in the sterile confines of the infant nursery. Not once did Ann venture down the long, antiseptic-scented hallway to view my sister and me through the windows of the nursery. No photos were taken of the three of us cuddling together either.

Five days after our birth, Ann signed away her parental rights, and my sister and I became wards of the state. Catholic Charities never heard from Ann again. Three weeks elapsed before the adoption agency placed my sister and me with our new family. During this interval we were legally orphans. The Daughters of Charity and the staff at St. Vincent's Infant Asylum on La Salle Street in Chicago cared for us.

Because my Catholic Charities adoption file is thin on details, there is no one to ask what happened during the first three weeks of our existence. And so, I'm left to imagine and suppose. How did we get from Lewis Memorial Maternity Hospital on the city's South Side to St. Vincent's orphanage north of the Loop? How were we cared for there?

Part of me wonders if Catholic Charities would have entrusted the transport of two newborns, each of whom weighed just over five pounds, into the care of a pair of nurse's aides from St. Vincent's orphanage. But then again, why not? We were just a few more of the city's abandoned children. Illegitimate. Born out of sin. Instead of nurse's aides ferrying us from the hospital to the orphanage, there is another alternative I fancy. Perhaps Sister Mary Alice, the director of St. Vincent's, dispatched two of her most trusted nuns.

I can see them now. A pair of the Daughters of Charity decked out in the prescribed habit of dark, bulky, full-length robes and crisp, white-winged headdresses that fluttered with every gesture. Yes, surely these were the messengers sent to shepherd two small, infant twin girls to their next home.

Whoever it was that drove the good sisters from St. Vincent's to the hospital would have had just a few miles to go, zigzagging first a few blocks, and then turning north on La Salle Street. Perhaps a Catholic Charities social worker accompanied the two nuns to gather our birth records from the hospital staff. Forms that would lay hidden in our adoption files at Catholic Charities and in the state of Illinois's Department of Vital Records for nearly fifty years. Paperwork that safeguarded the privacy of our birth mother, protected our adoptive parents' parental rights, and hid the stain of our illegitimacy from the public's damning shame.

In the hospital nursery, I envision the nuns from St. Vincent's unpacking two sets of warm travel gear donated by the faithful parishioners of the Archdiocese of Chicago. I'd like to think that the hospital nurses quarreled lightly with the nuns as to which set of women would feed us before our departure. Perhaps the nurses won out and marched to the corner of the nursery, where empty rocking chairs sat waiting. The nurses might have held my sister and me close, warming us with their own body heat, and we'd have settled to the rhythm of their hearts while sucking on bottles of formula.

Because of our sweet natures and big curious eyes, perhaps these staff nurses had developed a fondness for my twin and me, a preference even. Maybe they secretly called us "their girls" while they hummed and rocked us in the crook of their able arms. Possibly these women entertained fantasies of *if only I could adopt these perfect baby girls*. When they whispered about us, I hope the nurses and nuns spoke of us as Ann Marie and Mary Ann instead of Baby Girl Jensen #1 and #2. I must wonder how it was any of these caretakers could discern which twin was which without the benefit of peeking at our hospital tags. I wonder, too, if our identifying bracelets remained fixed throughout our stay at St. Vincent's—and when it was that we were freed from them.

I suppose that once my sister and I had been fed, changed, and dressed for the frigid February Chicago air, the nuns from St. Vincent's returned with us to a warm and waiting car for the short drive north. At the orphanage, we were whisked out of the vehicle and through the black-enameled wrought iron gates surrounding the orphanage. The nuns bustled us up that singular lobby elevator to the infant nursery, where I wonder if we were placed in one bassinet or two.

If my sister and I were given our own cribs, did the nurses scoot our bassinets close so we could see one another and hear each other's cries? And if we were in proximity to one another and howling with hunger or fright, might one of the nurse's aides broken the order of things and put us in a cradle together? If a compassionate soul nestled us into the same bassinet to soothe and bond with one another, did she receive a scolding for breaking protocol?

With the endless cycle of feeding and changing and caring for us during numerous shifts of nurses, aides, and care technicians, I wonder to whom we bonded during those first three weeks of life. As we were dressed to go home with our new parents on March 6, 1959, did the nurses and aides who took a liking to us tear up just a little? Who was it that pinned the customary Miraculous Medal to our breasts as we left with our new parents for home? Was it the director, Sister Mary Alice, who assumed this precious honor, or was it one of our favorite caregivers?

It would be nearly five decades before I learned of the Miraculous Medal and the tradition of pinning this blessed medal to the chest of each infant who left St. Vincent's Orphanage beginning their life as an adopted child. The French saint Sister Catherine Labouré, also a Daughter of Charity, is reputed to have received direction from the Blessed Mother herself in creating this unique medal.

In quizzing my adoptive mother about my Miraculous Medal, she is uncertain of what happened to the ones my sister and I received on our adoption day. While I cannot be sure I ever received one, I do feel that I was blessed. Thanks to Catholic Charities' policy of keeping multiple birth siblings together, my adoptive life included the steady companionship of my biological sister. She and I have belonged to one another before our births and every day since, and even though we never felt the embrace of our birth mother, we were welcomed into the arms of a couple eager to start the family of their dreams.

2

Coming Home

Spring 1959

While our physical lives began on a cold February afternoon at a South Side Chicago hospital, our family life and true sense of belonging started on Adoption Day, March 6, 1959. On this date, Jeanne and John "Jack" Ryan—the childless couple whom Catholic Charities had selected to become our adoptive parents—came to St. Vincent's Infant Home to pick us up.

During this period of closed adoption history, Catholic Charities matched babies to their new parents based on the biological parents' physical features, ethnic background, education, and religious preference. This suggests that both our mothers had dark hair and eyes, while our fathers shared wavy, reddish-tinged locks and blue eyes. Catholic Charities' policy of aligning physical appearances meant a child "fit in" with their adoptive families. And it spared both the adoptive parent and adopted child from the stigma of explaining about infertility issues and illegitimacy. Although my parents were given no information about our birth parents, it was assumed that they had finished college, were practicing Catholics, and of Irish and German descent, because this matched my adoptive parents' profiles.

When we left St. Vincent's orphanage, pinned with our Miraculous Medals, we became Jennifer Anne and Julie Anne Ryan, the names our adoptive parents selected for us. Once our adoptions were finalized in the fall of 1959, our original birth records were sealed, and I would not receive access to mine until 2011 when Illinois's adoption laws changed. In the fall of 1959, our parents, Jeanne and Jack Ryan, received redacted birth certificates showing our new names alongside their personal details.

So, instead of the play-by-play of what happened on February 11, the day Jenny and I were born, the events of Adoption Day have become the family legend trailing us into adulthood. My mom's vivid retelling of the day she got "the call" from Catholic Charities has become so real to me it's almost as if I were in the room with her when she picked up the phone.

Mom had been immersed in a lesson with her busy third-grade class at St. Cletus in the western suburb of La Grange when someone knocked at the classroom door. The school secretary poked her head in.

"You have a phone call in the office," she said.

The entire staff at St. Cletus knew my folks had experienced a half dozen miscarriages during their five-year marriage. At twenty-six and almost twenty-eight, my adoptive mom and dad had been waiting nearly two years to adopt.

As the story goes, Mom left the school secretary in charge of her class and rushed down the wide hallway. With each hurried step, Mom felt more certain that the phone call she was about to take was the one that would change her life. Breathless, she paused at the door of the school office. The principal glanced up from some paperwork, saw Mom's flushed face, and jabbed her finger toward the school secretary's phone. Mom darted to the adjacent desk and stopped, staring at the rotary dial phone with its flashing red "hold" button. She squeezed her eyes shut and sent off a quick prayer. Then, Mom lifted the receiver and punched the red button.

"Hello," she said, "this is Jeanne Ryan." Her voice was soft, questioning.

"Jeanne? This is Marge Duffy calling, the social worker at Catholic Charities."

"Yes . . . hello, Marge." Mom readjusted the phone, as if moving it closer to her ear would hurry the delivery of the message she craved.

"Sorry to disturb your school day, Mrs. Ryan, but we had a question about your adoption paperwork."

"Yes?" Mom frowned. She wondered why the social worker had pulled her out of a busy classroom to ask a question that could have been posed in the evening hours.

"In your adoption paperwork, you checked the box next to 'twins.' Did you mean to do that or was it an error?" Marge's tone was friendly, almost casual.

Mom did remember putting a neat little checkmark in the box next to "twins," but in all truthfulness she wasn't sure why she had done it. The youngest of twelve, Mom yearned for a big Catholic family like the one in which she'd grown up. Declaring that she and my dad would welcome twins had been spontaneous, but the decision still felt right.

"Yes, I meant to check the box for twins. It was no mistake." Mom shrugged at the nearby principal as if to apologize for the delay in returning to her classroom.

"Well, in that case, we need to set up a time for you to come to St. Vincent's Children's Home. To pick up your twin daughters."

Mom's whoop of joy startled the principal and could be heard in the outer offices. She slumped into the secretary's chair. "Twin girls? Really? They're ours?"

When Mom hung up, the principal and everyone within earshot swarmed around my sobbing mother. The principal helped her dial my dad's office number. In a shaky and tearful voice, Mom informed Dad they were about to become parents—of twice the family for which they'd prayed during the last five years.

On March 6, a week after Mom received the phone call at St. Cletus, my adoptive parents pulled their sedan out of the detached garage behind their two-bedroom ranch in Western Springs, Illinois. Mom fidgeted with the diaper bag, then folded and refolded the identical pink blankets she'd brought for this occasion. She quizzed Dad numerous times about the traffic and how long it would take to reach St. Vincent's on the city's North Side. Throughout Mom's nervous chatter, Dad kept his eyes on the road. As was his way, he offered a corny joke to diffuse Mom's nerves.

"What do you call twins before they are born?" he quizzed.

"I don't know, Jack. What?"

"Womb mates." Mom's giggle was all my dad needed to pull out another jest from his stash of humorous material.

"What do you call twins after they're born?"

Mom couldn't help herself. She was already chuckling. "I dunno. What?"

"Bosom buddies!"

After the twelve-mile trip east on the chaotic Eisenhower Expressway, my parents arrived on the city's developing Gold Coast. Dad maneuvered the sedan into the private lot behind the massive, red-brick structure at 721 N. La Salle Street. Mom scooped up the baby gear she'd packed, and they walked hand in hand around to the main entrance. They strolled through the shiny, black-enameled gates, joy etched onto their young faces. Inside the spacious, marble-floored vestibule, the security guard directed them to the elevator. Shivering with new parent nerves, Mom and Dad took the elevator from the lobby up to the fifth floor.

When the elevator doors opened, Sister Mary Alice Rowan

waited for them. Sister had dedicated her entire career to running the infant and children's home. Her reputation as a competent administrator and hard-nosed advocate for the city's poor and downtrodden reached beyond the city's limits. It was said that the monsignor at Holy Name Cathedral need only open his office window, a city block to the north, to hear Sister's booming voice issuing orders to her staff.

The stout, heavily robed nun ushered my soon-to-be parents into her office. She signaled for them to sit in the two chairs facing her large wooden desk, and then she rambled around it, settling her large frame into a chair across from them. Over the years, Mom confessed to me that Sister Mary Alice intimidated her. Seated behind the massive desk, Sister's commanding presence in her dark robes and white, winged headdress did not invite idle chitchat. She was all business. In this final interview of the eighteen-month adoption-vetting process, Mom committed the ultimate sin of daring to ask Sister Mary Alice a probing question.

I can just see my mom, her dark brown eyes shining, her manicured brows furrowing. Her unbridled enthusiasm for this chance at motherhood propelling her desire to know more about the infant girls she would soon call her daughters.

"Sister, can you please tell us a little about the girls' background?" Mom asked.

The ruddy-faced nun sighed loudly. She heaved her bulky frame close to the desk, placed her palms on the desktop, and leaned toward my mother.

Through a thin smile, Sister Mary Alice asked, "Do you want these girls or not?"

Knowing my mother as I do, she squirmed in her seat, her eyes flicking first to my dad and then at the fearsome nun. She swallowed hard, squinted up into the prioress's flashing blue eyes, and nodded her head vigorously.

"Yes, Sister. We do. We desperately want to be the parents of these two babies."

A look of satisfaction lit up Sister's face as she fixated on Mom. "Then there will be no more questions. Understood?"

Mom swallowed again and nodded. After that exchange, she let Dad do all the talking.

Sister cleared her throat. "Have you decided on names for your new daughters?"

Dad shared our new names, and Sister Mary Alice nodded her approval. As the nun transcribed our names onto the forms, her winged headdress bobbed like a bird taking flight. "Anne is a perfect middle name," she said. "Anne was the mother of the Blessed Virgin Mary. And it is one of the names given to the twins by their birth mother. I'm pleased that you will be honoring that connection."

As Sister Mary Alice delivered her little speech, she gave my mother a kind look. Inwardly, my mother sighed. She took Sister's demeanor to mean that she'd been forgiven. Mom allowed herself to relax just a little. It appeared that Sister held no grudge toward her, and that the adoption would go off without a hitch. Mom slid her hand inside my father's elbow and squeezed his arm.

When the paperwork was complete, the nun gathered up all the documents and put them into a large envelope. She slid the bulging envelope across the desktop to my father.

"Besides the adoption paperwork you have signed, inside this packet you'll find the girls' baptismal records. Their baptisms have been certified by Holy Name Cathedral, the seat of the Archdiocese of Chicago."

Sister sat back in her chair and regarded my parents as if anticipating pushback about the two of us having already received our first sacrament.

"Here at St. Vincent's, we baptize our babies as soon as possible.

It's important to free them of the original sin that mars their newborn souls. Before they go out into the world."

Dad picked up the envelope and set it in his lap. He shrugged at my mother. Mom lowered her eyes, dug her fingernails into her palms, and willed herself not to cry. Her sister, Addie, and my father's dear friend, Bob, had agreed to be our godparents. Now that the sacrament had already been administered, a ceremony at my folks' home parish, St. John of the Cross, was unnecessary. The party planned in their home following our baptisms also became irrelevant.

The brief look that my parents shared encompassed all these small disappointments, but it meant something so much more. As new parents and devout Catholics, they had missed out on witnessing our initiation into the Catholic faith.

"Now that the paperwork is all set, it's time to meet your daughters." Sister Mary Alice beamed.

She moved briskly around the massive desk and motioned for my parents to follow. Like chicks following a mother hen, my parents trailed her down the glistening linoleum hallway toward the chapel.

The director hovered near the entrance to the chapel. "You will wait inside the chapel here. The babies will be brought to you shortly."

Sister held open the door and directed them to sit in any one of the dozens of pine pews, and then she bustled off to the elevator, which took her to the first-floor infant nursery.

This time alone, waiting to receive their first children, must have felt like hours to my folks, but within minutes the chapel doors glided open again. At the sound of Sister Mary Alice's booming voice, my parents sprung up from the pew in which they had been kneeling and praying. The nun charged down the chapel's center aisle, the smile on her face as broad as a Halloween pumpkin.

Behind her trailed two young nurses dressed in clean, starched white uniforms and caps. Each held a blanket-wrapped bundle.

Sister Mary Alice stopped at the end of my parents' pew.

When the nurses joined Sister Mary Alice, she nodded at the pair grandiosely. "You may hand the babies over to their new parents. Congratulations, Mr. and Mrs. Ryan. You are now the parents of two perfect little girls."

My parents' faces gleamed as they received Jenny and me into their arms. Finally, the family that they had prayed for over and over.

On the car ride home, Mom settled into the back seat with a tightly wrapped bundle in each of her arms. As Dad navigated the busy expressway, his eyes often met my mothers in the rear-view mirror. They shared a loving, knowing look that meant, *We did it. We've achieved our dream. We're no longer an infertile, childless couple. We're building our American family, like our siblings and peers are doing, but in a unique and beautiful way.*

Since that first day of parenthood was precious to them, my parents chose to forgo a large welcome party. Instead, Dad parked the sedan in the front of their ranch-style home, unlocked the front door, helped my mother out of the car, and flicked on the lights in the living room. While my mother changed our diapers in the nursery, Dad retrieved two bottles of formula from the fridge. He placed them on the stove in a saucepan filled with water and watched the clock on the wall as the bottles heated for the prescribed time. He brought the bottles into the nursery where he and my mother settled into rockers and fed us for the first time.

"Now that you're mine," Mom cooed, as she covered us with blankets in our matching cribs, "I'll love you for the rest of time."

Later that evening, once my sister and I had been fed and settled into our matching white cribs, my mother retrieved the packet from

Sister Mary Alice. She pulled out the stack of documents, fingering them until she found the ones that she was after—our baptismal certificates. Her finger traced the words *Holy Name Cathedral* and the seal of the Archdiocese of Chicago. *What an honor to be baptized there*, she thought.

In truth, we had not been baptized at the magnificent marble font on the side altar at the cathedral. Instead, our indoctrination into the Catholic Church occurred in the modest chapel on the fifth floor at St. Vincent's where our parents received us. Ours was not a private ceremony with pomp and circumstance. Instead, we were one of many infants baptized in rapid succession by Rev. Coughlin on a day that fit his schedule. The nurses who had cared for us on the first floor brought us to the chapel, stood in as our godparents, and witnessed our initiation into the Catholic faith. It would be decades before the misunderstanding regarding where we had been baptized came to light.

Mom studied our baptismal certificates. When her eyes landed on the baptismal date, her hand flew to the center of her chest.

She gasped. "Jack! Come here! Quick."

Dad found her at the small round table in the corner of the cozy but tidy kitchen. Mom's soulful eyes glistened with tears. "Look. It says here the girls were baptized on February 27."

Mom pushed the certificates across the pine table and pointed to the date.

"Your birthday?" Dad's clear blue eyes locked with my mother's dark ones.

Staring at the date, Dad rifled through the reddish-brown curls tickling his forehead. "Incredible!"

Mom's face glowed with high emotion as she learned forward. "I believe this is a sign that the twins were meant to be ours."

Dad's ruddy cheeks dimpled. "It's probably just a coincidence, honey." When my mom's smile faded, he added, "I'd like to believe it's a sign, too."

As Mom threw her shoulders back, her chin jutted out. "I think it's a sign from Our Lady, telling us that she heard our prayers when we visited the shrine at Lourdes all those years ago."

"You're probably right, dear." Dad held his hand out to my mother. "Come. Get some rest. They'll be up soon for another feeding."

On the way to their bedroom, my parents stopped at the second bedroom, which had been quickly converted into our nursery. Mom put her finger to her lips, shushing Dad, and then she pushed the door open wide enough for them to see our cribs.

Jenny was on her tummy facing my crib, her forehead pressed against the pink bumper tied to the rungs of the white frame. A few of my sister's small fingers had snuck under the pads and curled around a wrinkle in the soft crib sheet. Two feet across from her, I mirrored my twin. I snoozed on my belly, one cheek pressed against a clean white crib sheet. My forehead with its tiny dark widow's peak had found the bumper pads, too. A few of my fingers poked under the soft pink cushioning as if reaching out to my sister.

"Aren't they precious, Jack?" Mom whispered. She leaned into his side, and Dad's arm went instinctively around her shoulders.

"I can't believe they're ours," Mom sighed.

My mother looked up at my dad, and he pulled her to him. "Perfect in every way," he said, his breath heavy. "Well worth waiting for."

"I can't help but think, they were meant to be ours," my mom said with wonder.

It would not be long before another detail emerged, one which eliminated all doubt in my parents' minds, affirming that Jenny and I were right where we belonged.

3

The Missal

Spring 1959

When my parents met, my father had graduated from Xavier University with an accounting degree. He was also a first lieutenant in the US Army. My mother was in college studying education and art; she planned on teaching elementary school after graduation. The two were introduced through their mutual friends Ginger and Dick, dated throughout my mother's senior year, and fell in love. They married in September 1954 at Saint Giles Catholic Parish in Oak Park, Illinois, and then moved to an army base in Darmstadt, Germany, where they spent the first year of their marriage. My mother suffered two miscarriages that year.

Having attended Catholic schools all her life, my mother was more than familiar with saints and their feast days, holy days of obligation, and religious sites where visions and miracles occurred. She knew that in 1858, a fourteen-year-old girl named Bernadette had been gathering firewood with her sister and a friend in the cave of Massabielle outside the town of Lourdes. Bernadette reported to her mother that she had seen a "lady" there, who spoke to her. Eighteen more apparitions of the Blessed Virgin Mary occurred that year. Once the Catholic Church sanctioned these visions, a church was built on the site, and Lourdes became a top religious pilgrimage destination.

Desperate to have a family, my folks planned a 1,400-kilometer journey from Darmstadt, Germany, to Lourdes, France, to visit the Blessed Virgin's shrine and pray there. When they arrived in Lourdes after a two-day journey by train, they joined hundreds of travelers visiting the holy place. Although there were many tourists interested in just viewing the shrine's church and the cave where Bernadette first saw Our Lady, many visitors, like my folks, needed a miracle.

My parents waited in the seemingly endless line and studied the crowd. Everywhere their eyes landed, they saw international travelers who suffered from poverty, illness, and deformity. People knelt at the statue of the Blessed Mother interred in her little grotto and prayed. Some wept as they pleaded for Our Lady to intercede. Most left behind alms, trinkets, and flowers.

As my parents neared the front of the line, Dad looked sheepishly at my mother. "What do you think?" he asked, gesturing at the multitude of visitors who surrounded them.

Mom knew what he meant. How could their meager request—asking the church's most important saint to help them start a family—compare with the apparent dire needs of the crowds? My mother took my father's hand. As they edged closer to the shrine, her heart quickened. They had traveled such a long distance. How could they come all this way and not offer the prayers they intended?

Mom whispered to Dad, "Let's pray for mercy for all these suffering souls . . . then, we'll ask for Our Lady's help in starting a family."

Dad squeezed her hand. "Okay. Sounds good to me."

My dad's deployment ended in December of 1955, and my parents sailed home to the United States on Christmas Day. Back in the Chicago area, where they had both been raised, they moved into their first house: a two-bedroom ranch on Woodland Avenue in Western Springs that would later become my first real home. My mom suffered three more miscarriages there, and the doctors offered a gloomy outlook about her chances at carrying an infant to full term. They made an appointment with Catholic Charities and initiated the adoption process. Two years later they received the call from Marge Duffy that changed their lives forever.

By this time, Dad had received his discharge papers from the army and became a salesman with Chicago Granitine Manufacturing Company, a washtub fabrication firm that his father, my Grandpa Joe, had founded. But due to competition and product obsolescence, Chicago Granitine was experiencing declining sales. Because my mother wanted to become a stay-at-home mom, the loss of her modest teacher salary would squeeze their tightening household budget. These concerns on top of setting up a nursery and caring for two babies instead of one put enormous pressure on my parents.

The first person they turned to when they got the call from Catholic Charities was my dad's mother, Grandma Mimi.

"Twins! Why, that's marvelous. How could we be so lucky?" Grandma Mimi's thrilled chuckle filled the phone line. "That nursery needs to be pulled together right away! Listen, I was in Marshall Field's the other day and saw the most beautiful crib. I had the clerk put one on hold, but now . . . shall I call her to see if they have two in stock? I know you'll love it. It's creamy white with a curved headboard and exquisite detailing . . ."

That phone call from my parents was all it took for Grandma Mimi's generous heart to bloom. Her desire to see my parents' dreams come to fruition—and her willingness to open her pocketbook—eased their worries about managing the mounting sudden expenses. My grandmother had a habit of doing this, sliding in at just the right moment and doling out a blessing, one that you couldn't offer yourself. It was her way. Each time she witnessed the surprised grin of a person whose life she made a little bit better, the dimpled smile she had in common with my dad punctuated her round face.

For my parents, the frenzied week of preparation following the call from Catholic Charities was like standing in the path of a fire hose. Mom prepped the teacher taking over her third-grade classroom at St. Cletus, while Grandma Mimi manned the house on Woodland Avenue. She took delivery of the Marshall Field's furniture and saw to it that our nursery was set up exactly as my mother specified. Between my mom's colleagues at St. Cletus—who surprised her one day after school with a baby shower—and the bountiful gifts from close friends and family, our nursery was ready in record time.

So, on March 6, when my parents pulled their sedan out of the detached garage to make the trip downtown to St. Vincent's, they had received everything that a nursery required times two. Once Jenny and I were established in our first home, the generosity continued. Someone was always dropping by or sending a gift to welcome the two of us into the Ryan family. By the time we were a few weeks old, Mom could barely shut the door of our nursery closet. Putting all the goodies away, sending out handwritten thank-you notes, and staying on top of our feedings occupied my mother for weeks. So it's not surprising that a month passed before my mother made the second discovery, "the sign" that confirmed her belief that my sister and I were destined to be their daughters.

As life settled down, my folks slid into the socially prescribed routine that was expected of married couples during the 1950s. Each morning, my mother waved goodbye to my dad as he pulled out of the driveway and headed to the office. Mom tightened her robe, had a second cup of coffee, and evaluated whether there was enough time to shower before we woke. One morning when my sister and

I were still sleeping, my mother sank into the living room sofa and reached for her missal.

I remember that missal.

As a young girl, I used to creep into my parents' bedroom and scrounge around till I found that little book. It was the size of a small paperback novel. Instead of an intricate plot, it contained Gospel readings, prayers, and a detailed listing of saints and their feast days. I'd usually find it resting under her rosary in the wood shelving framing her side of my parents' double bed. Once I located the missal, I'd sink to the shag carpet, lean against the frame of the big bed, and hold the prayer book in my small hands.

Mom's missal was nothing like the scuffed, dog-eared hymnals in the pews at church. This book was a treasure. The spine, front, and back covers were inlaid with an elaborate mother-of-pearl design. Stiff and highly polished, in my palms it was as heavy as a change purse full of nickels. Next to my mother's beaded lace wedding gown—stored in a special garment bag in the hall closet—the missal was the most beautiful thing my young eyes had ever seen.

Knowing my mother as I do, it's not hard for me to conjure what happened next. My sleep-deprived mother needed a dose of spiritual guidance to buoy her. She picked up her favorite prayer book and held it. She sighed. The sight of its magnificent bindings soothed her. Mom opened the pearl cover and fingered the first velum pages. A thought flickered.

What is the saint's feast day coinciding with the twins' birthday?

When she flipped to the entry marked February 11, Mom's heart took off like a released balloon. Our birthday was the feast day of Our Lady of Lourdes. A shocked smile erased the tired lines around her eyes. She reread the date and corresponding feast day again and again. Then she closed her eyes, pressed the prized missal to her drumming heart, and let the tears come.

Our Lady did hear our prayers at Lourdes. The girls were meant to be ours!

To my parents, our birthday coinciding with the feast day of Our Lady of Lourdes did more than prove that Blessed Mother had interceded on my parents' behalf. It solidified their belief in the power of prayer. It served another purpose as well. It eased my mother's insecurities about her inability to carry a fetus to term. Our Lady's show of faith in her as a mother, someone who could handle the parenting of twins, reduced her shame, buoying her confidence as a new parent. Mom had suffered, shown patience, and been both faithful and prayerful. For those virtues, she'd been rewarded. Twofold.

I often reflect upon the spiritual energy that swirls around my beginnings. While I do not believe that our lives are predetermined, I'm curious about how ethereal forces like saints and angels, as well as the energy of prayer, influence its trajectory.

Mom often says to Jenny and me, "If in the past, I had carried those other babies, we wouldn't have you. I can't imagine life without you."

Whether my parents' prayers influenced Jenny and me joining the family they assembled, I can't be sure, but I don't discount it. The validation that my mother experienced on the day she picked up her missal propelled her into a lifelong devotion of Our Lady.

After my parents adopted Jenny and me, they remained on the lengthy adoption list with Catholic Charities, hoping to receive a third child, possibly a little boy. A few months after Jenny and I celebrated our second birthday, another social worker from Catholic Charities phoned. A three-month-old blonde, blue-eyed little boy was theirs if they wanted him. They named him after my grandpa Joe Ryan, but because he scooted around so fast, the nickname *Skeeter* stuck.

My brother's adoption meant my parents' prayers to Our Lady had been answered once again. Their dream of building a big Catholic family was falling into place, a goal that would continue to challenge a tight budget, create constant chaos in our small home, and pressure each of us to forge our own sense of identity and belonging.

By Father's Day 1961, my parents had three children under three: two girls and a boy. At twenty-eight and thirty years old, they had the makings of a perfect—albeit small by 1960s standards—Catholic family. Most importantly, my mother still had Our Lady's ear. Over the years, she would rely on her time and time again.

4

Chosen

Fall 1963

In one of my earliest concrete memories, Jenny and I were four years old. It was a sunny but chilly November morning. The two of us played quietly together on the floor of the den, while Mom, Dad, and Grandma Mimi watched TV from the red leather sofa.

My grandmother turned to my dad. "Jack, the screen is fuzzy. Can you fiddle with the antenna again?"

Sometime after Catholic Charities called to say that our new brother, Skeeter, was waiting for them at St. Vincent's Orphanage, my parents swapped houses with Grandma Mimi. Within weeks, our swelling family left the small ranch-style home in Western Springs and moved into my grandmother's three-bedroom Dutch Colonial across from Waiola Park in the nearby town of La Grange.

The move benefitted everyone. Grandma Mimi assumed a lifestyle that meant fewer stairs and a smaller home to manage. My parents gained a house with more bedrooms to fill. The big bonus from the move was that my siblings and I landed in a neighborhood that would leave a permanent imprint on our hearts. A place all of us would remember fondly. And at a time when our family life was content, chaotic, and untouched by deep loss.

After a few twists and tweaks, Dad stepped back from the TV. "Is that better?"

From her end of the long, red sofa, Grandma Mimi sighed, "Much better."

Dad scooted past Jenny and me where we sat cross-legged on the carpet—our naked Barbie dolls, colorful outfits, and matching plastic stilettos lay sprawled out around us. Our dad sank down at the opposite end of the sofa next to Mom. He stretched his arm out along the sofa's carved wooden back, his elbow resting on the crest where an eagle's beak rose out of the dark wood. His fingers curled around the puffy shoulder of my mother's crisp white blouse.

Mom's gaze remained fixed on the TV screen. Like Grandma Mimi, she sniffled and dabbed at eyes wet with tears.

"I still can't believe all this happened," she murmured.

Jenny and I dropped our dolls into our laps. Like skittish birds on the lookout for danger, our eyes darted back and forth between the adults on the sofa and the scene playing out on the television. A large, black vehicle—Mom called it a hearse—led a parade of cars through a lush green park set with rows of upright white stones. In a sorrowful voice, Grandma Mimi explained that it wasn't a park like our Waiola Park—"The Park," as we called it—but a cemetery near our nation's capital where important people and war heroes are buried.

Grandma Mimi dug out the lace-trimmed hankie from the sleeve of her voluminous print dress. "It's called Arlington Cemetery, pets," she said, swiping at tears. "Such a dark, sad day for our country. What's the world coming to?"

"I dunno, Mom," Dad said. He pulled my mother in close, and she rested her dark head against his crisp blue work shirt. "The world seems to be chock-full of crazies."

Perhaps it was the confusing scene scrolling across the TV and the information my grandmother offered. Or maybe it was simply the deflated moods of everyone in the room that caused that day and that moment to stick irrevocably in my mind. The combination of those factors must have troubled both Jenny and me, for suddenly, the carpet felt too hard on our bottoms. We abandoned our dolls in their various stages of undress. Jenny scrambled over to the sofa and slid into the narrow space next to our mom. I wandered over to Grandma Mimi and tried climbing up in her lap. The heavy scent of her favorite Yardley perfume tickled my nose.

"Give me a minute, pet," Grandma said, blowing her nose with such force that the numerous strands of beads around her neck rattled against her large bosom.

I slipped past my grandmother to the only window in the room and fiddled with the painted wood shutters. Sunbeams poked through the narrow slats and pierced the darkened room. Out in the yard, I spied my green tricycle parked next to Jenny's pink one by the side door. As I stared at our bikes, I lifted the end of my pigtail and sucked on the light brown cluster of hair. I longed to go outside. We'd been stuck inside most of the weekend. One news show after another had been running since Friday, interrupting all regular programming to inform the country that President Kennedy had been assassinated in Dallas.

"Close that shutter, pet," Grandma Mimi said softly. "We can't see the TV properly with the glare."

I snapped the shutter closed. "Why can't we go out to play, Mommy?" I asked.

"Not now, honey." Mom reached for a tissue from the box on the coffee table. "We're watching this show right now. When your brother wakes from his nap, we'll go to The Park. I promise."

Jenny slid off the sofa. "Let's play some more."

She tugged me over to where our Barbie dolls lay in a mess. Before we dropped to the floor, Jen nabbed a few tissues from the box. I watched as she folded one, draping it around her Midge doll just like our mom did with fresh towels when we emerged from the bathtub. I grabbed some Kleenex, too, copied my twin's efforts, and then used another tissue to fashion a turban around my Skipper doll's long brown hair.

"Oh, gosh. Just look at those poor sweet kids," Mom cooed. "Caroline is so stoic, so brave, her reddish hair just like JFK's."

Grandma Mimi shoved her hankie up the sleeve of her dress. "And that John-John," she said, making the clucking sound that always caused my sister and me to share a private snicker. "How cute is he with those knobby little knees poking out below his coat?"

Jenny and I glanced up from our play and studied the children on the black-and-white screen. A boy and girl. Children around the same ages as us.

"What're they doing, Mommy?" My dark green eyes implored her to offer an explanation.

"Those two children lost their father."

I wagged a finger at the TV screen. "Is their mommy gone, too? Will they get a new mommy and daddy like we did?"

I glanced at my mother. Her eyes smiled and so did my grandmother's. Their reactions infused me with courage, so I shared the first thing that bubbled up in my childish mind.

"Were they picked by their mommy and daddy? Just like you and daddy picked us?" I asked.

Mom let out a big breathy, tired sigh. "Maybe one day those two kids, Caroline and John-John, will get a new daddy, but they still have their mommy." She gave me a warm smile and patted her lap. "Come sit with me."

As Mom hoisted me up, she gave Dad one of her looks and nodded in Jenny's direction. He coaxed my sister to leave her doll and climb into his lap. As we sat there, our parents' arms pulling us in close, their slow breaths ruffling the errant wisps of our fine brown hair, my mind replayed the "chosen" talk Mom had given Jenny and me months before, about the time we turned four.

We had just finished our nighttime routine: warm sudsy baths, reading picture books from the stack on the nightstand, and reciting our bedtime prayers. Mom perched between us on the edge of Jenny's canopy bed.

"I think you girls are old enough now to understand something very important."

My mother explained that my sister and I were adopted, which meant when we were born, we had come out of another mommy's tummy. Her eyes closed as she described how she and Dad had tried for years to have babies without any luck. They prayed hard and began working with Catholic Charities for help in starting their family.

"And then one day, a nice lady from Catholic Charities called. She said the two little girls we said we always wanted were waiting for us at St. Vincent's. 'Come pick them up,'" Mom said, squeezing us hard. "Your dad and I can't believe how blessed we are. We waited a long time for you girls, and your brother, too. God chose you for us. And I want you to know how much we wanted you. How very loved you are."

That night my mother hugged us a long time. "Do you have any questions?"

When we shook our heads no, she tucked us into our matching canopy beds, kissed our foreheads, and gave us a big, warm smile as she closed the bedroom door.

Mom's loving words about being "chosen" filled my body with a warm feeling, but the other stuff about "being adopted" and "another mommy's tummy" made me twist and turn under the covers. I looked over at Jenny. She was fast asleep.

If she isn't bothered by any of this, then why should I be? I reasoned.

A little voice inside me said, *You don't need to think about this. You're right where God wants you to be.*

Next to me on the sofa, Grandma Mimi's booming voice shook me out of remembering. "Oh, would you look at that. What a sweet boy. John-John's saluting his father's casket."

I heard the marvel in my grandmother's voice and wondered if Jenny and I could teach Skeeter to salute like John-John. I stole a look at my father and mother.

My lips twitched in a silent prayer, *Please, God, don't let us be like those kids on TV. Don't take my mommy or daddy away from me.*

It didn't seem to matter to my parents whether we were adopted or their biological children. Their shared goal was to build a large Catholic family. They professed to love us all equally. But for me, it wasn't so simple. I would spend a lifetime wondering about what happened to my family of origin, and why closed adoption took me away from them. I would also harbor an inner fear that if I wasn't good enough, if I didn't obey every rule and fulfill every expectation, then my adoptive parents might consider giving me away like my first family had done.

I promised myself I would work extra hard to please Mom and Dad, to be perfect in every way possible. And in turn I hoped the God I prayed to every night would continue to bless me and my family, safeguarding us from sickness and harm.

5

Nothing Under the Tree

Winter 1963

Before setting out to the far southern suburbs to attend the annual holiday dinner and gift exchange with my father's family, Mom helped Jenny, Skeeter, and me pack up things to play with in the car. As she did so, her face puckered in a frown.

Those gatherings with my father's family stressed Mom and set her on edge. She put enormous pressure on herself to select just the right gifts for everyone, dress my siblings and me in attractive holiday outfits, and present herself as an attractive, organized, and classy woman. One who was also the perfect wife and mother.

"You can bring these same toys into Aunt Helen's house for playtime with your cousins before supper. After we eat, we'll gather around the Christmas tree and open presents," Mom said.

As Skeeter, Jenny, and I scurried about selecting toys to pack up, Dad appeared in the doorway of the den. He towered over us like the Jolly Green Giant. His breath came out in puff-puff chugs, like the freight train sounds we heard in the early-morning hours. Dad's normally rosy cheeks flamed, and chunks of snow clung to the cuffs of his overcoat.

"We need to get on the road, Jeanne. The snow we got this morning is gonna make the drive to Helen and Ned's slow going."

Melted snow dripped from my dad's auburn curls and snuck down his forehead. He wiped it away with his coat sleeve.

"I shoveled the walkway. The car's warming up. Ready?" Dad said.

Mom's pretty face crinkled. Her eyes flashed first at my dad and then flicked over to Skeeter. My almost-three-year-old brother jammed fistfuls of Matchbox cars into the blue carrying case he dragged everywhere.

Mom grabbed his wrist. "No more!" she said firmly.

Her red-painted lips flattened into a thin line. I hated when Mom's voice hitched like that, moving in an instant from soft and sweet to sharp and gruff. Mom raised her voice most with Skeeter, less so with Jenny and me, and hardly ever with Dad. But whenever my mom's temper flared, Jenny and I gave each other a look, moved closer toward one another, and if we could, we slipped out of the room. My mother's desire for everything to run smoothly ramped up the tension in our household. The net result was that we were put on notice to be on our best behavior.

"We're almost ready, Daddy." My words were soft as my eyes beamed up at my dad.

He winked at me.

I never tired of looking into my dad's blue eyes; there always seemed to be the suggestion of a smile lingering there, a tease coming, or a joke forming.

Mom stood and massaged the small of her back. When she fussed with her boxy white blouse, straightening it over her growing midsection, I spied the wide elastic panel at the waist of her black skirt. The thick black hose she wore barely contained her swollen ankles. At Thanksgiving time, Mom and Dad had told us that in the spring we'd have a new brother or sister. On some level, I guess I realized the baby would be my parents' first biological child, but my folks weren't focused on that. Because of her long history of failed pregnancies, there was more fuss around my mother being careful and carrying the child to full term than anything else.

I wasn't sure how another new sibling was going to affect me really. Something would change, but at almost five I was more interested in the suede pumps mom had on. I mused about how great they'd be for playing dress-up with Jenny.

Mom coaxed Skeeter up from the floor. She tucked his crisp white shirt into red corduroy slacks and buttoned up his plaid Christmas cardigan. He fidgeted and tried escaping, squealing, "I wanna play. Don't wanna go!"

Mom grabbed his pudgy hand. The smile she gave my dad didn't show her teeth. "Okay, dear. I think we're ready to get in the car."

While Mom helped the three of us into our dress coats—the woolen ones that we wore only to Church on Sundays—Dad placed the stack of gifts Mom and I had wrapped into the back of the green station wagon. When Mom and I put tags and ribbon on the presents earlier in the day, she explained how a gift exchange worked. Our family would give a package to everyone in Dad's family. Each of us would receive three gifts in return: one from Aunt Helen and Uncle Ned, one from Aunt Rose and Uncle Pat, and one from Grandma Mimi.

"All loaded up," Dad said. "Let's get the kids in the car before the snow makes the roads even slushier than they are already."

Inside Aunt Helen and Uncle Ned's cozy, ranch-style house, Jenny and I scrambled over to say hello to Grandma Mimi first.

She scooped us up into a tight hug where she cooed over our matching green dresses. Squirming free of her big-hearted embrace, strands of our wispy brown hair snagged in the chunky costume jewelry around her neck. As we tried fleeing the room in search of our cousins, Mom stopped us short with one of her sharp looks. So we crept over to our aunts and uncles and whispered a hasty "Merry

Christmas." After tossing our coats on the large heap in Aunt Helen's bedroom, we chased each other down to the rec room where our older girl cousins waited.

During all this mayhem, Dad traipsed back and forth from the car with the gifts for the family gift exchange. Aunt Rose and Aunt Helen placed them under the white-flocked Christmas tree anchoring Aunt Helen's living room. Mom corralled Skeeter away from the tree bedecked with glass ornaments and plopped him on the floor next to her place at the end of the sofa. When she nodded at him, Skeeter grinned and dumped out his entire car collection.

With most of us occupied in the rec room, Grandma Mimi and my two aunts got dinner underway. They fussed with the silver settings on the "adult" table in the dining room, folded linen napkins at every place, lit tapered candles in the candelabra, and placed steaming food into Aunt Helen's fancy set of china on the buffet. In the kitchen, Aunt Rose placed folding chairs around the maple table where the cousins would eat together.

When the special Christmas meal was ready, Aunt Helen marched to the steps leading to the lower level, hollering, "Dinner is ready. C'mon up, everyone! Before the food gets cold."

Jenny and I raced our cousins to get seats side by side at the kids' table. Even though mouth-watering smells drifted from the buffet, our steps slowed when we saw the stack of gifts under the Christmas tree. Toward the front of the tree skirt was an array of small Christmas gift bags, each with a card and a candy cane peeking out. As I got older, I would come to recognize those as Grandma Mimi's signature gift. Each envelope held a check, which we were expected to deposit into the savings account she and Grandpa Joe had set up for us.

Dinner at the kids' table was lightning fast. We couldn't wait to gather around the tree and find the packages marked with our names. We snarfed down the food and beelined into the dining room, where we pestered our parents until they set down their wineglasses. In the living room, my older cousins encouraged the younger ones to sit quietly on the floor, cross-legged around the large pine tree, while the carefully labeled gifts were passed out.

The evening was shaping up to be idyllic, just as my mother imagined it would be. Both of my father's sisters had complimented Mom on how adorable Jenny and I looked in our outfits—the matching green velvet dresses, lace-trimmed anklets, and shiny black patent leather Mary Jane shoes. Even Skeeter received praise from Aunt Helen on how nicely he'd played on the floor next to Mom before dinner.

When Aunt Rose commented to Mom over dinner, "You look so trim and beautiful. No one would even dream you're five months pregnant," my mother's face glowed.

The abundance of flattery made what was about to happen even more painful.

After all the presents were distributed, Jenny, Skeeter, and I each had only two gifts in front of us. We looked at our cousins. All of them had a stack of three presents. I looked bug-eyed at Jenny, and she shrugged. Before we could get my mother's attention, Grandma Mimi sauntered over.

She whispered in my mother's ear. "I'm not sure what happened. I see that Skeeter and the girls ended up with only two gifts. Whose gifts are they missing?"

Mom huddled over Jenny and me and read the gift tags on our packages. It turned out there were no presents from Aunt Helen and Uncle Ned. While Mom scoured the tree skirt for the missing gifts, Grandma Mimi cornered Aunt Helen. As they conversed quietly by the kitchen door, the color of my grandmother's face flushed such a deep crimson that it blended in with her garnet-colored blouse. Whatever my grandmother said to Aunt Helen sent my aunt fleeing into the kitchen.

Grandma Mimi draped her arm around my mother's shoulders and explained that with all the holiday fuss and prepping for the big family meal, Aunt Helen had neglected to buy gifts for my sister, brother, and me.

"She'll make it up to them later in the week," my grandmother said.

When my mom whispered this to Dad, his face grew bright red. "Jeanne, leave it alone. Let's deal with it later," he whispered.

But this "leaving her kids out" didn't sit well with my mother. Having grown up as the youngest of twelve—a role that meant she was often left out or left behind—my mother championed those ailing, hurt, or mistreated. As my relatives oohed and ahhed over their gifts, Mom sat perched on the edge of Aunt Helen's loveseat, her shapely lips pressed into an angry line. I don't know what was harder to watch, my mother's face or my cousins squealing with delight over their new toys.

I edged closer to Jenny. The questioning look we shared meant, *Who's in trouble now?* While we knew we hadn't done anything wrong, we realized that whatever was going on was not something to giggle about.

After what seemed like an hour but was a matter of minutes, my mother turned to my dad and said, "Jack, it's time to get the children in the car."

When we were bundling up in our coats and saying our good-byes at the door, Aunt Helen squeezed in close to my parents.

"My goodness. I'm sorry I forgot to get the kids a little something. I have a dollhouse in the garage. Stay for a moment while I clean it up and then you can take it home for the girls."

Mom straightened the collar on her tweed coat, her soulful brown eyes flashing as she looked Aunt Helen in the eye. "Not necessary. They're getting a brand-new dollhouse from Santa."

With that retort lingering in the stale foyer air, my mother leaned over, buttoned Skeeter's dress coat, and marched us out the front door. Dad closed the door with a little extra oomph. On the long car ride home, the only noise filling the station wagon was the steady *vroom-vroom* sound of my brother racing a new Matchbox car along the seat.

It has never been clear why my aunt acted as she had. My parents believed she wished to call attention to the fact that my sister, my brother, and I were brought into the Ryan family, not born into it. While I knew how much my parents wanted my siblings and me to be part of the family they were putting together, it is startling to consider that their extended family harbored a different perspective about adoption. If Grandma Mimi was privy to Aunt Helen's mindset, she never let on. And rather than fan the fires, my parents chose to let the flames of my aunt's inconsiderate act die out.

While my aunt's motives were questionable, I have never doubted how my parents felt about my sister, brother, and me. Whenever my mom relives the painful turn of events from that family Christmas party, her message is unwavering.

"We love you. We desperately wanted you. Your place in the family we have put together is secure and important."

Adoption has the potential to produce great joy and love, and it also holds stigma. A child adopted in the 1950s was assumed to be either the product of an illicit union, from an impoverished or uneducated family, or unwanted for other reasons. I credit my parents for not letting my aunt's cruel behavior sever their ties with my father's family, but Aunt Helen's insensitive actions are something my family has never forgotten.

6

The Sickly One

Spring 1964

It's common in multiple births for one infant to be born larger than the other, but over time the smaller twin usually catches up. Sometimes though, one infant continues to be healthier than the other for no remarkable reason.

Jenny and I were considered healthy, full-term twins. My sister was five pounds, nine ounces at birth, and I weighed in at five pounds, eleven ounces. As we developed, we maintained that slim margin of difference. Throughout adolescence, we never deviated more than a half inch in height or a few pounds in weight. One month Jenny might be taller, and then the next month, we were dead even again. Despite this equal start in life, I have always been the sickly one. This important difference between Jenny and me highlighted vital questions, ones which my parents could not answer due to our closed adoption.

Who am I like? What is my family medical history, and where did I come from?

One of the first ways I set myself apart from my sister was the time I became very ill and entered the hospital. Shortly after my new baby brother, Patrick, was born in the spring of 1964, I lay delirious in the children's ward at La Grange Community Memorial

Hospital, sweating and shivering. My fever refused to dip back to normal. For forty-eight hours, I remained oblivious to my parents' fearful looks and the round-the-clock shifts of medical staff trying to control my temperature and determine the cause of my illness.

When my lab tests came back, my family learned I had nephritis, a kidney infection.

I've been told that when I finally emerged from my delirium, it was Grandma Mimi who kept vigil next to my hospital bed. Like my mother had done during her shifts by my side, my grandmother fingered a strand of rosary beads, praying to Blessed Mother, beseeching her to empower the antibiotics to knock out the nasty bacteria infecting my young kidneys.

As much time as I've spent with my grandmother, I have no trouble imagining the scene. Grandma Mimi sitting close to my bed so she could hear me breathe. Her large, bulky frame drooping over the edges of the inadequate hospital guest chair; her quaff of thin, gray hair teased up high and held in place with a thick spray of Final Net. No doubt she wore one of the vibrantly colored muumuus she favored, those loose housedresses that floated like a shirt from her broad shoulders down past her gnarled, arthritic knees. Even with profound worry rattling her insides, Mimi's green-blue eyes would have held their twinkle and special gleam, and her thin pink lips would have curled in the pleasant smile she shared with my dad.

As I stirred in that hospital bed, my fever ebbing, something happened that made my grandmother smile with wonder and her twinkly eyes tear up.

I muttered to her, "Don't worry, Mimi. Saint Thérèse says I'll be all right."

Grandma Mimi sat there uncharacteristically speechless, trying to take in what I had said. "Saint Thérèse? Saint Thérèse, the Little Flower? She came to you in your dreams, pet?"

"Yes, Grandma!" I gave her a weak smile. "She said I was going to get better. And I do feel better."

That assurance from a sick five-year-old to a fatigued and fear-addled grandmother launched a flurry of phone calls, questions, and conversations. It also instigated the purchase of a slew of statues, stories, relics, and holy cards featuring, Saint Thérèse, the Little Flower.

After my hospital stay, I learned a lot more about Saint Thérèse, a small Carmelite nun who died from tuberculosis at twenty-four. She had been severely ill as a young girl with symptoms suggesting a kidney infection. And like me, she loved roses. Even though she was dying, she believed her mission had just begun.

She explained: "After my death, I will let fall a shower of roses. I will spend my time in heaven doing good upon earth." According to the religious brochures, "Shortly after her death, the rain of roses began. Sometimes roses literally appeared, and sometimes just the fragrance of them."

One of the items Grandma Mimi purchased for me was a round ceramic statute of Saint Thérèse. I placed it on the nightstand between the canopy beds in the room I shared with Jenny. About the size and weight of a baseball, it fits in the palm of a hand. On the front, Saint Thérèse's likeness is painted in pastel colors, and on the back side is a small opening, like a window, which holds a relic, a small section of a rose petal from the shower of roses that supposedly fell when Saint Thérèse took her place in heaven.

In the days that followed my recovery, my grandmother and parents quizzed me many times. "Honey, how did you know about Saint Thérèse?"

I shrugged. "She came to me in my dreams."

I couldn't explain how I might have known about that saint. At five years old, I was not enrolled in school yet. Mom didn't recall reading to me about her from one of the many religious booklets populating the coffee tables and bookshelves in our small house.

It's possible that I overheard a network news segment about the new retreat center opening in a nearby suburb dedicated to Saint Thérèse. But I like to think that because I was a young child whose mind was not yet clouded by the details of everyday life, I was open to such things as angels and visitations from the heavenly worlds.

As a young girl who was constantly home sick from school, I welcomed Saint Thérèse's help in combatting the frequent upper respiratory and ear infections that plagued me. Much like my mother and her relationship with Blessed Mother, I have called upon Saint Thérèse for special needs and requests. I still have the small figurine my grandmother purchased for me.

Just before my eighth birthday, Dr. Welford, our family pediatrician, consulted with my mother. Because of my frequent bouts with strep throat and ear infections, he convinced her that I needed a tonsillectomy.

When Dr. Welford explained the procedure to me, I said, "Well, since we're twins, then my sister Jenny needs this, too."

He glanced at my mother, chuckling. "No. Jenny doesn't need surgery. Not yet anyway. But you sure do."

I looked down at my Keds sneakers and frowned. While I didn't mind having a few different experiences from my sister, I still wanted her by my side during important moments.

I thought a diet of ice cream and Popsicles sounded cool, but I worried about how much my throat would hurt. My heart boomed all the way up into my ears as I considered spending the night in the hospital, alone, away from my parents and twin sister. At eight years old, I had done sleepovers at Grandma Mimi's and my cousins' homes, but Jenny had always been right there with me.

I whispered to my mother, "Even if she doesn't need surgery, Jenny can come. She could sleep in the bed next to me just like we do at home!"

Dr. Welford's forehead wrinkled. "Healthy kids can't take a bed away from a sick person who needs it."

"Besides," Mom said, giving me one of those sweet, pretty smiles that always chased the butterflies out of my stomach, "you won't be alone in the room, honey. You'll have a roommate. It just won't be your sister. And you'll only be in the hospital for one night. It'll be okay, I promise."

I nodded okay to my mother, but inside my stomach tickled as it always did on the first day of school. Later that week when Grandma Mimi came over for dinner, she brought one of her suitcases, the small pink polka-dotted one with brass latches that you had to line up just right to get closed.

The night before my mom and dad took me to the hospital, I packed my favorite fleece flowered pajamas, some coloring books and crayons, a few Little Golden Books to read, and the cuddly, stuffed Steiff rabbit Santa brought at Christmas. On surgery day, Dad took the day off from work, and then he and Mom drove me to La Grange Hospital. Even though I wished Jenny was going through this with me, it felt good to have my parents to myself.

Dad kissed my forehead and Mom squeezed my hand when the nurse came to help me onto the gurney for surgery. "We'll be right here when you wake up, honey," Mom said.

Before I could reply or smile or cry, the cheery nurse inserted herself into our conversation. "We'll take good care of her, don't you worry."

As she tucked the white sheet around my legs, she said, "And you, young lady, the procedure will be over before you know it, and then you're going to get all the ice cream you want. Wave goodbye to Mom and Dad. Off we go."

When the orderly wheeled me back into a room after surgery, my parents were waiting. Along with the hand-made crayon colored get well cards from Jenny, Skeeter, and Patrick, they brought chocolate-chip ice cream and a box each of the banana and root beer popsicles I loved.

The young nurse smiled. "You can call for one anytime you want."

I watched as she positioned the white call button box by my pillow, admiring the little white hat that set atop her head. It had a red cross on it. Right then, I decided I wanted to be a nurse for Halloween.

Once visiting hours were over, Mom dug into her purse and pulled out a clump wrapped in white tissue. It was the Saint Thérèse statue Grandma Mimi had bought me after my bout with nephritis. She placed it on the bedside table and kissed me good night.

"Saint Thérèse will watch over and keep you safe tonight." Mom kissed my forehead. "I'll be back to see you first thing in the morning."

After my parents left, I remember crying a little. My throat hurt a lot—more than any strep throat I'd ever had—and I missed my bed at home, the one I slept in across from Jenny. I wiped my wet cheeks with the bed sheet, slipped out of bed, and peeked around the tall curtain that separated me from my roommate. What I saw troubled me. The girl in the next bed had casts on both legs that went all the way up her thighs. I gulped hard as I studied her. The heavy white casts were connected by a bar above her ankles.

Yikes, I thought, *she has it way worse than me.*

I scampered back to bed, pulled the stiff sheet and thin white blanket up to my chin, and rolled on my side away from my roommate.

I stared at the Saint Thérèse relic, pleading, *Please, please, please make sure I only spend one night in here.*

I was pretty sure I could count on Saint Thérèse for that simple request. She'd already come through for me with the kidney infection. But just to be certain, I recited the good-night prayers I had learned years before. Once I had "God blessed" all the members of my family, I braved another peek around the curtain at the girl with the casts. With stunning ferocity, I squeezed my eyes shut and added that girl to my list of God-blesses. She needed more prayers than I did. For good measure, I adjusted the Saint Thérèse statue, making certain that nothing blocked its view of my roommate's bed. I wanted Saint Thérèse to look out for her, too.

This moment was a turning point for me. Up until then, I had prayed only for the well-being of the people in my family. Witnessing sick people firsthand made an impression on me. I realized the importance of praying for those outside my inner circle. I belonged to my family and my twin sister, but I also belonged to the world.

7

Fear

Spring 1965

There wasn't much I was afraid of as a kid.

In the thirteen years that my family lived in our yellow brick house bordering The Park, I don't recall anyone who stirred up serious "stranger anxiety." As a young girl, I felt safe in our community, but I think part of the reason I harbored a false sense of security was due to my fearless younger brother, Skeeter. Because of him, the tough guys in the neighborhood never bothered my siblings and me.

As my brother matured, he developed a reputation as a kid not to be messed with. He had a great throwing arm, which made him an excellent Little League shortstop and football quarterback. This skill also meant he could land a good punch and throw a rock with unerring accuracy. Skeeter may have seemed like a bully to some, but I was never afraid of my brother.

As the only adoptees in our growing family, Skeeter, Jenny, and I had an unspoken understanding. The three of us were members of the same tribe: kids adopted through Catholic Charities in Chicago. None of us had any clue about our respective families of origin, but by a stroke of luck or due to spiritual guidance, we became siblings. That common experience bonded us as tightly as blood kin, maybe tighter. If I ever did tattle on Skeeter, it was not very often, and only to protect him from injury or harm. In turn, I knew that he had my back whenever trouble popped up in our neighborhood or beyond.

At some point in my younger years, I might have worried about the dark or unknown, but as I matured, the dusk's advancing gloom wasn't the reason my siblings and I rushed home each evening when the streetlights came on. It was my mother's temper. All of us feared the angry, punishing side of my mother's personality, because when it came out, she became someone else. A stranger.

Sauntering home after dusk, mouthing off, or not finishing every crumb Mom put on our plates might mean we'd be sent to our room or given an extra set of chores. Those punishments were not so bad, but if she was already in a foul mood due to the challenges of the day—and if we had already gotten caught disobeying—we were marked. We knew that soon we would be on the receiving end of a loud, vicious verbal dressing down. And maybe a face slap, an earlobe tug, a body shove, or a hair yank. When Mom lost it, she didn't just scold. She grabbed and slapped until everyone within range was a shivering, howling, sobbing mess.

Sometimes, none of us kids knew what we had done to set Mom off, or who would bear the price of the demons unleashed. And it seemed that whenever Dad was around, there were fewer ugly scenes, and more peace. Dad had a knack of diffusing my mother's negative energy. He knew when to head it off, and how to steer Mom away from a blowout.

He did this just by saying, "Now, Jeanne. Do you think all that yelling is necessary? Let me take 'em up to their room and give 'em a talking-to."

It was usually Skeeter who triggered my mother's fury. He was, as Grandma Mimi often said, "a real dickens." When Mom took him to the pediatrician because of his frenetic energy, the doctor labeled him "just another busy boy." Back then, I thought Skeeter addled Mom on purpose, to get her to give in, because on occasion that worked. At times, I believe my brother pestered, poked, and mouthed off simply to see how far he could get before Mom blew. It occurs to me now that perhaps his age and undiagnosed ADHD were the reasons he didn't think through the consequences of his behavior.

Witnessing my siblings on the receiving end of my mom's often senseless temper was not just about being scared; it was humiliating and demoralizing. It also troubled and confused us. One minute Mom was this loving, compassionate parent, and the next second, she was a demon to be reckoned with. Knowing what I do now about how hormones influence emotions, I believe PMS (premenstrual syndrome) played a significant role in my mother's irrational outbursts.

I was six when Mom was brushing my hair one morning in the bathroom off the den where we watched television on Sunday evenings together. I suppose we were hurrying off to be somewhere, like school or an appointment. My mother towered over me, and her breath came out in short puffs as it did when she searched for the car keys. She grabbed the comb from the counter and parted my hair on the left side just as I liked it. And then she ran the hairbrush under the faucet so that the fly-a-ways would cooperate with the pigtails she intended. On the counter lay my favorite set of hair ties: elastic bands with plastic knobs at each end, which twisted around and snapped into place through a loop.

When I noticed one of the hair ties was skating toward the edge of the countertop, I lunged for it, hoping to catch it before it disappeared to the linoleum tile. I jerked forward, and Mom yanked my head back so hard I felt as if I'd been scalped like one of the American pioneers on *Bonanza*, my favorite Western. I let loose a piercing scream, and she whacked my scalp with the bristled brush. As my hands flew up to protect my head from another pelting, I knocked the brush from her hand.

My freckled cheeks now exposed, Mom slapped both and launched into a verbal assault that began with, "You kids are so ungrateful . . ." This reproach stunned and hurt like a punch to the gut. Mom had spent a lot of time coaching us on appropriate behavior and good manners—like when to say "please" and "thank you"—so I didn't think my siblings and I appeared ungrateful to her. My mom's angry admission felt like an additional slap. But as quickly as she snapped, she came out of it, apologizing profusely. But the damage had been done.

Over time, I developed a coping strategy to deal with the nasty side of my mother's personality. I detached. When it was my turn to receive a scolding, I willed the tears to stay in. It was pride, I suppose, that caused me to refuse to let her see how much her actions hurt me.

Besides detachment, I had another secret weapon: Jenny. My biological sister has always been my backstop, my safe haven. She was the person I bonded with long before we became our mother's daughters; I have relied on her since the moment of our conception. Knowing Jenny felt as I did about our mother's dark side provided great comfort to me. Without that support, my mother's behavior might have affected me more than it did. Even now, I don't think Mom ever understood the power of our twindom. We were a united front. Our belonging to one another is a superpower. It has fueled us through much adversity, and we have never taken it for granted.

Corporal punishment like spanking, slapping, and shoving was commonplace in households during the 1960s and '70s. It was how many people parented during that era to get their points across and establish order in the home. Time-outs and "using words" to reasonably point out wrongful behavior in children didn't come into vogue until I parented my own kids in the 1980s. My mother's frequent bouts of slapping and screaming didn't sit well with me, and I vowed to never treat any of my children like that. I would be a different mother than the one who raised me. Calmer, gentler, and reasonable.

Because of angry episodes like the one with the hairbrush, I developed an inner voice, which I would later call my "wronged-adoptee voice." At first the voice only whispered in my head. When I matured and developed a rich fantasy life about my first family, the voice spoke louder, saying things like, *Your other mommy, your real mom, wouldn't do something like this. She would never hit you or scream at you like this.*

As I came to pay more attention to it, the voice became indignant, protective, claiming that, *Someday, your real mommy will come back for you. And when that day comes, things will be so much better, perfect even.* I would lie in bed at night imagining who my birth parents were, what they might be doing, and when they might come back for Jenny and me. Each time I heard the voice's mantra, the more I believed the truth in its words: *Your real mother wouldn't treat you like this.*

The more my adoptive mother scolded and slapped, and the further I withdrew from her, I placed my phantom mother, my birth mother, the mother I knew nothing about, high on a pedestal. I started to believe *that* mother could do no wrong. I convinced myself that when *that* mother lifted a hairbrush, she would brush my hair gently and compliment me on how shiny it was, what a lovely shade of light brown. I believed that my other mother wouldn't dish out so many chores, require that I finish all the peas on my plate, or lose her temper so rashly.

Still, another part of me knew that I was fooling myself, pretending, and suppressing. The reasonable side of my brain informed me: Our *other* mother had done the unspeakable. She had given two babies away to strangers to raise in her place. At the time, I didn't think about this failing, this disturbing truth, and wouldn't consider or dwell on it for many years to come.

My fear of my mother's temper taught me something else. It confirmed in me the need to be better to avoid punishment. Because if I were more perfect, then I wouldn't deserve any reprimands. I would only earn my folks' favor and respect. And, if I worked hard every day, I could achieve the goal I visualized before falling asleep at night: the dream of being perfect enough to be wanted.

8

The Talk

Winter 1967

"Are you two enjoying your birthday?" Grandma Mimi asked Jenny and me.

"Yes, Grandma," I said. "And it's not over yet!"

Jenny and I giggled as we pointed to two stacks of wrapped presents at the end of the long buffet behind my grandmother's dining room chair.

"Run to the hallway, pet, and get my pocketbook," Grandma said to Jenny.

My sister did what my grandmother asked, and I watched starry-eyed as Grandma Mimi reached into her purse and pulled out two white envelopes. I understood what they held: a check, which meant that on Saturday morning our dad would take us to the bank to deposit the money into our savings accounts.

Next to me, Dad got up from his chair at the head of the table and freshened Grandma's Manhattan cocktail. I watched, amazed, as the cherry sunk to the bottom.

When he returned to his seat, Dad said, "Girls! Help your mother clear the rest of the table, please."

In the kitchen, Mom was at the sink, where she hand-washed the "good china" dinner plates and set them neatly on a drying rack.

The full-length apron she wore camouflaged her navy slacks and starched white blouse. My mother's tummy was flat again. When Jenny and I began second grade the previous fall, my mother had suffered another miscarriage, her first pregnancy since Patrick was born nearly three years before.

Patrick had been my parents' first biological child, and while I suppose his arrival was a huge milestone for my folks, I don't recall them making a fuss over it. Given my mother's history with failed pregnancies, I imagine they were relieved all went well and that their little family was growing. Another boy meant they had achieved the perfect balance of two boys and two girls. As I think about this now, I marvel at my mom's energy, mothering and caring for four busy children under the age of eight.

Mom's recent miscarriage had made an impression on Jenny and me. In retrospect, I don't suppose my siblings and I would have known about it at all if Mom's doctor hadn't ordered bedrest. Because of this, Dad hired Mrs. Seitz, a widow they knew from church, to keep the house running until Mom was back on her feet. Those were some scary few days as we watched my mother recuperate in the double bed she shared with Dad. None of us were used to seeing her face look so pale or her feet propped up on pillows instead of charging around the house. If she were ever to become pregnant again, I hoped nothing would go wrong. It was hard on all of us when my mother was sick or out of sorts.

By year's end, I'd get my wish. On December 30, my mother would deliver a healthy baby girl. My parents would name her Elizabeth Anne, a version of Grandma Mimi's first name, Elsie. We would call her Lizzie for short.

As Mom turned away from the sink, dish suds slid down her forearms, turning the rolled-up cuffs of her pretty white blouse a pale gray.

"Girls, we're almost ready for cake. Is the dining room table all cleared?"

Jenny and I both nodded. "Yes, Mom."

Mom dropped the intense look she had worn throughout our special dinner and gave me one of her prettiest smiles. I felt my whole body relax. It was our birthday—Jen's and my special day—and I wanted it to go off without a hitch. If my mom was enjoying herself and managing the stress of taking care of the four of us kids, then everyone in our household was happy, too.

So far, so good.

"Back to the table with you, birthday girls!" Mom said.

Jenny and I shared wicked grins with one another. We knew what came next. Within minutes, Mom emerged through the dining room's big swinging door. She set a large cake with white icing from Kirschbaum's Bakery in front of us. The cake top read: HAPPY 8TH BIRTHDAY JENNY & JULIE. Because our birthday fell just three days before Valentine's Day, little pink hearts decorated the edge. Dad whipped out a cigarette lighter from his trouser pocket and lit the candles, and then in a beautiful soprano, Mom led my dad, Grandma Mimi, Skeeter, and Patrick in singing "Happy Birthday."

"Make a wish and blow out the candles. On the count of three. One, two . . ." Mom said.

I leaned over the luscious cake and peeked at Jenny to see if she was ready. Her big white front teeth gleamed back at me. Our birthday. My wish was simple. Jenny and I had both asked for new ice skates and a set of big fat yarn pom-poms to tie on the laces. While Mom cut the cake into even slices, I glanced over my shoulder through the large dining room window toward The Park, our favorite place on earth. The ice rink was lit for evening skate time. Even though it was a school night, I hoped our parents would let us try out our new ice skates once dinner was over. That privilege would cap off a perfect birthday.

I poked Jenny's thigh. She nudged me back with such vigor that her ponytail swished from side to side. Mom had utilized the same white grosgrain ribbon she used on my braids to tie a neat floppy bow at Jen's crown. She had also purchased the same pullover for us to wear for our birthday dinner. Jenny got the purple one, and I took the pink one. Mom knew we hated dressing alike. Switching up the color of our matching outfits was something we were slowly getting tired of, too.

"Okay, time to open your gifts, girls," Mom said.

"I think I know what's in the big box!" I grinned joyously at Mom and Dad.

Jenny and I stared at one another. "Ready, set, open," we shouted, ripping the wrapping paper off the boxes to expose shiny white figure skates.

After leaping up and hugging our parents and grandmother, we returned to our seats to admire our gifts. The room grew as quiet as if it was a Sunday Mass.

"Jack, are you alright?" Mom asked.

Gone were Dad's dimples. Instead, tears collected in the corners of his blue eyes.

Jen poked me again, but I refused to look at her. Dad stared at us, studying us in a familiar loving way. I had an inkling about what he might say next.

"The day we picked up you girls at St. Vincent's was one of the happiest days of our lives," he said. "Wasn't it, Jeanne?"

Across the dining room table, Mom and Dad shared a knowing look. I stayed rooted in my chair, my face flushing. I didn't dare glance at Jenny.

I hope they're not going to repeat our adoption story. Going into it again, on our birthday, will spoil the evening for me.

Something about the adoption conversation always embarrassed me. Maybe it was because my folks got all schmaltzy and emotional as they relived the call from the Catholic Charities social worker. Every time it was retold, I was left feeling confused and exhausted. I couldn't understand why if they were so happy, I felt like curling up in a ball and taking a nap.

Dad took a sip from his tumbler of Scotch. "Girls, take your gifts up to your room. When Mom is done in the kitchen, we'd like to talk to you in the living room."

Uh-oh!

I looked over at Dad to see what expression his face held. I couldn't read his eyes because his head rested against the chair back. He inhaled the cigarette and blew a smoke ring up to the ceiling, and then he did another one and another. Jenny and I giggled. Whatever it was that our parents wanted to discuss, I hoped it wasn't something that would disrupt our lives, like switching schools or moving away from our friends and The Park. Any of those things would not just ruin our birthday, they would wreck our lives.

As Jenny and I galloped up the front staircase to put our presents in our room, Gigi, our white poodle puppy, followed. I scooped her up and scratched her behind the ears. Jen and I sat cross-legged on the fluffy green shag carpet for a few minutes, admired our gifts, and chatted about all the special things that had happened on our eighth birthday. Recapping our day was something Jenny and I always did before falling asleep each night. We lingered. Neither of us was in any hurry to join our parents in the living room, a place that was usually off-limits. It was where breakable glassware lived in locked cabinets and the spot where grown-ups gathered for cocktails before one of my mother's dinner parties.

Jenny sighed. "I guess we'd better see what they want to talk about."

I followed my twin down the stairs, and we paused at the wide entrance to the living room. I sidled up close to her. Dad had taken his cigarette and ashtray with him from the dining room and made himself comfy in one of the overstuffed armchairs by the fireplace. In his right hand, he swirled a fresh tumbler of Scotch whiskey.

"Come in, girls!" Dad's expression was serious and thoughtful.

He gestured to the cream damask sofa with its perfectly placed velvet pillows. Jenny took the end with the rust-colored pillows, so I plopped down in the middle near her. When Mom appeared in the doorway, she gave my dad a quick nod. He leaned over the coffee table and stubbed out his cigarette in the ashtray. Mom untied her apron and sat down in the matching armchair across from my dad.

Beside me, Jenny pulled the white ribbon from her ponytail and retied it. My eyes glued onto my mother as I balled my hands and hid them in my lap. My mother's face had that tight look it got when she handed over the last dollar in her wallet to the A&P clerk.

Mom nodded at my father. "Please begin, dear."

I scooted in tight to my sister. Our thighs nearly touched, and I heard her breath coming in quiet puffs. Being close to Jenny made the flip-flopping in my belly settle down. I lowered my head, hiding my disappointment. It didn't seem as if Jenny and I would have time to try out our new skates.

Dad uncrossed his legs and swiveled toward Jenny and me.

"Your mother and I wanted to have a little talk with you. It seems fitting since it's your birthday. Remember our other talks about the two of you being adopted?"

Jenny and I glanced at one another and then back at our parents. Out of the corner of my eye, I saw Jenny nod, so I did the same. I swallowed hard and wished I could dart into the dining room and finish the glass of milk I'd left on the table.

Why did our special day have to end like this?

"You know we love you both very much, right?" Dad said.

We nodded again.

"That we desperately wanted you to be our girls?"

I jumped on this. "Yes, Dad. We know all that."

I had answered so fast that I worried my voice showed how annoyed I felt inside. Dad's sentiment was one we heard often enough on special occasions, particularly after our folks had enjoyed their evening cocktails.

"We love you, too," Jenny said, picking at the cording on the edge of the cream sofa.

Can't we be done with this already?

Dad's smile vanished. He glanced at Mom and continued. "If someday . . . you decide you want to look into your adoption, we'll help you."

With that said, the tears that had appeared on Dad's face at the dining room table made a comeback.

"Are you girls happy?" Mom asked.

Suddenly, it felt as if there was no more air in the room. I wanted to roll my eyes at Jenny, prod her, and run back up to our room. I didn't dare. Instead, I just sat there, gaping at my mother.

When my mom asked that strange question, her head tilted to one side. She watched Jen and me. Her manner made me wonder for a second if she was a mind reader. Sometimes when Jenny and I lay in bed at night whispering to one another, we invented stories about our birth parents. About what they looked like, where they lived, what they might be doing, and why they had chosen adoption for us.

Had Mom been eavesdropping on us? Is that what this was about?

Thank God Jenny answered my mother's question for both of us.

"Yep. We're happy. And we don't need to look into the adoption stuff."

Jenny's answer brought instant smiles to my parents' faces. Relief washed over me. I liked making my parents happy. Besides, they didn't need to know what Jenny and I talked about in our room. That was between us. Private stuff, like what I wrote in my journal.

The look Dad gave Mom seemed to say, *I told you so.*

Jenny's words pleased me, too. She'd spoken for both of us. I hoped we were done with this icky conversation once and for all. I just wanted to get up to our room, lace up my new skates with the cool pom-poms, and get them ready for tomorrow so we might skate at The Park after school.

Dad blew us each a kiss and picked up his Scotch. "Okay, that's all we wanted to talk about."

"Can we go back up to our room now?" I asked.

Mom nodded, her smile warm and friendly as it had been when she led our family in the "Happy Birthday" song.

"We'll be up later on to say good night," she said.

Jenny and I stood, grinned shyly at one another, and raced upstairs where we snickered over how awful the talk with our parents had been. Discussing our adoption was not what either one of us envisioned for our birthday.

As an eight-year-old, the notion of poking around into my closed adoption seemed dreadfully complicated. Even though I was curious, I feared disappointing and alienating my adoptive parents. Jenny, Skeeter, and I didn't know anyone else who was adopted, much less anyone who had launched an adoption search. In retrospect, I wish there had been someone to talk to about the conflicting emotions I often felt as an adoptee. On one hand there was the loyalty and love I felt toward my adoptive family, and on the other hand, there was my curiosity about our adoption circumstances and a bewilderment as to how adoption had happened to us. It would be years before I explored adoption literature, where I discovered that the ideas Jenny and I shared in our room at night were not unique. Fantasies surrounding birth family members, feelings of curiosity, and righteous adoption anger were commonalities shared by many adoptees.

As far as the fantasy I indulged in every now and then about our birth parents coming back to look for Jenny and me? While I wasn't pining for this to transpire, I resolved that I would be curious to meet them if they showed up. If they didn't make the effort though, I convinced myself I wouldn't lose sleep over it. My parents made me feel loved and wanted, but the real contentment I felt was due to the special bond I shared with my twin sister. Jenny and I relied on one another and took great comfort in our likeness, shared mindset, and similar interests. And as our parents continued adding to our family with their own biological children, I realized the privilege I had been given. Despite being placed for adoption, I was growing up with a full biological sibling.

9

Sleepover

Winter 1969

On a frigid and overcast January afternoon, Jenny and I trudged in through the back door from a full afternoon of ice skating at The Park with our neighborhood friends Erica, Lisa, and Kathy. The five of us had been outside since lunchtime practicing our twirls, jumps, and skating backward. When I made sharp turns, it thrilled me hearing my blades grind and see ice shavings spray up into the frosty air. If it hadn't been for fatigue and our near-frozen fingers and toes, we'd have remained out there perfecting old tricks and trying new ones.

As we flicked off our gloves and untied our snow-encrusted skates, Mom called out to us from the front of the house.

"Girls, after you hang up your things, c'mon in here. I need your help."

We hollered back. "Okay, Mom."

We found our mother in the living room crouched on all fours, stuffing Christmas ornaments and tree trimmings into carefully labeled cartons. Even with the chic black headband tamping her dark hair away from her forehead and cheeks, her hair was a mess. So were the living room's rust-colored carpet and the faux-brick linoleum leading up to the front door. Threads of silver tinsel, fluffs of white flocking, and dried needles from the Douglas fir our family had selected from the A&P grocery store tree lot were everywhere. Before Dad left for work that morning, he'd lugged the withered Christmas tree to the curb, leaving a trail of debris in his wake.

"Give me a hand here, girls," Mom said. "Lizzie is down for a nap, and I want to get these decorations into the storage room before she gets up. I'll make you a hot chocolate when we're done."

My fingers and toes were still so numb from the hours outside that I struggled to hold the box my mother handed me. By the second trip to the basement, my fingertips had started thawing, but as they warmed it felt as if pins and needles pricked my skin. All I wanted to do was run my hands under warm water or wrap them around a cup of hot cocoa, but Mom was like a sergeant major commanding a small army of two.

"I can't wait till the boys are old enough to help with this kind of stuff," Jenny grumbled under her breath.

I rolled my eyes and nodded. At four and seven years old, Patrick and Skeeter were forever screwing around, shouting and bickering, making simple things harder than they needed to be. Because of that, Mom preferred our help to that of our younger brothers, but I wished that the lion's share of helping our folks didn't fall on Jenny and me. Sometimes, all I craved was more quiet time in my room with my library books and journal. As much as I loved having Jenny as a built-in best friend, I dreamed of having my own room, but that would mean moving from the house across from The Park to a bigger home, something I knew my parents couldn't afford. My dad had just started a new job selling business forms to accountants and small businesses. Money was tight.

I sighed. It was just as well. The larger homes in La Grange didn't border Waiola Park like our cozy, yellow-brick Dutch Colonial. Leaving our beloved elm-lined, block-length park with its large playground, multiple baseball diamonds, bike paths, and basketball court was something none of us Ryan kids wanted. It would be like losing a limb.

Jenny fetched the broom and dustpan, and I dragged the Hoover upright from the basement. By the time the two of us finished tidying up the living room and foyer, one-year-old Lizzie was up from her afternoon nap. Mom put Lizzie in her highchair, sprinkled Cheerios on the tray, then set steaming mugs of hot chocolate on the kitchen table for Jenny and me.

"Do you want marshmallows, too?" she asked us.

"Yes, please!" we said in unison.

Mom handed us the bag of mini marshmallows as she sat down at the table. "Some people have a birthday coming up!" Her grin was wide, the way it got when Dad rattled off one of his corny jokes. "I can't believe you girls will be ten next month! Where has the time gone?"

Besides having a family dinner in the dining room as we did every year, Mom asked if we wanted to invite friends over for an in-home birthday party. She suggested an ice-skating party at The Park or an afternoon of games and arts and crafts. Jenny grinned at me, and I winked back.

Jen peered across her mug of hot cocoa at our mother. "How about a sleepover party!"

I held my breath and watched Mom's sculpted eyebrows arch. She dropped another handful of cereal on my sister's tray. Lizzie squealed, shaking her strawberry-blond curls with delight. It confounded everyone that blue-eyed Lizzie looked more like Skeeter than her red-headed biological brother, Patrick.

Mom turned and looked at Jenny and me. I set down my mug and matched my mother's serious expression.

"Mom, we're way too old for 'pin the tail on the donkey' and musical chairs with prizes for the winners. That's for the younger kids. Not us."

Beside me, Jenny's greenish-brown eyes gleamed.

Bolstered by my twin's support, I continued. "If we had a sleepover, like on a Friday night, we could use the Ouija board I got for Christmas. Jenny's Twister game, too."

Jenny chimed in. "Pizza and popcorn and watching a scary movie downstairs in the rec room. That's what we'd like for our tenth birthday party."

I leaned over the tabletop toward my mother. "We'd be quiet. No way you'd hear us on the second floor. I swear."

Mom sat back in her chair and crossed her arms over her chest. "You can do most of those things in a few hours on a Sunday afternoon, too."

Jenny wrinkled her nose. "That doesn't sound as much fun as a sleepover."

"Mom, we don't have to invite a lot of kids. Maybe one or two friends each." My eyes pleaded with my mother.

"Yeah, and everyone can bring a sleeping bag and a pillow. It'll be easy. We promise we won't stay up late. Please, please, please," Jenny whined.

"I'll have to talk to your father," Mom said.

In hindsight, I wish my mother would have said, "Let's wait until next year. When you two are a year older."

If she had been that decisive, perhaps I'd have been better prepared for the uncomfortable situation that unfolded.

After a week of badgering and bargaining, our parents agreed to let us host three friends for a sleepover party. We picked the Friday night that followed our birthday: February 14. Jenny invited Lisa, the studious, thin girl with glasses from her fifth-grade class at St. Cletus. I asked Lucy, the dark-haired new girl in my class. Mom insisted we include Erica, the third grader with a pixie haircut who lived next door. She said it was the right thing to do, since we spent a lot of time at Erica's house. Jenny groaned about this, but I didn't care. Erica was shy and awkward, but she was also sweet and thoughtful. She almost always went along with the crazy schemes my twin and I dreamed up when we grew bored with conventional toys and games.

Like most years, our birthday party food and decorations were Valentine's Day themed. This time Mom baked chocolate cupcakes, decorating them with vanilla icing and pink and red sprinkles. In the basement rec room, Jenny and I strung pink crepe paper streamers and taped up red paper hearts on the walls and cabinets. We loaded the Formica countertop with our favorite drinks: Coca-Cola, Hires root beer, and Orange Crush. Mom supplied a big wooden bowl, which we loaded with sweets selected from the penny candy store in town. Turkish Taffy, Red Hots, Chuckles, Lemonheads, nonpareils, candy cigarettes, and licorice whips all made the cut. As excited as Jenny and I were and as hard as we worked to get everything just right, I would soon regret pooh-poohing Mom's idea of a simple afternoon celebration.

When Lisa, Erica, and Lucy rang the front doorbell, Jenny and I hurried them downstairs away from the chaos of our family. For the first hour, the five of us giggled through sessions on the Ouija board, posing simple questions like "Will I be famous when I grow up?" "Will I marry the man of my dreams?" "Will I get to travel the world?" After several rounds of silly tangling in the game of Twister, Jenny switched on the black-and-white TV mounted in the rec room cabinetry. We found a Vincent Price horror flick that wasn't too scary.

At 10:30 p.m. sharp, Mom appeared in the rec room doorway. "Time to close the party down. Lights-out, girls!" she ordered.

One look at my mother's face informed Jenny and me that we didn't dare argue for more time. Mom's dark eyes were piercing. I knew from experience that a stern warning like "Don't make me regret letting you have a sleepover" was only one breath away.

I swallowed my disappointment. "Okay, Mom."

Hands on her hips, my mother hovered in the room, watching as we spread out our sleeping bags. "I've left the hall light on upstairs, so you can find the bathroom if you need it. Good night, girls."

"Good night, Mrs. Ryan. Thanks for having us!"

Something about our easy obedience or our friends' good manners softened my mother's no-nonsense attitude. She wove through our makeshift beds and planted a kiss on both Jenny's forehead and mine.

"Happy birthday. I hope you had a good party," she whispered.

After Mom dimmed the lights, I zipped myself into my sleeping bag, squirming to find a comfortable position on the shag rug. Across the room Jenny whispered with Lisa in the dark. Lisa had taken off her glasses, which made her look smaller than she really was. She and Jenny were too far off for the rest of us to join their conversation. I figured they were talking about our latest Camp Fire Girls project, since we met at Lisa's house after school once a week to do crafts and service projects. Lisa's mom was our group leader, and she was always pestering Mom to become her co-leader. Erica yawned and waved shyly at me from several feet away. Her head found the pillow, and she turned away from Lucy and me.

Lucy moved her sleeping bag inches from mine, pulled out the rubber band in her ponytail, and shook out her long brown hair. Because my friend had joined our class late in the fall, she had a lot of questions about the kids in our fifth-grade class. I explained the in-group of boys and girls. Lucy and I chatted about how these kids barely spoke to the rest of us, a dynamic that would shift in a year or two once puberty set in. When a pause settled between us, I shifted to one side, nestling deeper into my soft pillow.

Beside me, Lucy was still. I figured she'd drifted off. Her dark brown eyes glistened in the dark.

"You and Jenny are adopted, right?" she whispered.

For a moment, my breath caught and held, suspended in time with Lucy's stunning question. Within seconds, my sleeping bag became an oven. My mind ordered me to yank down the sleeping bag's zipper and provide relief to my sweaty torso and flaming cheeks, but my fingers refused. Instead, I lay still, hot with shock and embarrassment. I debated whether to feign sleep or respond to my friend.

I abhorred Lucy's question. It was more than an unbidden intrusion into my privacy. It was a slap, a wake-up call, and a reminder. At ten, I was no longer a child, an innocent who lacked the mental constructs to consider how adoption affected my sense of self and belonging. Compartmentalizing my adoption and the internal confusion it wreaked was no longer a luxury I could indulge.

Up until this moment, I had yet to widen the adoption conversation outside the inner circle of my folks, my Grandma Mimi, and a few aunts or uncles. Until this sleepover party, no friend of mine had ever broached the subject. In my naivete, I had supposed that my friends were oblivious and didn't know that Jenny, Skeeter, and I were adopted. But on this night, I got a reality check. Lucy's question meant my classmates, friends, their respective parents, and probably my teachers were aware that Jenny and I were not our parents' biological kin. Lucy's query also suggested that the community had gossiped about my family's dynamics. The realization made me feel sick to my stomach.

I squeezed my eyes shut and whispered to Lucy, "Yeah. We're adopted."

I rolled over onto my other side, facing away from Lucy, hoping she got the hint that the conversation was over, but Lucy scooted closer. I could feel her hot breath on my neck. I cringed, thinking about what she might ask next.

"So, what happened to your *real* parents?"

"I dunno," I mumbled. "I'm tired. Good night, Lucy."

As I lay there going over the uncomfortable questions in my mind, a few tears trickled down my freckled cheek, dampening the pillowcase. Lucy's question may have soured my party, but it served a purpose. I vowed to be better prepared for the next time it happened. I couldn't wait to tell Jenny. Together, we developed a well-rehearsed response to rattle off.

"Yeah, we're adopted. We've always known about it. And we don't know any details. Our mom and dad are our *real* parents."

After our canned spiel was delivered, we learned to change the subject right away.

As I look back on the many uncomfortable adoption conversations I've had over the years, I believe the reason they have stuck with me is because of unrecognized shame. My closed adoption was outside my control, but I was embarrassed to have no information about my background, my birth parents, or why I'd been placed for adoption. I wasn't uncomfortable about belonging to the Ryan family. I loved my parents and siblings, but I hadn't started off life with the Ryans. I had belonged somewhere else, to someone else, and those people had chosen not to keep my sister and me. Admitting to myself that perhaps we had been unwanted was one thing, but discussing something so deeply personal and humiliating in public was another thing entirely. At ten years old, I lacked the skills to do so.

As a budding preteen, I was more concerned about fitting in and being accepted by my peers than I was in discussing how I was different. That night, my friend Lucy's innocent curiosity had shone a spotlight on what I deemed a shortcoming, one that placed Jenny and me outside what was considered "normal." If during our sleepover Lucy had asked, "What is it like to be a twin?" I would have had a different reaction, because for me my twindom was positive. I loved my sister. Since I understood what being a twin entailed, I could have spelled that out for Lucy with a smile on my face.

Because the facts of my adoption were a mystery, I viewed it as a secret, a stigma. Just like Jenny and I did on the frozen pond across the street from our home, all I wanted was to keep up with my friends and excel at our shared interests, whether it was ice skating, cheerleading, theatre, or school. In my mind, if I was good enough, if I was perfect, maybe other people wouldn't judge me for being adopted. Maybe I wouldn't judge myself either.

10

April Fool

Spring 1970

In late March, the week before my brother Mark Edward was born, the seven of us—Mom, Dad, Jenny, me, Skeeter, Pat, and Lizzie—gathered in the kitchen around the oval table as we always did for supper. As soon as we finished saying grace together, Mom sliced into her homemade meatloaf, placed the first piece on Dad's plate, and then began serving the rest of us.

"Jack, make sure the kids get a good serving of carrots," Mom said. "Skeeter, pass the biscuits and butter around to your brothers and sisters."

As my mom stood at my father's end of the table, plating up the hefty portions the five of us kids were expected to finish, she informed Dad about the events of the day. Six-year-old Patrick, who inherited Dad's quick wit, made Mom laugh in the middle of her scolding him about forgetting his lunch again. Skeeter fought with his third-grade classmate Chuckie during lunch recess, and they had to clap erasers together after school. Lizzie, not quite two and a half, mastered the alphabet puzzle. Jenny and I received our wood fairy parts in the La Grange Children's Theatre spring production of *Hansel and Gretel*.

After all that, Mom drew in a deep breath. "Ginger called this morning. To see how I'm feeling. If we're up for it, she and Dick would like to have dinner Friday night."

Jenny lifted her napkin to cover her mouth as she whispered to me, "Guess we're babysitting tomorrow. Again."

I rewarded my twin with an eye roll. At eleven years old, she and I were getting tired of being our parents' go-to babysitters. Believe me, it took two of us to handle getting our siblings, aged nine, six, and two, to bed without issues. Most of the time, Jenny and I had to pretend we had our folks on the telephone to get the boys to obey us. Hassling with my younger siblings had convinced me I didn't want kids when I grew up.

Across the table from us, Dad's eyes smiled at my mother. "If you want to, hon. Dinner out sounds good."

Mom nodded at him. She picked up the last dinner plate, filled it with what was left in the serving dishes, and then walked to her end of the table. She hesitated before sitting down.

"What is it?" Dad asked, his craggy eyebrows knitting together.

My mother's free hand caressed her enormous belly, stopping only to smooth out the wrinkled band of the support hose she wore to control the varicose veins that had plagued her during this, her third full-term pregnancy.

"Probably nothing," she sighed. "But . . . I thought I heard a strange noise this afternoon." She pointed to her belly.

My eyes shot up from the carrots I was shoving around my plate. I nudged Jenny under the table.

Did this mean something was wrong with the new baby?

Mom's statement made me feel slightly guilty about all the whining Jenny and I had done about babysitting. I sat up straight in the hard pine chair and tuned in to my folks' conversation. My brothers were oblivious. They continued bantering with one another about their new Little League teams.

Dad set his fork down on his plate. "What kind of sound?" he asked, fingering the clump of religious medals around his neck.

Mom's eyes drifted, landing on the pots and pans soaking in the sink.

"Sort of like . . . one of the kids snapping a wad of bubblegum."

Dad's big belly pressed into the edge of the table. "Good Lord, what do you think that means?"

Mom swiped at a tiny bead of sweat trickling into the brunette pin curls covering her ears. She held Dad's look with those saucer-like brown eyes of hers—the ones that one minute glared, freezing you dead in your tracks, and the next minute swallowed you up with sympathy and love. When she finally spoke, her voice was deep and hoarse, the way it got after hollering at one of us kids.

"I don't know, Jack, whether it's anything to worry about at all, really. I'll mention it at my doctor's appointment tomorrow."

Dad gave my mother a brief expression of shock and worry, and then he did what he always did. He diffused the heavy moment with his own brand of humor and optimism.

"The baby's been kicking like an Olympic swimmer. I'm sure it's nothing."

Mom studied the food on her plate. "I hope you're right, dear," she said.

Jenny's eyes were wide as she handed me the vegetables to pass to Mom. "Oh, boy!" she whispered.

And that was it—the end of the conversation. Mom cut Lizzie's meatloaf into small bites. Skeeter argued with Patrick about which one of them had the better knuckleball pitch, and Dad nabbed the last biscuit, smothering it with butter and strawberry jelly. Through-out this predictable dinner mayhem, I snuck peeks at my parents.

I didn't know what to think of my mother's quiet announce-ment or my parents' reactions. They seemed concerned, but my mother had brought up the subject over family dinner. Normally when my folks had something serious to talk about, they sauntered into the living room with their cocktails and chatted so softly we kids couldn't hear a word.

To be honest, I really didn't want to think about pregnancy, babies, or childbirth at all. I was still reeling from the "birds and bees" talk my mother had given Jenny and me a few months before when we turned eleven. The whole subject of where babies came from, how they got there, and why women had to wear bulky, cumbersome pads once a month had traumatized me. Jenny and I found the whole subject gross. So even though I was interested in what was going on with Mom and the new baby, I adopted my father's approach. I shrugged away my mother's concern with a nervous giggle and inwardly deemed her a worrywart.

As it turned out, we were all wrong.

Mom was not an anxious, overreacting expecting mother. She had experienced enough problematic pregnancies to know something unusual was going on with this one. When Jenny, Skeeter, Patrick, and I came home from school the following afternoon, Mom didn't greet us at the door with the typical "How was your day?"

Instead, she gave us a nonchalant wave from the family room carpet, where she sat cuddling and reading books with Lizzie. It was as if we'd just popped in for a forgotten lunch rather than having been absent for an entire school day.

"Mom's being weird," Jenny said as we hung up our jackets.

Neither of us thought to ask about her doctor's appointment, and she didn't volunteer any details. Instead, she issued an order.

"Girls, help your brothers with a snack. I made chocolate pudding. It's in the fridge."

As soon as she heard the garage door go up at five o'clock, Mom rushed out of the kitchen where Jenny and I sat practicing our vocabulary words. I watched as she waited for my dad in the family room near the entrance to the garage. When he opened the door, Jenny and I heard them whisper. We could not make out any of what Mom said, but Dad's booming response was unmistakable.

"No heartbeat? Is the doctor certain?"

For the next five days, the tension in our household was as thick as overcooked oatmeal. My mom reported to her doctor's office every day. The obstetrics team couldn't find a heartbeat, and Mom admitted, "I can't feel the baby move anymore."

The doctors apprised my parents that if my mother didn't go into labor and deliver the baby on her own, she might need "a special procedure."

My family reacted the way we always did in tough moments. We prayed.

When Dad led us in the mealtime blessing, he began, "Bless us, our Lord, and these thy gifts," but before he got to the "amen," he added, "and please, Lord, we also ask for a small miracle. That our new baby will be born alive and healthy." At nighttime, when our parents came in to kiss us good night and to witness our bedtime prayers, they tacked on a special intention to our God- blesses. "And God bless Mom, so her body can withstand the risks of carrying this baby, and that she will not be harmed during its birth."

On April 1, when we came home from school, Mrs. Seitz, the babysitter who had stayed with us during mom's miscarriage, stood in our kitchen wearing Mom's apron, spreading chocolate icing on a pan of warm brownies. Mrs. Seitz greeted Skeeter, Jenny, Patrick, and me with a somber smile.

We barraged her with questions. "How's Mom? Did she have the baby? Boy or girl? Did we get our miracle? Is it alive?"

Mrs. Seitz ignored our pestering. "Your father called. He'll be home soon. Until then, how about a chocolate brownie and a nice cold glass of milk?"

Jenny and I looked at one another, hung our heads, and took a seat at the kitchen table. As I bowed my head over a warm brownie, I dropped my hands into my lap and prayed silently. *Dear Lord, I hope you granted that miracle we've all been praying for. We sure could use a break here.* And then I tightened my hands and scrunched my eyes tight, willing tears back in. *And, please, please, please. I'm begging you. Let my mother be okay. We need her! I promise I'll stop whining so much about babysitting.*

I couldn't imagine what our lives would be like without my mother. If she died because of the poison in her body from carrying a dead baby, what would my father do? Would he find another mother for us? With five kids under twelve, how easy would that be? And how could he work at his new job selling those business accounting systems while managing our care? Would Mrs. Seitz fill in? I guessed I wouldn't mind having her around to keep the house going. Even though Mom's dark moods often scared us kids, I'd miss her boosting us up when our spirits sagged, her electric laugh, and how easily she corralled the five of us into singing with her in the car.

Another notion wedged itself in among all those thoughts. Jenny and I had already lost one mother due to our adoption. My chest lifted, and I let out a sigh. I turned away from that thought as I would from a bad odor. I didn't want to think about being adopted or *that* other mother. I was too consumed with the possibility of losing *this* mother, my mom. That loss would rock my world.

Life couldn't be that unfair, could it, to lose two mothers by age twelve?

When I lifted my head from silent prayer, I studied Mrs. Seitz as she poured out cups of cold whole milk from the glass gallon jugs the milkman brought most mornings. She caught me staring and looked away. I wondered how much Mrs. Seitz knew about my mother and the baby, and why she wouldn't answer our questions.

It felt cruel to have our hearts twisted in knots as we waited for Dad to come home from the hospital. I couldn't have known it then, but this would not be the last time a trusted adult would serve as a gatekeeper withholding vital family news.

By the time we heard Dad's car pull into the garage, it felt as if hours had passed instead of minutes. The worrying had done us kids in. Lizzie played listlessly with her stuffed animals in the corner of the family room. Patrick and Skeeter lay sprawled against one another on the sofa, taking in another rerun of *Bewitched* while Jenny and I pretended to do math homework at the kitchen table.

When my father burst into the family room, his face flushed from the cool spring air, he tossed his overcoat across the arm of the sofa.

"Scoot over, boys," he said as he plopped down between my brothers, and then he patted his legs and called out to Lizzie. She climbed onto his lap, her strawberry-blond pigtails splaying out against his chest. Jenny and I dropped to the braided rug and sat cross-legged at my father's feet. Our dog Gigi scrambled over and crawled into my lap. We repeated the questions with which we'd barraged Mrs. Seitz not quite an hour ago.

Dad closed his eyes. When he opened them, his blue eyes were bloodshot, and his smile thin and forced.

"Your mother's going to be fine. She's tired. She'll need to stay in the hospital for a few more days to catch up on her rest. Mrs. Seitz will be here until then."

He gave my brothers a sharp glance as he threaded his fingers through his wavy auburn hair. "You'll cooperate for her, won't you, boys?"

They looked Dad in the eye, their faces solemn, and nodded.

"Good," Dad said, and a hint of his usual dimpled smile

emerged. "I promised your mother we'd call her after dinner. Wouldn't you like that, Lizzie?"

Dad stroked my sister's soft hair for a second, and then he forced out unwelcome news. "Kids, you have a brother, Mark Edward. The doctors were right. When he was born this afternoon, he wasn't breathing."

I stiffened as Dad choked up and pulled the boys tight against him on the sofa. His chin dropped and nuzzled the top of Lizzie's head. Seated on the floor, I moved closer to Jenny, our shoulders and arms touching. We stared at our father. None of us knew what we should say.

When my dad spoke again, his voice was thick, measured.

"Tomorrow, I'm going to pick up all of you from school. Then we're going to the funeral parlor to make some arrangements. I'd like your help."

The boys blinked up at our dad, while Jenny and I gaped at one another. None of us knew what this entailed. None of us had the nerve to ask.

"Sure, Dad," Jenny and I managed to get out.

The next day, instead of walking the eight blocks home after school like we normally did, the five of us congregated around the flagpole at St. Cletus. As we piled into the family station wagon, my brothers argued about who got to ride shotgun.

"Neither of you get it. Both of you climb into the way back," Dad shouted.

We weren't used to Dad losing his cool. So, for the three-block car ride from St. Cletus to Hallowell & James Funeral Home, none of us spoke. In the parking lot, we trailed after him like a brood of ducklings. Inside the poorly lit waiting area, we clustered around him until Mr. James emerged from the back office to shepherd our family through the process of burying a loved one. As the funeral director explained the process, Jenny and I blinked at one another. Our personal brand of Morse code telegraphed how unwelcome and shattering we found this experience to be.

When it came to choosing a casket for Mark, the brother we'd never met or held, Dad looked first at Jenny and me. I liked the white one and said so right away. Jenny agreed. Something about the purity of that stark white casket seemed appropriate for a soul that had never committed an earthly sin.

"It's decided then," Dad said to Mr. James. "The white one, please."

My father picked up Lizzie and held her, his eyes filling. "Now you kids have an angel in heaven to look out for you."

I liked how that sounded: an angel looking out for us. Much kinder than what the doctors had said: a perfectly formed full-term male child, strangled by the cord meant to give him life.

After the casket selection, we traipsed after Dad and Mr. James up to the front desk. My dad signed some paperwork and wrote out a check, and then we piled back into the dusty station wagon. But instead of heading in the direction of home, my dad surprised us and drove two blocks down Fifty-Fifth Street to the Highland Dairy Queen.

In the parking lot, Dad dug out his wallet, handing Jenny and me a five-dollar bill.

"Let the kids order whatever they want. Order me a vanilla sundae with extra hot fudge. Nuts, too. I'll be waiting here in the car."

Jenny and I smirked at one another. Dad sure loved ice cream and chocolate.

The family outing to Dairy Queen is the last thing I remember about my brother Mark Edward's death. I don't remember trooping off to the family cemetery or witnessing the small white casket being lowered into the unforgiving, hard spring ground, but I know that happened. I also don't recall whether my mother was present for the burial or missed it as she convalesced. If the typical two-day Catholic wake or funeral Mass occurred, that memory is blocked, too. But I do know this: Grandma Mimi arranged for one of the full-sized Ryan family cemetery plots to be used for Mark's internment.

Her comment over dinner one night still rings in my ears. "You know, the cemetery director said there's room enough in that plot for another small casket, should the need arise."

My mother fiddled with the gravy boat while my siblings and I stared open-mouthed at our parents and grandmother.

Dad's face was beet red. "God forbid, Mom."

My grandmother's sentiment, while seemingly insensitive, was offered in good faith. Grandma Mimi hailed from a generation that prized frugality. They found a purpose for everything. If something was broken, you didn't toss it in the trash, you fixed it. So, as I consider Grandma's comment now, I have no criticism of her. What I hate is that my grandmother's statement would someday require serious consideration.

Over the last five decades, I have often visited the Ryan family burial site and stood over my brother's grave marker, which reads MARK EDWARD RYAN, 4-1-1970. While no one ever said it, the thought must have crossed everyone's minds: April 1. What a cruel April Fool's Day joke for life and God to play on my parents and family. As I reflect upon the tragedy, I believe it may be the pivotal moment when I began questioning the tenets of my Catholic faith. How is it that a loving and forgiving God allows bad things to happen to good people?

After burying my brother, I also wondered if my parents were done adding to our family. When I lay in bed and pondered the trauma unfolding around me, I hoped for two outcomes. First, that the heartaches my parents had faced in building their American family would come to an end. I also wished they could look at the family they had assembled and say, "This is enough." Because I wanted us to be enough. Each of us could have used more of our parents' time and attention, their guidance in developing our interests, honing our identity, and discovering our sense of purpose. But because our folks' energies were spread thin, we were often left to our own devices. Some of us— Jenny and me in particular—thrived under this regime of independence, but several of my siblings hit some big speed bumps later in life.

Over the years, I have also considered my father's request for the five of us to accompany him to Hallowell & James. I don't know if it was our parents' idea to include us in the funeral arrangements, or whether it was a suggestion made by a health professional. Regardless, it provided closure, bonded us to one another in a heartbreaking way, and strengthened us as a family unit. Despite our disparate ages, each of us understood that our baby brother, Mark Edward, had been born, and that he had died. He hadn't just disappeared. Not one year has gone by without our acknowledging his birth and date of death.

A few days after my mother returned from the hospital, I came upon her in the dining room. She sat alone, staring out the front window at The Park, her brown eyes weary, and her mood morose.

I asked her, "What's wrong, Mom?"

She fingered the rosary beads in her lap and said she was thinking about Mark. My heart melted. After we hugged, Mom studied the veins on her hands and shared details about my brother's death. These images remain with me still. She bowed her head as if offering a quick prayer for the repose of his innocent soul.

My mother looked up at me. "The doctors said the cord had wrapped around Mark's neck several times. It cut off his breathing. Perhaps that was the popping sound I heard."

And this is the part that has stuck with me, the wisdom that I have had to draw on so often in my own life.

Mom reached for my hand, her dark eyes wide and serious, and said, "Julie, life is a fragile gift. We're not in charge of how long we live, or when we join our Lord in heaven."

My mother's faithful words rang true then. Today, they still do.

Over the course of my life, I have considered how lack of control relates to many things, including my adoption. Much like the circumstances causing my brother's death, adoption happened to my sister and me. We had no say in the matter, just as my mother could not affect the circumstances of Mark's life or death. Mom's attitude of accepting what we cannot change allowed her to cope with the many losses she experienced in building her American family. It provided an example for me with respect to my adoption and a useful philosophy with which to approach life. If we accept that we lack full control over the events in our lives, frustration and anxieties loosen their bind, acceptance and forgiveness are possible, and the road to joy and gratitude becomes less fraught.

Even though he had died before we knew him, my brother Mark had left his imprint on this life after all.

Part Two

BELONGING

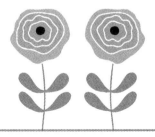

11

Crash

Spring 1971

When Jenny and I came down for breakfast dressed in our white blouses and red plaid uniform skirts, it was not our mother clanking around in the kitchen setting out cereal boxes, bowls, spoons, and small juice glasses on the table. It was Dad—perhaps a clue that the day was not going to unfold like every other school day.

I tugged at a loose thread on my skirt. "Where's Mom?"

"She'll be down before you leave for school." Dad pushed his large tortoiseshell glasses up the bridge of his nose. "She was up late doing laundry."

I glanced at the clock mounted on the wall by the refrigerator. Frowning, I wondered if my mother's sleeping in meant we were going to have to bag our own lunches. Jenny shrugged at me, pulled out a chair, and poured herself a huge bowl of Frosted Flakes. I debated about the Cap'n Crunch but grabbed the last package of Brown Sugar Cinnamon Pop-Tarts instead. Skeeter would be mad; they were his favorites, too. I peeled back the silver cellophane, popped both pastries into the toaster, grabbed a glass of orange juice, and then returned to the counter to guard my breakfast.

A few minutes later, Skeeter bustled into the kitchen. His white oxford shirt was not yet tucked into his navy trousers.

"Morning, Son," Dad said as he slipped off the green rubber band wound tightly around the morning edition of the *Chicago Tribune*. "Is Patrick up?"

Skeeter mumbled a feeble "yeah" to Dad and yanked a chair out from the table. As he dropped into a seat, I noticed his white-blond hair had curled up into little *C*s at the nape of his neck. My brother's blue eyes narrowed, darting around the display of cereal choices. When he spied the empty Pop-Tart box on the counter next to me, he smirked.

"Hey, let me have one of those, would ya, Jules?"

Before I could say, "Too bad. I got to 'em first," Dad interjected, looking straight at me. "Share with your brother."

I scowled at Skeeter but didn't offer any pushback to my dad. I was annoyed. Throughout the exchange, Dad sat reclined in his chair at the head of the table—his short auburn curls wet from his morning swim at the YMCA—while he perused the *Trib*'s front page. As irritated as I was with my father's nonchalance and my brother's insolence, I swallowed my feelings. Dad hated it when any of us bickered at the kitchen table.

"How did the White Sox do in their opener?" Skeeter asked with his mouth full.

Even though Skeeter did not have my father's genes, he and Dad shared an insatiable love for sports, particularly football and baseball. Dad snapped open the sports section.

He whistled, beaming at my brother. "They swept the A's. Beat 'em in both games of the double header at Oakland. The team's off to a great start. Spiffy new road uniforms, too."

As I peeked over my dad's shoulder at the photo of the White Sox's new powder-blue-and-red-trimmed travel gear, Lizzie's preschool babble and my mother's scuffing slippers could be heard on the staircase. When Mom ambled into the kitchen—her nubby blue robe cinched tight around her trim waist and her short dark hair matted down in the back from sleep—the drawn, melancholy look on her face made my heart sink.

Oh, man, she's still in a bad mood. This has been going on for days.

After Mom experienced my brother's stillborn death the year before, she had been quiet, serious, and distracted through the entire summer. By Christmastime, she was pretty much back to her old vivacious and energetic self. But when a blue mood captured my mother, everyone around her grew edgy. One look at Mom's sour face sent us scrambling to execute the chores expected of us, tasks we knew may or may not be rewarded with an appreciative smile. I swallowed hard as I watched my frowning mother shuffle into the kitchen with my three-year-old sister in tow.

"Should I start making the lunches, Mom?" I asked.

"That would be great," she said with a tiny smile.

"I'll help." Jenny jumped up and placed her cereal bowl in the sink.

We all wanted to make Mom smile, giggle, and laugh. Because when she did, we felt better about ourselves and the whole day seemed bright with promise. Over the past week, it seemed our mom barely noticed us when we entered the room. If she did, she brushed us off with a quick comment like "That's nice, honey," or "Put that on my desk. I'll look at it later." I also noticed she sighed long and hard at everything. She sighed when she cut up the food on Lizzie's plate. Even when Patrick made that silly farting noise with his hand and armpit.

I walked behind Dad's chair to get lunch meat out of the fridge and noticed the date on his newspaper: April 8. I sucked in a big gulp of air through my teeth. *Oh, man! Now I get it.* One year ago, my brother Mark had been born dead, an event whose details none of us would ever forget. The trip to the funeral parlor. Picking out the little white casket followed by zebra swirl ice cream cones at the Highland Dairy Queen. Reliving those heartbreaking moments soured my stomach.

"Jen!" I jabbed a finger at the wall clock. "We've got fifteen minutes. We told Carol we'd walk with her to school today."

I rushed through bagging my lunch, grabbed my book bag, and slipped on a light windbreaker at the back door.

"Bye, Mom. Bye, Dad. See you after school," we shouted.

During the three-block walk to the spot where we planned to meet Carol, Jenny and I discussed Mom's mood and the anniversary date of Mark's death. I had no way of knowing that later in the day I'd be grateful for every little inconvenience my family had presented me that morning.

"Yep. That explains it, all right," Jenny said. "Hope Mom comes out of it quick." She pointed to the corner of the next block. "There's Carol."

Carol was one of the cool sixth-grade girls, a member of the in-group with the cutest, most athletic sixth-grade boys. Tryouts for the seventh-grade cheer squad were coming up, and Jenny, Carol, and I had been assigned to the same practice group. Carol wanted to talk about the routine on the way to school.

When Jenny and I caught up with Carol at the corner, her soft brown perfectly styled shoulder-length hair—no doubt set in rollers by one of her older sisters the night before—whipped around in the gusty spring breezes. Carol waved us in close. Her lightly freckled face was rosy and animated.

"Did you hear about the Feys?" Carol's thin eyebrows arched, nearly disappearing into her light, fluffy bangs.

Jenny and I stared at one another.

"No, what?" Jen asked.

"You know Chris Fey?" Carol said.

"Yeah, he's in my class," I said.

"You're not going to believe this." As Carol's face drew closer, I could smell the orange blossom lip gloss she wore. "His parents are missing."

Jenny's mouth hung open. "How do you know?"

During the remaining six-block walk to St. Cletus School, Carol dispensed the facts she had gleaned from one of her sisters. The parents of our classmate, Chris Fey—the oldest of the five Fey kids—had been reported missing. The private plane Mr. Fey piloted, which carried his wife and two other couples, had flown over the Appalachian Mountains and mysteriously gone down. Search parties were combing the area, but due to the altitude and dense forest, the aircraft and its six passengers had yet to be located. By the time we got to school, I was so shell-shocked from absorbing the grim story I felt more like going home than I did elbowing my way through the crowded halls to homeroom.

In Mrs. Meyer's sixth-grade class, she opened the day with the same news. Even though we obeyed Mrs. Meyer and bowed our heads in prayer for the affected families, every head in the room eyed the empty desk where Chris Fey normally sat. At recess, the plane crash was all anyone could talk about. St. Cletus Parish was a tight-knit community made up of large Catholic families like the Feys. With a Fey child in nearly every grade, the tragedy affected everyone in a profound and personal way. It came as no surprise when the principal came on the loudspeaker during announcements and cancelled all after-school activities.

After the dismissal bell rang, Jenny and I trudged alongside one another off the school grounds. We stopped every block or so to chat with our classmates before they peeled off by bike or on foot toward their homes. All of our conversations held a similar refrain.

"I can't believe this happened. Poor Chris, and his brothers and sisters, too. I wonder how long it'll be before the parents are rescued?"

Just as Jenny and I reached the last block of our long trek home, Skeeter caught up with us at the southeast corner of Waiola Park. The Fey family lived one block away, at the western edge. From where we stood, we could see their home.

My brother pointed toward the Feys' house. "Man, can you believe it? I can't imagine what it would feel like to be one of the Fey kids right now, can you?"

"Nope, I can't either." Jenny shook her head sadly.

Per usual, Skeeter had to have the last word, but one that rung true to me. "Glad Mom and Dad were not on that plane."

As I considered my brother's comment, my mind reeled back to the scene that morning in our kitchen. The day hadn't started off as it usually did—with Mom's moods and all—but I'd take it, withstand all of it any day of the week, when compared to what my classmate Chris was enduring.

With empathy instead of fear, the three of us contemplated the playground where just a few days before the Fey kids cavorted carefree among us on the swing sets and slides. Like us, they were neighborhood kids—kids we knew, who lived and breathed the pleasures of The Park, and who deserved to luxuriate in the innocent womb of childhood just a little bit longer. Little did we know how close we came to living the Fey kids' nightmare.

As we gathered for dinner that night, Mom led us in a special intention before grace, her hands resting heavy in her lap, and her large brown eyes cast downward.

"Dear Lord, we pray for those who are missing in the plane crash, for the search parties' success in locating them, and for everyone's safe return to their loved ones. Amen."

When Mom looked up from prayer, her soulful dark eyes filmy

with emotion, she met my father's grave glance, and then she uttered the words I'll always remember.

"Thanks be to God, we decided not to go with the Feys on that trip after all."

My eyes opened wide as my mother's words sunk in. I set my fork down beside my plate. Mom's announcement vanquished my appetite. None of us had any inkling our folks had been invited on the excursion with Mr. and Mrs. Fey. I locked eyes with Jenny across the table, swallowing hard.

My question popped out before I could consider it. "Why didn't you go?"

Mom got up to check that the burners on the stove were turned off, something she often neglected to do.

"Dad?" My voice rose.

My father cleared his throat. "Your mother . . ."

Mom turned back from the stove with a stony look.

Dad picked up his napkin, refolded it, and replaced it on his lap. "Your mother thought it would be too hard to leave you kids . . . at this time of the year."

At twelve and a half, I didn't have any trouble reading between the lines and making assumptions. My mother's sadness, which had understandably surfaced around the one-year anniversary of my brother's death, had saved my parents from being involved in a horrific accident. I pushed the chicken and green beans around my plate.

After Jen and I helped Mom with the dishes, I tore up to our room and lay down on my bed.

Shutting our bedroom door, Jen asked, "Are you okay?"

"Yeah." I rolled over on my side and eyeballed my twin. "What a day, huh?"

"Yep. Too weird for words." She stretched out opposite me on her bed.

I smiled. Jenny had a way of summing things up that squeezed the pain up and out. Sort of like popping a pimple. When I started giggling, so did Jen. As the two of us lay there chuckling over nothing but words and our own brand of silliness, my world felt a whole lot lighter.

Within weeks, the remnants of Mr. Fey's downed aircraft were recovered, and the community mourned the shocking news that no one had survived its crash. The Fey kids never returned to St. Cletus School. Via the grapevine, we learned that one of Chris's aunts and uncle had moved the Fey children into their own home and planned on adopting them. By summer's end, the Feys' two-story brick home on the edge of Waiola Park was sold to a new young family. The home's solid presence served as a constant reminder. The Fey family tragedy had rattled our community. On its heels, we rallied in support, drew closer, strengthening our core. Unknowingly, what we learned because of the plane crash would brace us for the next wave of community misfortune.

I felt deep compassion for Chris Fey and his siblings because of the shock and trauma thrust upon them in the prime of their childhood. Their parents' deaths meant they had to move away from everything they knew: their friends, home, church, neighborhood, and most importantly, The Park.

Regarding their adoption, unlike my sister and me, Chris and his siblings had benefitted from knowing their biological parents before their familial bonds were severed. Since my adoption occurred within weeks of my birth, I was not afforded that privilege. The family adopting the Fey children were blood relatives, people who could pass on important family medical history, genealogy, pictures, and stories. They were folks who could memorialize the Fey children's biological parents and keep them alive in spirit.

Chris Fey never returned to our class to collect the things in his desk. If he appeared in our vibrant neighborhood, I don't remember having the chance to express my sympathies. If I had met up with Chris, I might have shared my mother's words: *Life is fragile. We are not in charge of when we are born or when we die.* Her wisdom may have offered him solace, as it continues doing for me.

12

The Sugar Bowl

Summer 1971

Jenny spotted our parents first. "They're here," she muttered to Lizzie and me.

I twisted around on my psychedelic Peter Maxx beach towel and shielded my eyes from the fierce July sun. Squinting hard, I scanned the slatted wooden boardwalk that began at the top of a heavily wooded ridge, threaded through a steep, sandy dune, and dumped onto the wide Clubhouse Beach where my siblings and I had been camped out for the last hour. Our parents had sent the five us to the beach with the promise that once the cottage was straightened up, they'd come down with beach chairs, cold drinks, and snacks.

"Finally!" I said.

Lizzie's large blue eyes lit up with the news. She dropped her red sand shovel into the pit she'd been digging and followed the line of Jenny's finger to the top of the boardwalk. When she spied our parents, Lizzie jumped up, her chubby little legs stomping and spraying sand all over Jenny.

With an angry scowl, my twin dusted off the fine grains coating her freckled cheeks, chest, and skimpy white bikini top. At twelve years old, my twin and I had just finished a major growth spurt, one that filled out our swimsuits and added shapely contours to our hips and long legs. The changes in our bodies were both exciting and scary. While I read every paragraph in the articles about dating in *Seventeen* magazine, I still fell asleep at night snuggling with the pile of stuffed animals on my bed.

Since school let out in June, Jen and I had been looking forward to our annual two-week family vacation at Grandma Mimi's cottage in Palisades Park, Michigan. We were eager to work on our tans, reread our stash of juicy teen magazines, and reconnect with summertime friends. Playing with Lizzie and "keeping an eye" on our brothers was cramping our style.

I cupped my hands and shouted to my brothers, who had wandered down the Lake Michigan shoreline.

"Hey! Mom and Dad are here," I yelled. "Come back."

Instead of acknowledging me, the pair continued their shoreline game. They darted in and out of Lake Michigan, scouring the beach for the smoothest, flattest rocks to skip off the lake's eerily calm surface.

"Aha! Gotcha, Pat. Seven bounces off that last one," Skeeter said.

I shook my head, mumbling to Jenny, "Poor Patrick."

It wasn't a fair game. Patrick had just turned seven. Skeeter was the best shortstop in La Grange's ten-and-under hardball league and a prized starting left-handed pitcher, too. A few minutes earlier, I'd caught Skeeter violating one of my folks' steadfast beach rules: You can go into the lake. But *do not* wade in past your kneecaps.

"Don't think I don't see you, Skeeter," I screamed.

Skeeter had spun around, his mouth lighting up in a mischievous smile.

As my brother bent to collect another flat rock, I'd continued my scolding. "And you're wrong if you think I won't tell Mom."

I straightened the corner of my hot pink and orange beach towel and plopped down, glowering at my twin.

"He's such a tough guy. Not afraid of anything. Not even Mom," I said.

Jenny offered a sympathetic smile. Both of us had been counting down the minutes until our folks released us from another babysitting stint. We longed to venture off on our own and visit our favorite summer haunts and walk down the long, sand-encrusted boardwalk connecting the north end of Clubhouse Beach to Circle Beach where all the action was. Both of us were dying to wander into the Soda Bar and order a Green River or Red Cream soda. We hoped our summer friends, Lori and Beth, were in Palisades for the upcoming Fourth of July holiday. And I couldn't wait to go to the Sugar Bowl.

Dashing down the middle of the Sugar Bowl, the large crater of sand located at the south end of Palisades, was a summer ritual. A local icon, the Sugar Bowl sand dune was accessible only by a steep footpath that wound up a narrow ridge shielded from view by towering oaks and thickets of gnarly bushes. It made for the ultimate afternoon adventure.

When Patrick and Skeeter spotted our parents, they hustled over. Giggling, they skidded to the edge of our beach towels, sending more sand cascading around us.

"You're not really going to tell Mom, are you?" Skeeter's blue eyes were as wide as saucers.

"Not if you sit here and play with Lizzie. Jenny and I need to go help Mom and Dad with all that stuff."

"Okay. Yeah," he said.

I ignored the gloat forming at the corners of my brother's mouth and charged through the warm sand toward the boardwalk. Mom handed Jenny a pile of bulky beach chairs and told me to help Dad. I tried not to giggle out loud. Our red-faced father looked like a camel. He had several beach towels bunched up around his neck and the large yellow and red canvas beach umbrella thrown over one shoulder. Everything our family did always felt like such a production. So much family time. So much togetherness. It wasn't easy for Jenny and me to just slip off and do our thing. Ever.

Once we finished our picnic lunch, Mom gave Jenny and me permission to head off to the Soda Bar.

"Be back in an hour so," Mom said. "And check in before you go anywhere else."

As soon as we stepped onto the boardwalk, Jenny and I folded in close. Our heads nearly touched as we walked side by side.

"Jeez, you'd think Mom would trust us to roam. Especially here at Palisades. We've been coming here every summer for most of our lives," Jenny said.

I smiled thinking about how safe I felt in Palisades Park. The unobtrusive sign off the exit from the highway. The single road in and the gated entry to which only owners possessed keys. The caretaker who lived in the house by the gate. No one could enter Palisades unless they owned a cottage, were invited in as a guest, or went through the board's rigorous rental vetting process.

"Yeah, I know," I said. "Next to The Park, I think Palisades Park is probably one of the safest places on Earth."

"I'm sick of all Mom's rules." Jenny tucked a strand of fine brown hair behind her sunburned ear. "Like, this is the first year she's allowed us to ride our bikes through the Hole and get ice cream at Baskin-Robbins."

When we were home in La Grange, Jenny, Skeeter, and I enjoyed the freedom of riding our bikes most places, as long as the destination fell within the tight geographical quadrant set by our folks. Recently, my parents had adjusted the perimeter to include a trip to the Garden Market Shopping Center, which meant we could ride our bikes through the Hole—an undeveloped and overgrown plot of land full of meandering trails wedged between a residential area and the south campus of Lyons Township High School. In the Hole, the prairie grasses were so tall that foot traffic was invisible from one path to the next. I loved zooming through there on my bike despite how isolated I felt when I made the trip alone.

I grinned at Jenny knowingly. "Yeah, that really surprised me. I consider going to the Sugar Bowl a whole lot safer than riding through the Hole."

In the Soda Bar's back room, we spotted Lori, a girl we knew from Western Springs, the village next to our hometown of La Grange. None of us had any quarters to play pinball in the back room, so we hung around outside the Soda Bar, finished our Green River sodas, and talked about what we'd been up to since the last time we'd all hung out together.

"Have you been to the Sugar Bowl yet?" I asked Lori.

"Nope. Let's go!" Lori's dark brown eyes sparkled.

Twenty minutes later, after checking in with my folks, the three of us dropped off the southernmost boardwalk and entered the parking area at the base of the Sugar Bowl. The early afternoon sun was screaming hot, and my shoulders glistened with sweat. Lori and I draped beach towels around our shoulders like capes.

Jenny grinned at Lori and me, pointing to the white skin around her bathing suit top.

"I'm working on my tan lines," she said, and tied her towel around her waist.

When we got to the mouth of the trail threading up the south end of the sand dune, I scrounged in the brush for a couple of thick branches to use as walking sticks. This had become a habit for my siblings and me. As we meandered along Palisades's narrow sandy roads, we poked at stuff in the brush, fascinated by all the critters and plants that thrived under a dense blanket of decayed leaves. Walking sticks also came in handy when we scaled the steep footpaths linking the Ryan cottage to the Circle Beach, the club-house, or the tennis courts.

I handed a thick stick to Jen. We pushed through the overgrown path leading to the top of the Sugar Bowl. In single file, Jenny led, and Lori followed me. As we climbed, the three of us chattered about music, fashion, and where we might be headed for high school. About halfway up, we clumped together while Jenny used her stick to knock away some dense vines hanging down over the trail.

"Well, well. What have we got here?" a masculine voice boomed.

The three of us froze, our hearts nearly bursting from the exercise and the shock of running into others on the trail. Boys!

Two feet in front of us stood two muscled-up older boys. They looked like high schoolers, maybe older. The pair were like a brick wall, obliterating our way forward. Jenny reared back and knocked into me, causing the towel around my shoulders to fall to the sandy path. The cute and skimpy navy-blue bikini I'd convinced my mother I had to have for our vacation was now in full view. I looked down at my bare midsection and wished that I was wearing last year's one piece.

I caught Jenny's glance. I knew what it meant: *Who are these guys and where did they come from?*

"I don't recognize them," I whispered to Jen. "Maybe they're renters?"

Panic built up in me, and I held my breath. Nothing like this had ever happened before. Two strange boys—who instead of stepping aside and letting us pass like anyone else would have done—blocked the only way up.

To no one in particular, I said in a quiet, hopeful voice, "We're going to the top. Let us pass."

In truth, I don't know where my courageous comment came from, but I hoped the boys would listen, and that it would be enough to get us out of what felt like trouble. The bulky, dark-haired guy with the shaggy haircut guffawed. A deep, creepy laugh forced his black bushy eyebrows to knit in one long line. His brown eyes looked wild and menacing.

"Oh, we'll let you pass, all right," he said, laughing again. "Once we get a peek at what's under there." He pointed to Jenny's white bathing suit top. "And there." He gestured at my navy bottoms.

Breathe. Remember what Mom taught you about strangers. Back away, run, and yell for help. Lori's mother must have coached her like ours had done because I no longer felt her breath against my nearly naked back. A twig snapped a few feet behind me. I hoped it meant Lori had snuck away.

"Not so fast, short girl," shouted the dark-haired guy. "Where do you think you're going?"

Lori didn't answer. I edged closer to my twin. Behind me, branches swished, and footsteps pounded the path. I sent a prayer off: *Be careful, Lori. Send help. Fast.*

"You girls from around here?" the dark-haired boy took another step closer.

The second guy, the shorter one with cropped blond hair, refused to look at us. He studied his bare feet and kicked the ground, carving a small trench in the trail.

"Leave them alone, Billy," he said softly.

Billy glared at the blond guy and turned back to leer at Jenny and me. I avoided Billy's predatory looks and his stupid question. I thought about all the times I'd been forced to stand up to my brother Skeeter to get him to behave. That knowledge gave me courage. When Billy was within arm's reach, I knew I had to do something. With one hand on my walking stick, I plucked up my towel and tightened it around me like a sarong. I glanced at Jenny and thrust out my walking stick, waving it in front of me like a weapon. Jenny did the same.

To the boys, I tried disguising the panic in my voice. "We're leaving." Taking a small step backward, I said, "If you try to follow us, we'll clobber you with these sticks."

I nodded at Jen. "Let's go!"

We took off racing down the treacherous path, clenching our towels and gripping our sticks. As we ran, the puffs of our breath came out heavy and thick like the snorts of wild animals. Once or twice, I glanced over my shoulder to see if the boys were chasing us. No sign of them. Were they really gone, or would they appear out of nowhere as they had before?

When we got to the parking area, Jenny and I doubled over and tried catching our breaths.

"Do you think we really lost them?" Jen asked.

"Let's keep moving," I panted.

Down by the boardwalk, we glimpsed Lori gesturing wildly to Skeeter. He ran to us like lightning, bending and scooping up rocks along the way.

"Where are they?" My brother's blue eyes bulged.

"What're you doing here?" Jen managed to get out between gulps of air.

"Mom sent me. Said you two had been gone too long. That I should find you," Skeeter said.

He dropped some of the smaller pebbles in his hand and picked up a few heftier ones. His eyes narrowed, zeroing in on the path that led to the Sugar Bowl.

He strutted to the mouth of the trail, muttering, "Those guys are gonna be sorry they messed with my sisters. Really, really, sorry."

Pride filled my chest. Relief, too. My little brother, the prized shortstop, pain in the ass, and perpetual bender of rules, had risen in stature in my eyes. I vowed that I would never rat him out to my mother again. As I watched him peer up the path, I felt oddly grateful. He had given Jenny and me plenty of practice in standing up to an antagonistic personality.

After several minutes, Skeeter relaxed out of his assault position, rolled the collection of stones around in his left palm, and returned to where Jen and I stood.

"I think those guys took another way out. But if you see them around again, make sure you point them out." He strutted off. "They're all mine."

Jenny and I shared a fond smile. As we headed back to the beach where our family waited, another of my mother's axioms burst into my head: *Family always takes care of family.* I chuckled to myself. I guessed my brother had absorbed more of my mother's preaching than I would have thought, more than he let on, anyway. No one was ever going to hurt my sister or me when Skeeter was around.

Our brush with assault was a true coming-of-age moment for my sister and me, one that put us on notice. Jenny and I were no longer children. We were young women. And with our budding maturity, we had entered a new stage of life, one with more complicated and nuanced joys and challenges where the only person who could keep you safe was you.

13

Trouble in the Hole

Fall 1971

It was mid-October, and the weather was unseasonably warm and dry. Over breakfast, Dad had read the weather report out loud, calling it an Indian summer.

"A glorious Sunday," he had said, "one to be spent outdoors enjoying the sunshine," and then he chuckled, "or indoors watching Sunday afternoon football."

If Mother Nature knew misfortune was lurking on such a gorgeous autumn day, she disguised it. At least for a few hours anyway.

Jenny and I had ridden our bikes home after cheering for the St. Cletus seventh-grade boy's football team. Our muscles ached from jumping around on the field and rooting for our Cardinals. Throughout the game and the mile-long pedal home, sweat seeped through our white polyester bodysuits, darkening the armholes of the fitted red jumpers Mom helped us sew over the previous summer. We couldn't wait to go to our room and peel off the sticky, suffocating outfits.

As the two of us slumped against the kitchen counter downing bottles of Coca-Cola, Skeeter and Patrick burst through the back door hollering, "Mom! Dad! Where are you?"

"Kitchen!" Mom yelled back.

When the boys bounded in, Skeeter screeched to a halt. His blue eyes were huge, as if he'd just sat through a scary movie.

"Mom! Girls!" he panted. "You're not going to believe this."

Mom turned away from the sink, a dark green dish towel over her arm. She smoothed out the wide, pleated midsection of her white blouse and let her hand rest there. She was pregnant again. After school started around Labor Day, Mom had come in to say good night to Jenny and me. When she lowered herself onto the edge of Jenny's canopy bed, her long, elegant fingers came to rest on the small mound of her belly.

"We're expecting a baby. In May. That's the good news." Mom sighed, but her grin disappeared. "I'm sorry. I had to tell Lisa's mom I can't lead your Camp Fire Girls troop. I know you're disappointed, but it's just bad timing." She reached out and patted our hands. "I hope you both understand."

We assured Mom we were fine with a different mother leading our troop. Jenny inched closer to Mom, concern etched in her greenish-gold eyes.

"What does the doctor say? Is everything okay with the baby?"

Mom patted our hands again. "The baby has a strong, healthy heartbeat. Everything's fine."

When the latch on our bedroom door clicked behind our mother, Jenny groaned. "I don't care about the Camp Fire Girls stuff, really, but another baby. Wow!"

I scrunched up my pillow and lay down with a thump. "When the baby comes, you and I will be thirteen." I spread my arms wide. "That's a huge age gap."

Jen was silent for a second. "I wonder where Mom and Dad plan on putting the new baby. In with Lizzie?"

"Makes sense." I snorted. "She's the only one of us with her own room."

Neither of us needed to say more. Six kids scrambling around in our small three-bedroom home—even with the first-floor den now converted into a bunkroom for our brothers—was a lot. If our dad's new job continued taking off, Mom had promised they'd look for a bigger house.

"One not too far from The Park," she'd said. "But until then, we all just need to make do."

The new baby and all the changes it would bring were not top of mind when Patrick rolled into the kitchen, out of breath, and planted himself beside Skeeter. Pat's brown eyes, dark like olives, flicked from Mom to Skeeter. At seven, he was still content to let his older brother do most of the talking.

Mom dried her hands on the green towel. "I'm listening," she said to my brothers.

"There are search parties going out. All over the neighborhood." Skeeter waved his hands wildly. "From The Park to the Hole. And over to LT South."

Mom stared into Skeeter's excited face. "Good Lord. Whatever for?"

Jenny and I set our empty Coke bottles down on the counter with a smack. Skeeter's stunning announcement felt like a shocking crack of lightning a hair's length away.

Skeeter tugged at his dirt-smudged tee. "You know the Fredians? Public school kids. They live down the street from the Feys' old house."

"Calm down, honey. Yes, I know the family. What happened?" Mom's hands slid to her hips.

Skeeter swallowed. "Okay, so Alan, the older boy. Sophomore at LT South. He's missing."

Mom's hands flew up and landed at the center of her chest. "Mary, Mother of God." She breathed heavily. "What else do you know?"

"The word at The Park," Skeeter pointed off into the distance, "is that Alan's parents called the police last night when he didn't come home after Homecoming. And get this! Coppers are all over the place."

Patrick chimed in. "They kicked us off the playground."

Skeeter stiff-armed Patrick, pushing him aside. "Yeah. They've taped it off. Said Waiola Park is off-limits for a while."

Mom's pretty face clouded over. "I wonder why."

"Cops wouldn't say. Told us to scram. But one of the guys I was shooting hoops with said he heard the cops talking about a pile of burnt clothing."

Mom's pink lips opened into a surprised *O*. "What? At The Park?" She jabbed a finger at my brothers. "You're not to go anywhere near there, hear me? Go tell your dad all this. He's got Lizzie with him down in the rec room watching the Bears game."

Mom surged toward the phone resting on the pass-through, a small niche in the kitchen wall that opened to the center hallway.

She picked up the receiver and started to dial. "I bet Dot knows something about this."

As our brothers raced to the basement to fill in our dad, Jenny and I fled to the dining room to peer out the front window into The Park.

"Mom!" Jenny yelled. "Don't call Mrs. Lofquist. I see her. She's outside in her front yard."

Mom joined us at the window. "Oh, my. I think the whole block is outside." She craned her neck to see beyond the crowd. "And I do see police cars down near the playground."

She rushed to the top of the basement stairs. Cupping her hands around her mouth, she shouted, "Jack! I think you'd better come up here."

When my dad and brothers stormed up from the lower level, poor little Lizzie trailed behind like the last kid picked for a game of dodgeball. Mom asked Jenny and me to take her upstairs with us while we changed into clean clothes.

"Your father and I are heading outside to hear what the neighbors might know." She threw us a pleasant smile. "We're having Arby's for dinner. Think about what you want to order."

As the door slammed, Jenny and I looked at one another. Of course, it was an Arby's night. It was Sunday. And after dinner, there would be homework to finish. That is of course if any of us could focus after listening to the evening news.

When the heavy wooden front door creaked open, Jen and I sprinted from our room and cornered Dad in the foyer.

"What's everyone saying?" I asked. "Did they find Alan Fredian yet?"

Dad shook his head, avoiding our probing eyes.

"There are just too many rumors flying around, kids. We'll have to wait for the six o'clock news to know anything for certain." He slid past us down the hallway, saying, "I'm going down to the basement to catch the end of the Bears game."

As Jenny and I turned to retrace our steps to our room, we glimpsed Dad taking a detour into the kitchen. Jenny put a finger to her lips and motioned for me to follow her down the hallway near the kitchen pass-through. We huddled close to the wall, our heads touching, while we strained to hear our parents' conversation.

"Jeanne, it's preposterous to me that a fifteen-year-old boy—a kid from a good family, a respected high school swimmer—goes out on a Saturday night to Homecoming and stops in the Hole to buy dynamite with a friend. So, they can blow up the high school? How can that be true?"

As Jen and I huddled in the passageway blind to our parents' gestures, I imagined Dad throwing up his hands in despair and letting them fall to his sides with a *thwap*. Jenny elbowed me in the ribs, smiled wickedly, and tiptoed about an inch from the pass-through. Her head darted back and forth, fast, garnering a flash peek into the kitchen. Her daring tickled my insides. When Jen turned back to me, she dragged her fingers down from her eyes to show Mom was crying, and then she pantomimed Dad hugging Mom and our mom laying her head down on his shoulder. I beamed at my sister's theatrics.

When we heard Mom's mournful voice nearing the pass-through, we jerked back.

"I feel for the Fredian family," she said. "All the ugly rumors. Their son missing all night. And now—if it's true what the neighbors are saying—he's dead! Found by a search party in that godforsaken place, the Hole. I don't want the kids going through there anymore, Jack."

I squeezed my sister's upper arm. She winced and pivoted. We stared into each other's eyes, our faces identical: eyes popping out and mouths so wide it was as if each of us were silently screaming. I pointed up. On tiptoes, we scampered off to our room before we got caught eavesdropping.

After the Bears got blanked 13-0 by the 49ers, Dad left with our brothers to pick up the Arby's order. Mom dragged out the TV tray tables from the back closet and set them up around the family room. When Dad arrived, he handed out warm foil-wrapped sliced beef sandwiches, packets of special sauce, and bags of potato chips. Mom passed out cans of A&W root beer and tumblers of ice. Even with the windows cranked open wide, the air in the family room was stale and still, heavy like a day when a torrential downpour was expected.

Before Dad sank down on the eagle-crested sofa to eat his meal, he lumbered over to the console. He flicked on the television set and tweaked the rabbit-ear antennae.

"We want to watch *Wild Kingdom*," Patrick squealed.

"Me, too," Lizzie yelled.

"In a few minutes." Dad turned the dial a few clicks. "First, we're gonna see what the news has to say."

As Dad landed on the network channel with the best reception, a headshot of Alan Fredian appeared on the screen. Mom hushed us. We stopped munching and stared at the solemn news anchor as he reported:

"We lead tonight with a tragic story. Fifteen-year-old high school sophomore Alan Fredian, from La Grange—a western suburb of Chicago—went to meet friends Saturday night at Lyons Township High School's South campus. Police say Alan Fredian, who is the son of a Loyola administrator, was found this afternoon. He'd been bludgeoned to death. His parents reported him missing late Saturday night, October 16, when he did not return home after LT's Homecoming festivities. Search parties went out early this morning."

"See, I was right," Skeeter shouted, interrupting the broadcast. "That's exactly what I told you, Mom!"

My mother put a finger up to her lips. Dad set aside his half-eaten sandwich and cranked up the TV's volume. Jenny and I eyed one another, our lips puckering into sad pouts. Even though we'd overheard our parents talking earlier, hearing the news on TV made it official. Someone we knew from the neighborhood, a guy not much older than Jenny and me, had been found dead. His murder wasn't hearsay or rumor anymore. It had really happened. Next to me, I heard the tiny whistle of Jenny's breath. Slumping back into my seat, I didn't think I'd ever feel safe again riding my bike through the Hole, at least by myself anyway.

But who would murder Alan?

As my family absorbed the sobering truth, we remained rooted in place, the litter of our half-eaten takeout growing cold on our TV trays. All eyes stared at the newscaster while he continued the broadcast:

"Alan Fredian's body was found in a shallow grave at an area the locals call the Hole, which is a wooded overgrown field just east of the 4800 block of Gilbert Avenue, or Willow Springs Road, and directly across from the LT South Campus. LT students cut through the Hole on their way to the Garden Market Shopping Center or to downtown La Grange. Sometimes they meet there to fight, drink alcohol, and smoke cigarettes.

Police reported that young Fredian's skull was crushed with either a block of concrete or a piece of four-by-four lumber or both. He was found by a search party. A motive for the killing is unclear and there are no leads or suspects at this time. However, rumors center on one of two possibilities: a drug deal gone bad, or a falling-out between former friends.

As this story unfolds, we promise to report the latest details."

Mom closed her eyes and rested her head against the back of the leather sofa. The shock of what we had learned muted us. We just sat around looking at one another. After a moment, Mom sat upright, nodding her head from side to side.

"Such a sad, sad thing," she murmured. "Senseless. An unimaginable loss for the Fredian family. We must keep them all in our prayers."

Cued, we mimicked our mother and dropped our chins to our chests in silent prayer. When my mother sighed and rose heavily, her mouth was set in a familiar, narrow line.

Once she had her feet beneath her, Mom zeroed in on my dad. "Jack, I think we've had enough of the news. Flip to a show the kids might enjoy." She shifted her stern gaze to the rest of us. "After the program, it's baths and bedtime."

Without another word, Mom gathered up the remaining dinner items and asked Jenny and me to put away the tray tables. Once the family room was tidied up, Mom's hands found her thickening waistline. "Who has homework to finish up?"

The boys each grumbled, "Not me," and Jenny muttered something about a civics reading assignment that "wasn't a big deal."

When Mom left the room, Jenny squinted at me. I nodded.

Was Mom serious? Who could think of anything else but the murder?

As the week wore on, the murder was all anyone talked about at school, on the playground, or at home. We were all obsessed. Before dinner, my parents, Jenny, and I listened to the evening news. In the morning, Dad hustled out to the curb to retrieve the *Tribune*, scanning the headlines for a break in the story. With all the local gossip, it became hard to distinguish what was fact, hearsay, or truths not shared with the police or the news media. Were the police on a wild goose chase? Had informants misled them? Or was there a deeper plot playing out that the police were in on? The common sentiment was that the police needed to make an arrest.

The issues of the dynamite and the alleged plot to blow up the high school were the subjects my peers latched on to. Everyone speculated whether "dynamite" meant drugs or explosives. Because there was no resolution regarding Alan's murderer, the entire town was pensive and edgy. Someone among us—another neighbor, a drug-crazed youth, or a stranger passing through town— had killed a boy we knew.

The entire neighborhood was looking over their shoulders. No one lingered on porches for friendly chitchats with a strolling neighbor. After dinner each night, Dad made a show of latching every window and locking every door. The only windows left open were the ones in our second-floor bedrooms. I'm not sure his efforts made us feel any safer. Mom and Dad set new rules, too. We had to come right home after school. We couldn't be outside after dark, and we were prohibited from riding our bikes anywhere except to school and back.

Alan Fredian's murder locked down our community and put fear in every heart. We became wary of everyone—strangers, neighbors, and even the police who had failed to make an arrest.

One evening, about a week after the murder upended our town, my mother invited Grandma Mimi for dinner. As Mom stood quietly over the stove stirring and prepping supper, my grandma sipped a Manhattan cocktail in a kitchen chair. Over the years, this had become a frequent scene. In a cheerful voice, Grandma would update Mom on what our cousins were up to, offer tales about her elderly friends' mishaps and maladies, and comment on the local news and gossip.

Jenny and I were within earshot in the adjoining family room, our textbooks and spiral notepads scattered around us. Because most of Mom and Grandma's chatter centered on the Fredian case, my sister and I struggled to concentrate on our homework.

My Grandma's lilting voice wafted through the doorway. "You know what they say?" She waited for my mother's response. "Bad news always comes in threes."

I pictured my mother turning away from the stove, frowning. "That's just an old wives' tale, Mimi. We're already on edge. Why bring something like that up now?"

Undeterred, my grandma spoke loudly and with confidence. "Well, first there was the Feys' plane crash. Now this. Gonna be something else. Mark my words."

My grandmother's comment caused me to stop midway through

a math problem set, my pencil hovering in the air. *Does bad news always come in threes?*

Jenny and I talked later in our room about Grandma's strange prophesy. We speculated if the trouble we had avoided at the Sugar Bowl—something we had not shared with our parents—qualified as the third thing in Grandma's rule of threes. Before I drifted off to sleep, it occurred to me our little neighborhood had lost a teen-ager, Alan Fredian, but it was gaining a new soul next spring—my new baby brother or sister. I thought about how we were adding to our family and how the Fredians had lost a member of theirs, and I wondered whether the lives of Alan's family would ever return to normal. Would arresting a suspect and learning the motive help the family cope and heal? Such deep thoughts for an almost thirteen-year-old. Ideas I would never have contemplated had it not been for the murder in the Hole.

As the leaves on Waiola Avenue's arching elms turned from mossy green to a kaleidoscope of warm color, I stopped focusing on the negative aspect of Grandma's saying. Instead, I convinced myself we had passed through the cycle of three bad-news items. As I mused in bed one night, I considered a positive play off Grandma's idiom: good things run in streaks of three.

I desperately wanted the blissful existence I'd enjoyed when I was much younger to return. I decided to put my trust in God and the universe that three wonderful events would come to fruition: Mom and Dad would get their healthy new baby, Dad's job would take off, and we'd move to a beautiful big house, one that was large enough for all of us to have our own rooms.

Over time, my positivity and patience would be rewarded. Two of those wishes would come true.

14

Oh, no!

Spring 1972

"It's a girl!" Dad bellowed as he flung open the door connecting the garage to the family room.

Late-afternoon light shot like a missile through the opening. The beacon spotlighted debris in our cozy family room: cookie crumbs and crumpled napkins at one end of the dining table, a missing puzzle piece below the sofa, and an assortment of library books stacked haphazardly on the end table. Things that if my mother hadn't been in the hospital would have been straightened or cleared away. But with all that was going on, Dad and Grandma Mimi could have cared less.

The five of us—Jenny, Patrick, Skeeter, Lizzie, and I—were spread out in the family room area much like we had been two years prior when our dad issued the grim news about our stillborn brother, Mark. This time, though, I didn't have the comfort of Jenny's warm body next to me. Instead, we sat opposite one another at the dark wooden table where we labored over our seventh-grade civics projects.

Four-year-old Lizzie bounced off the sofa, dragging her Raggedy Ann doll behind her. "Yay! Another sister!"

She rushed over to my dad, who lifted her into his arms. Lizzie laid her head on his shoulder, and the blond braids Jenny had plaited that morning before Grandma took us to Sunday Mass thumped against his broad chest. I watched my dad and sister, wondering when it would dawn on Lizzie that the prized position of "youngest" now belonged to someone else.

As we all clustered around my father, his grin widened, deepening his dimples. "We're going to call her Susie." Dad's face flushed as he set Lizzie back on the floor. "Suzanne Margaret. After Mom and her mother, your grandmother Nana."

Grandma Mimi bustled in from the adjoining kitchen. The voluminous, blue-patterned housedress she wore fluttered around her thick, bowed knees.

"How's Jeanne? The baby?" she asked, wiping her knobby fingers on Mom's apron, the one with the hand-embroidered hearts around its edges.

I let out a big breath, grateful my grandma posed the question that had nagged all of us since learning my parents had left for the hospital before any of us got up.

Dad nodded solemnly at Grandma. "The delivery went fine. No issue with the cord." He closed his eyes for a second. "Like what happened with Mark."

My grandmother pulled a tissue out of her pocket and dabbed at her eyes.

"Praise the Lord," she said as she touched two fingertips in rapid succession to her forehead, chest, and each shoulder. The sign of the cross.

Now that the waiting was over, and our new sister had been born alive and healthy—and Mom was okay, too—the air in the house felt breezier, aromatic even, as if someone had lit a candle. I felt lighter somehow, too. Suddenly, I had the urge to move, go outside, maybe take Gigi for a quick walk in The Park. While I didn't make the sign of the cross like my grandmother, in my head I mumbled a quick thanks to Saint Thérèse for looking out for everyone.

I glanced back at the table where I had sat across from Jenny. When Dad had burst through the door, I'd wedged my pencil into the metal spiral of my civics notebook. I couldn't wait to finish it and turn it in by tomorrow's deadline. I sighed. Our seventh-grade year was almost over, and the rest of May was chock-full. Cheerleading tryouts were in two weeks. With that realization, my smile vanished. Even though I'd served as the squad's seventh-grade captain, that honor didn't guarantee a spot on the eighth-grade team. The tryout routine was intricate, loaded with jumps and split combos that I had yet to master. I couldn't imagine what life would be like if I didn't make the team. All the "cool" seventh-grade girls were on it.

Glancing over at Dad, I sidelined my teenage worries and took a step closer to him. "When's Mom coming home?"

"A couple of days. Maybe Wednesday." Dad gave in to a huge yawn. "The doctors want your mother to rest. They also want more time to evaluate your new sister."

The way he said that—his hand rifling through a crop of reddish-brown curls, and the quick glance at Grandma Mimi—made we wonder if something was wrong with my new sister. *Susie. Such a cute, girlish name.* I liked it. It fit with the rest of our names. And it sounded nice with our last name, Ryan.

But before I could ask what he meant by needing more time to check out Susie, Dad clapped his hands together.

"How about Arby's for dinner tonight, kids? It's Sunday. Our usual thing. What do ya say?"

When Jenny and I burst through the back door a few days later, Grandma Mimi was pulling out fresh fruits and vegetables from several large A&P grocery sacks.

I dropped my schoolbag onto a kitchen chair. "Where's everybody?"

Jenny sauntered up beside me and grabbed an apple. "Yeah, I thought Dad was bringing Mom and Susie home from the hospital today?"

I tittered at my twin. "That's gonna get stuck in your braces."

She pouted and put the apple back. While I felt bad about the agonies my sister endured with her new metal braces, I was glad to be spared. My teeth were straight and hadn't shifted like Jen's. Maybe I would need braces in a few years, the dentist had said, but not yet.

My grandmother peeked around the door of the fridge. "They were delayed," she murmured. "The doctor ordered additional tests. Something to do with your sister's eyes. Don't worry, pets. By the time you change out of your uniforms, your folks will be driving up."

Uh-oh, was my new sister okay?

If she wasn't, it meant the hopes and dreams I had set for our family last fall—the ones I'd been praying about ever since Grandma said, "You know, bad news comes in threes"—were in jeopardy. I wanted Susie to be healthy, for Dad to be successful at his job, and for us to move to a bigger house near The Park. I wanted those things to happen with all my heart.

Within the hour, the tan Buick sedan my father drove to his new job with Safeguard Business Systems pulled up in front of our house. Even with our bedroom door closed, Grandma's shout was hard to miss.

"Kids! They're here! Your mom and dad are home with the new baby."

Jenny and I scrambled down the front stairs, giggling and dragging Lizzie between us like a monkey. When the boys stampeded out of the family room, Skeeter edged out Patrick and took the lead. We converged on Grandma Mimi in the foyer. Skeeter whipped open the bulky, black-enameled wood door that Jenny, Lizzie, and

I had decorated with a *Welcome Home* sign. Before the boys could send the outer glass storm door flying, Grandma pulled them back by the necks of their T-shirts.

"Stay here, pets. Let your folks get out of the car and into the house first. We don't want to jostle that tiny new sister of yours."

Grumbling, they gave my grandmother sour looks. "Okay, Grandma."

So instead of the five of us rushing out and encircling our parents on the front walk, we trudged after Grandma Mimi into the front room, a formal space off-limits to sticky fingers and fidgety limbs. With our noses pressed against the glass of the large picture window, we watched as Dad ran around to Mom's side of the sedan. He opened the passenger door. Our mother handed him the tightly wrapped pink quilt she had cozied in the crook of her arm. *Susie.*

We watched Mom emerge from the car. My dad kissed her on the forehead and returned Susie to her arms. Mom stood there for a moment. Still. Her dark and solemn eyes peered into the soft blanket. The line of her thin pale lips moved ever so slightly, and I wondered whether she whispered to Susie or sang a lullaby to settle her. Shielding my sister's face from the bright spring sun, my folks ambled up the walk, my father's arm wound tightly around my mother's shoulders. To my teenage eyes, my parents looked more tired and tentative than they did joyful.

Lizzie jumped up and down on our side of the glass storm door, pointing at the *Welcome Home* sign.

Even though our mother was not in earshot, Lizzie shrieked, "Mommy, we made a sign for you. See! I did it with the twins."

Mom must've sensed the commotion because her face lit up as soon as she saw Lizzie.

Skeeter stepped in front of Lizzie and opened the glass door. "Hey, Mom 'n Dad. Hurry up!" he shouted. "Grandma said we have to wait here inside."

When Mom stepped into the foyer, her eyes gleamed. "Here she is. Your new baby sister, Susie." Mom dipped the pink bundle so all of us got a peek.

Patrick's brown eyes looked up into Mom's. "She's so small."

Dad chuckled and ruffled the crown of Patrick's reddish-brown head.

"Let's go into the family room." Mom switched Susie to her other arm and started down the hallway. "Each of you can hold your new sister in there."

We traipsed after our parents into the back of the house. Dad dragged two chairs away from the table and motioned for Grandma Mimi to take a seat. He pulled the other chair closer to the sitting area. My mother settled into the center of the eagle-crested red leather sofa, and Lizzie clambered up, snuggling in tight against my mother's warm body. Patrick and Skeeter jockeyed for the spot on the other side of Mom. Jenny and I took positions next to one another at the end of the sofa, which gave us a good angle.

"She's got dark hair like you, Mom," Jenny mumbled. "Dad's blue eyes, I think."

"Yes, I think so." Mom's dark eyes glanced away from Jen and landed on Dad.

Dad cleared his throat. The sound was loud and grumbly. Puzzled, we turned to look at him. His dimples had faded, and his broad, freckled hands whitened as they spread around the arms of the chair.

"Kids, your mother and I have important news. About Susie . . ."

Jenny's elbow found my ribs. I winced and stepped aside, settling one hip on the rolled end of the sofa. My heart quickened as we waited for Dad to continue.

Dad swallowed hard, his Adam's apple quivering. "The doctors detected something wrong with Susie's eyes. Your sister has something called cataracts. In both eyes."

Mom's forehead creased into tiny pleats as she explained more about cataracts. "They're milky white capsules that have formed inside Susie's eyes, behind the clear outer lens. They prevent her from seeing clearly."

"What? That's crazy," Jenny moaned. "Is that normal?"

Mom's voice dipped into a monotone. "No. Not normal." Her chin lifted and dropped with a sigh. "The doctors think I must have been exposed to rubella—German measles—when I was pregnant."

I thought about the many class parties and events at which Mom had volunteered or attended at St. Cletus during the previous winter. School-wide cupcake sales. Our interscholastic volleyball games and cheer competitions. Skeeter's basketball league. She could have picked it up anywhere, or she might have gotten it from one of us. I grimaced. *So unfair.* Mom had been punished for being an active and involved mother to the five of us. *Where was that good and merciful God, the one Sister Hillary ranted about in religion class?*

I looked over my mother's shoulder and studied Susie's eyes. "I don't see what the doctors are talking about."

Dad got up. "Watch Susie's face." He switched off the family room lights and then flipped them back on right away. "See, she didn't squint at the bright light like newborns should."

Our reactions ranged from "Wow," from Skeeter, "Oh, no!" from Jenny and me, and stunned silence from the others. Grandma Mimi dabbed at her eyes.

Suddenly I felt guilty about fretting over the upcoming cheerleading tryouts. This was a much bigger deal. My little sister couldn't see any of us.

Skeeter's voice pierced the muted mood. "The docs can fix it, right?"

Dad's voice trailed off to whisper as he said, "She'll need surgery to remove the cataracts."

Surgery? She was so little. Years younger than I was when I had my tonsils taken out.

I leaned in close. My eyes flicked from Susie's face to my mother's profile. Even if I'd been able to look right into my mother's face, I'm not certain I could have guessed what she was thinking. I imagined she was in shock over Susie's impairment. I'm sure she worried about surgery and the days and years ahead. One look at Mom's pale complexion told me she was tired. Besides fatigue and distress, perhaps there was disappointment and frustration with the god to whom she devoutly prayed and believed in.

Dad turned to my grandmother. "Mom, would you like to be first? Hold your newest grandchild?"

As Grandma Mimi held out her large fleshy arms and snuggled Susie against her generous chest, my mind skipped back in time. To the previous October. To the rule of threes and wanting positivity in our life. I thought we had completed the cycle of bad news. With Susie's cataract diagnosis, it appeared a new cycle of mishaps and misfortune had begun.

15

How Dare You?

Spring 1972

I had forgotten my library book on the end table in the living room. As I left my bedroom and descended the front staircase, I grinned. Mom and I had finally reached an agreement. She allowed me to read in the living room—a place reserved for special occasions—if I promised not to rest my ponytail against the back of the flocked olive club chairs. It was a win that deeply satisfied me. The living room was the only spot in the house where I could truly be alone to read, journal, and muse about my teenage goals and dreams. But there was to be no daydreaming or reading in the living room that day. When I was halfway down the carpeted front stairs, Mom's voice filtered through the funnel of the kitchen's pass-through, resounding into the hall and stairwell.

"What makes you think Jack and I would *ever* entertain such an idea?" Mom said. I could hear the anger in her voice.

Whoa! Who is Mom talking to?

The underlying emotion seeped out, making her delivery clipped, crisp and tart like a Granny Smith apple. Whomever my mother was speaking with had made her blistering mad. But just as she had coached us many times, Mom contained her fury "like a lady would do."

Afraid to make a sound, I crouched down on a step.

I knew I shouldn't eavesdrop on such a private conversation, but I couldn't help myself. I wanted to know who had irritated my mother and what they had proposed. Above me, Jenny's footsteps creaked on the landing. I put a finger to my lips and patted the spot next to me. She plopped down, her face scrunching up with questions. I jabbed my finger in the air and pointed at the kitchen pass-through a few feet away.

Mom's voice rose, her wrath too fierce to tame. "Just *who* do you think you are to suggest such a thing?"

Jenny turned to me. Our mouths opened in a silent *wow.*

We scooted close to the staircase railing, our faces peering through the banister.

Like a train leaving a depot, mom's speech accelerated. "Now, you listen to me. Susie's impaired vision is a challenge we'll weather as a family." As Mom paused, I envisioned her gathering the necessary energy to complete a counterattack. "No one, do you hear me? *No one* but Jack and me will raise our precious little daughter."

When Mom hesitated again, Jenny and I glanced at one another, our eyebrows raised. "Hiding Susie away in an institution is not an option. This conversation is over."

My breath felt trapped inside my chest. *Who would have the courage to suggest our parents put our new baby sister in an institution?* Before Mom slammed down the receiver, my eyes crinkled with doubt. I turned to Jenny and mouthed Grandma Mimi's name. Jenny shook her head. We stared into each other's eyes and then whispered the same name in unison: Aunt Helen.

When we heard Mom hustle into the hallway powder room, Jenny and I double-backed to our room and softly closed the door.

My twin sunk onto the edge of her canopy bed, staring into my eyes. "It just had to be Aunt Helen. Remember the story of when you, me, and Skeeter were the only ones who didn't receive gifts from her at Christmas?" Jen's mouth puckered in thought. "I think Grandma's too kind and loving to suggest putting sweet little Susie away."

I hung my head. The conversation we'd witnessed had left me feeling wounded. "I can't imagine Susie growing up anywhere else but *here*. With all of us."

Jenny teared up, her hazel eyes brightening to a vivid green. She and I didn't know it then, but the caller's suggestion was not an uncommon practice for the times. There was precedent for families to send children off to special care facilities to receive treatment and therapies, such as the dreaded lobotomies. Even famous people like the Kennedys had institutionalized a daughter with learning disabilities.

Jen's face was bright pink. Clenched fists lay balled up in her lap. "Mom did the right thing telling off whoever that was on the phone."

I squelched a snicker. "If it was Aunt Helen, I bet she never brings it up again."

The corners of Jenny's mouth turned up. Anyone who knew our mother was aware she could be quite the force if pushed too far. I didn't say it aloud, but my heart pounded with pride. Our mother had taken a strong stance against institutionalizing our sister. It was clear she wouldn't give away her child to someone else to raise. I sighed. Not like my birth mother had done.

Within weeks of Susie's cataract diagnosis, my parents scheduled appointments with a vision specialist and a surgeon at Children's Memorial Hospital in Chicago. To increase her chances of leading a normal life, the doctors proposed cataract surgery on both eyes, a groundbreaking procedure for a newborn. Susie would undergo the first surgery at six weeks old, and the second one for when she was three months old—about the time Jenny and I would begin our eighth-grade year at St. Cletus. I wondered if Susie's fussiness would interfere with the surgeon's ability to remove her cataracts, and when her vision improved, I hoped she kept the bright blue eyes she had in common with Lizzie and Dad.

Over one of our typical Thursday-evening spaghetti dinners, Dad grabbed a second slice of bread, slathered it with creamy butter, and repeated something else the doctors had shared. "Well, one good thing has come from all these talks with doctors. They say we should consider ourselves fortunate. Children affected by rubella often have serious heart problems, too."

My mom interrupted Dad, her face tired and pinched. "Susie was spared a serious heart issue, as far as they can tell, dear. Surgery will remove the cataracts, but they can't predict how good her eyesight will be."

Mom stood to clear the leftovers. "Post-surgery, she's going to need glasses."

Jenny elbowed me. I had a hunch what she was going to say next.

"We want to go with you, Mom," Jen gestured at me, "to pick out Susie's glasses. We don't want you getting frames that'll make her look like a dork."

Dad roared at Jenny's comment, the buttons on his blue dress shirt pulling tight across his belly.

As our family waited for the day of Susie's first surgery to arrive, our household did not function as it had before her birth. Mom was not sleeping well due to late-night feedings, so Grandma Mimi stopped by most evenings to help. Jenny and I pitched in with chores like folding laundry, sorting socks, and putting away dishes. Our brothers were tasked with keeping the family room picked up and the trash taken out. Despite all this, my mom was often short-tempered. It felt as if we were all walking on eggshells.

On top of the issues at home and keeping up with our school-work, Jenny and I were anxious about the upcoming cheerleading tryouts. My heart sunk when the gym teacher and tryout coordinator, Mrs. Halpern, announced the number of girls competing for a spot on the twelve-person squad had doubled from the previous year. Instead of a single day of tryouts, the new plan stretched over two days. Even though I'd led the seventh-grade girls as their captain, making the eighth-grade team would be twice as hard. There would be no room for error.

When the tryout times were posted, I reread the list several times. I couldn't believe it. Jenny and I had been split up. I was slated for the first day, and Jenny on the second. The outcome unnerved me. I was used to my twin being by my side in everything we tackled. *Who would help calm my nerves while I waited my turn to go out on the floor?* Separating us felt wrong, cruel, like an unwarranted punishment.

As it turned out, my angst was warranted. Partway through the tryout routine, there was a required stunt that involved jumping into the air and finishing on the floor in splits. I had no problem executing the jump, but when I hit the gym floor, I felt a searing pain in my groin. I struggled to get up and execute the next sequence of moves. The throbbing pain grew intolerable. It became clear I could not complete my routine, so Mrs. Halpern escorted me off to the bleachers.

When the gym teacher returned with an ice pack, she said, "I tried calling your home, but no one answered. I'll try again in a little bit."

Where was my mother when I needed her?

As I sat with my ice pack watching my classmates complete their tryout routines, my spirits plummeted. Grandma Mimi's rule of threes was one of the first thoughts to cross my mind. *You were an idiot to think a positive attitude could ward off trouble.* I hadn't completed my tryout. I knew my chances of making the eighth-grade squad were nil.

Since Jenny wasn't there with me, the only comfort I received was from Mrs. Halpern and a few friends. Because my mother hadn't answered the phone, I faced a grueling eight-block walk home. Alone. Injured. I had never felt so defeated and abandoned.

With each painful step, I sobbed, repeating over and over, "Where is my mother and why is she always unavailable when I need her?" Snot dripped down my face as I cried, envisioning Jenny and our friends cheering for the eighth-grade boys in the fall while I watched from the crowd. I wasn't certain which was worse—the injury or the idea of being left out of the fun.

When I hobbled through the back door, I found Mom in the dining room nursing Susie. I pulled out a chair and gingerly lowered myself onto the seat. At that point, my self-pity was so profound that no detail, no thought, was too small to share.

I unloaded on my mother.

"The one time I needed you to answer the phone because I'm really, really hurt, you don't." I wiped away fresh tears and blew my nose as noisily as I could into a tissue. "It's like this all the time, Mom. We all hate it." My mother did not look up; her eyes stayed riveted on Susie's face. Glaring at her, I continued. "When you finally get around to picking us up from one of our activities, you're so late that we're the last ones waiting in the parking lot. It's so embarrassing."

Exhausted from the walk home and spent emotion, I slumped against the seat back. I stared at my mother, blankly, mutely, waiting for her to respond. I hoped she understood how neglected I felt and the ramifications of my injury.

After I finished my little woe-is-me speech, Mom flipped a white cloth diaper over one shoulder and raised Susie up, patting her back. When Mom's dark eyes finally met mine, they were tired pools of sorrow and regret.

"I'm so sorry you're hurt, honey." Susie burped and Mom rubbed her back some more. "I didn't answer the phone because I was napping. I had a rough time with your sister last night."

Mom got up and laid Susie in the bassinet in the corner of the dining room. "Let's get you an ice pack and some aspirin."

While I appreciated my mom's apologies and her care for my injury, it did little to lift my dejected mood. I'd bombed the cheer tryouts. Nothing could fix that. Soon, I would be an outsider looking in at the cool girls, my twin sister among them.

Several days later, when Mrs. Halpern posted the eighth-grade cheerleading roster on the gym doors, Jenny's name was hard to miss at the top. She'd earned enough points to be named co-captain.

I tried smiling as I elbowed Jenny. "Look at you, Miss Co-Captain. Way to go."

I held my breath as I scanned the list, steeling myself for the inevitable disappointment.

Beside me, Jenny pointed to the bottom of the list, a big smile brightening her face. "You made it! I told you not to worry!"

"What? Really? How could that be . . ." I mumbled as Jenny threw an arm around my shoulders.

I blinked hard to squelch the brimming tears. My heart soared with relief. I wasn't going to be left out or left behind like I'd imagined. I found out later that Mrs. Halpern had gone to the cheer judges and explained my unique situation: I had served as the team's previous captain, my tryout routine had been impeccably executed up to the point of injury, my injury would heal, and I would be an asset to the squad.

Three weeks later, my parents took Susie down to Children's Memorial Hospital in Chicago, and she had the cataract extracted from her right eye. Mom and Dad had explained how tricky the procedure would be. Susie needed to lie still, and she'd come home with a patch that would need to stay on. Infection was the biggest concern. When my folks brought Susie home from the hospital with a perforated metal patch taped around her right eye, my heart melted. Something switched on in my teenage brain, too.

Because of those frequent "adoption talks" between my parents, my sister, and me, I knew that infertility was the reason my folks chose adoption to build their family. Although my parents often marveled how miraculous it was that Patrick and Lizzie were born to them, I never gave the significance of their births much thought. At the time, I had been too young to consider the facts. It was only after Mark's stillborn birth and the news of Susie's impairment that I realized the significant hardships my parents faced in realizing their dream of a big Catholic American family.

Once the reality sunk in that our family included a visually impaired child, I couldn't help but wonder if my parents were done adding to our family. As I held my baby sister after her surgery, I knew family life as we had known it was a thing of the past. Susie was going to need so much of my mother's time and attention. Raising five healthy children was one thing, but adding a child with a profound disability was going to affect all of us, not just our parents. Mom's failure to pick up the phone on the day of my cheerleading injury was not the only time she would neglect one of us—or all of us.

On that day of Susie's first surgery, I retrieved my journal from its hiding place between my mattress and box spring and headed straight to the living room to scribble my thoughts. Below the date, I wrote about holding Susie, her eye patch, and how I worried about what her life would be like, and because I could write honestly between the lines, I speculated.

If my parents had stopped adding to our family after adopting Jenny, Skeeter, and me, they'd have been spared so much heartache. Why hadn't we been enough?

16

All Are Welcome

Spring 1973

"Does my hair look okay?" Jenny asked.

As my sister turned, tucking an errant strand behind one ear, I got a whiff of the fragrant Prell shampoo we both liked. I stopped fussing with the clasp on my white satin graduation gown and scrutinized my twin. Her glossy, fine brown hair was parted neatly on the left side, like mine, and settled in a clean line across her shoulders. A few minutes ago, our entire eighth-grade graduating class had left St. Cletus school and filed into the back of church.

"Yep. Hair looks nice. But"—I started giggling— "you got something stuck in your braces. Right there," I said, pointing.

"Oh, man. You're so lucky you don't need braces." Jenny picked at her tooth with a fingernail. "Did I get it?"

I nodded and spied two of our eighth-grade teachers approaching. They cruised down the double line of graduates, eyeballing our class, and making sure for the umpteenth time that caps and gowns were being worn properly. We'd been lined up, not by last name, but by height. As had been the case throughout our grammar school years, Jenny and I—still known as "the Ryan twins," a nickname I hoped we'd lose once high school began—were paired together. Because my twin and I had matured early, already close to our adult height of five feet seven inches, we took positions near the end of the graduation procession.

Mrs. Murphy, our history teacher, smiled at Jenny and me as she glided past, stopping beside the pair of boys behind us.

"Dennis, you'd better tie that shoelace, honey. You don't want to wipe out when Father Gallagher hands you that hard-earned diploma."

Everyone around us cracked up at the image of six-foot-tall Dennis sprawled across the marble steps leading to the altar. Leave it to Mrs. Murphy, a favorite among all the eighth graders, to use gentle humor to lighten everyone's nerves.

As our teacher strode away, Jenny caught my eye. We scooted a few feet out of line to peek through the main doors of the church. Every pew on both sides of the center aisle was jam-packed with families. The alcoves, too. Even though the side doors leading to the rectory, parking lot, and schoolyard were propped open, the worship space was warm and close, mimicking the hot and humid June day beyond.

"Do you see them?" Jenny asked, referring to our family.

My hazel eyes narrowed as I scanned the crowd. "Nope. Bet they're off to the side. In case Susie gets antsy."

Jenny sent me a look that was part smile, part frown. "Or because they were running late, per usual."

I spotted Father McGinnity and Father Gallagher emerge from the sacristy adorned in their matching full-length green vestments. I yanked Jenny back into line as the parish priests threaded through the church and took the lead position in the line of sixty-some graduates. The priests couldn't have been more different in appearance, demeanor, and approach to ministering to our parish. Father McGinnity, with his warm, pleasant manner and handsome features, towered over our wiry, dark-haired, and stern pastor, Father Gallagher. Even though he was the associate pastor, most of the

Masses Father McGinnity celebrated were standing room only. Yet, one could often nab a seat near the front of the church when Father Gallagher said Mass.

As the opening notes of the processional hymn "All Are Welcome All Belong" filtered into the church vestibule, the excitement and anticipation leading up to Graduation Day coalesced, making me feel giddy and silly. Nostalgic, too. My twin sister and I had attended St. Cletus School with most of the sixty-plus students filing ahead of us into church since kindergarten. Alongside our class, we'd received our sacraments. During special all-school Masses, we'd mourned the assassinations of Martin Luther King, Jr., and Robert Kennedy, and thanks to teachers like Mrs. Murphy, we became aware of current events like *Roe v. Wade*, the end of the US involvement in the Vietnam War, Watergate, and the signing of the Paris Peace Accords. Together, we'd also prayed for the Fey and Fredian families. Now that a suspect was finally on trial for Alan's murder, we'd all breathed a collective sigh of relief.

Because of our years at St. Cletus, Jenny and I had honed our study skills and developed a love for sports like volleyball, softball, cheerleading, and track. Over the past year, my twin and I had begun to differentiate ourselves, honing our identities to fit our unique personalities. Jenny had become more social, sillier, and more spontaneous than me. I had gained a reputation as being the "serious" twin, more reserved and studious. In the classroom, both of us were inclined to tackle extra-credit projects, stay after class to help a teacher, and volunteer to lead group assignments. While Jenny planned on playing volleyball in high school, I had set my mind on trying out for the girls' tennis team.

As excited as I was to attend Benet Academy—a Catholic coed high school run by the Benedictine monks eleven miles from home—I would miss the easy familiarity, sense of shared history, and belonging I'd enjoyed at St. Cletus. Most of our graduating class was headed off to the local public school, Lyons Township High School (LTHS). Only a handful of students, like Jenny and me, were attending Catholic high schools in the greater Chicagoland area. To me, our graduation day was like the closing chapter in a good book. Part of me wanted to linger on the last page, and the other part couldn't wait to pick up the sequel.

I smiled shyly at Jenny as we took our first steps into the main church. The entire congregation was on their feet watching our graduating class—the girls bedecked in white robes and the boys in red—parade in. With so many bodies packed into the worship space, the church had become stifling. Many folks used the mimeographed program booklets to fan themselves. As the pamphlets fluttered in the flat air, they reminded me of little flags cheering us on. I tried not thinking about the sweat moistening the chic mini dress beneath my white gown, or how slippery the soles of my feet felt in new white strappy sandals.

Instead, I concentrated on the prescribed spacing between the students in front of Jenny and me. Once I landed in our assigned pew, all I wanted was to soak in the pageantry of the moment and try locating our family. After that, the rest was easy. Mass followed by diplomas and the announcement of the leadership awards, which we had voted on as a class. I had tried not dwelling on those honors, mostly because I assumed members of the "cool" crowd were destined to receive them.

Jenny tapped my arm. "Mom and Dad and everybody are over there on the left side. A few rows back. Near the confessionals."

I located my family in the spot Jenny described. My stomach tickled at the sight of them smashed together and consuming an entire church pew. Lizzie—looking so grown-up in her appliqued sundress and golden hair wrapped in a tight chignon—slouched next to Grandma Mimi at one end. Grandma patted a wadded-up hankie to her forehead and temples while instructing Lizzie how to craft a fan out of the program booklet. The nine-year age gap between Lizzie, and Jenny and me meant that just as my twin and I entered high school, Lizzie would begin her schooling at St. Cletus. The last year had been one of great change and transition for Lizzie. She'd started kindergarten, lost her status as the spoiled youngest child, and gained a roommate and a baby sister, but one whose needs demanded more and more of Mom's time.

Next to Grandma, Dad was wedged between my brothers, both of whom sported sour looks. I giggled softly at the sight. No doubt, the pair had bickered in the car over some slight, maybe even dared to argue with Mom over the matching crisp shirts and seersucker slacks she'd selected for them to wear. Unfazed by my brothers' poor attitudes, Dad slipped out of his khaki blazer, draped it over his lap, and handed each of my brothers a missal to follow along with the order of Mass.

Jenny whispered with friends seated in the row in front of us. I tapped her knee. "Look at Patrick and Skeeter's faces."

She covered her mouth, stifling a laugh. "I know they'd rather be at the ballpark. Both are missing a ballgame to be here."

Jenny went back to sharing whispers with the girls, and I gazed back at my family. At the far end of the pew, Mom sat with Susie on her lap. My sister's dark hair was gathered up in a wispy pony-tail, several plastic butterfly barrettes capturing the loose tendrils near her flawless heart-shaped face. Last month, we had celebrated Susie's first birthday in the dining room with everyone gathered around. It felt good to be well past Susie's surgeries. Other than her severe vision issues, she had developed normally, crawling and walking right on schedule.

Before I turned my attention back to the altar, I watched Mom and Susie snuggle close, singing along with the entrance hymn. I imagined my mom's lovely soprano voice mixing with my sister's soft babbles as they sang the refrain:

All are welcome in this place, behold love's amazing grace, all are welcome.

Bring your hopes, bring your dreams, mercy flows and love redeems, all are welcome, all belong.

Whether it was the song's powerful message, the stifling warmth in the church, or the conflicting emotions I had about beginning the next phase of my life, I suddenly felt weak and tired. But as I shuttered my eyes, the organ stopped, and our pastor, Father Gallagher, barked stiff words of welcome into the microphone. I jerked awake.

Jenny gave me a sidewise glance. I knew what her gesture meant—*He's so strict and boring.* I nodded my agreement.

Instead of tuning in to Father Gallagher's monotonous recap of our years at St. Cletus, I constructed my own personal list. I relived significant moments from the previous year: Susie's healing; the passing of my beloved pet, Gigi; Jenny's success at the cheer squad's co-captain; my speedy recovery from the groin injury; and Mom's suggestion that Jenny and I deserved a room makeover.

When she brought that up, our faces gleamed with surprise. I had pounced on Mom's idea. "I'd love a more modern, teenage bedroom. Wouldn't you, Jen?"

Jenny's smile spread from ear to ear. "We need proper study desks. More room to spread out."

My mother's face brightened. "Yes, I do think the canopy beds are more appropriate for Lizzie and Susie. We could shop for colorful fabrics. Now that you two know how to work the sewing machine," Mom pointed at Jenny and me, "you can make the accessories."

Mom's suggestion snowballed. At the fabric store, we selected vivid check and polka dot fabrics in greens, yellows, pinks, and purples. We chose yards of snazzy trim like zigzag grosgrain ribbon and clusters of pompoms. When we swapped rooms, Lizzie and Susie inherited the white canopy beds, the all-white bedding, and green shag carpeting. Jenny and I took over their bedroom at the front of the house where Dad installed an L-shaped work area with open shelving overhead. As thrilled as we were to settle into fresh spaces, we weren't as electrified as we would have been with a larger bedroom, a room each to call our own, or a bathroom we didn't have to share with four younger siblings.

As the Mass moved through its predictable rituals, my mind continued to wander. I thought about the dinner conversation the previous fall when Dad announced, "Girls, it's time to start looking at Catholic high schools. Your mother and I have decided that LT is not an option."

Jenny and I had grumbled. "But Dad, Mom, all our friends are going there. Please . . ."

Perhaps it was the Fredian murder, the frequent arrests of "greaser" types who hung out smoking in front of the school's south campus, or the news reports of widespread drug use that pushed our parents in the private school direction. No matter what arguments we threw out, nothing we said swayed them to change their minds.

Dad's face had been solemn, not a hint of his usual lighthearted manner. "Girls, as we see it, your choices are Nazareth or Benet."

Jenny exploded. Her face became so red it erased all evidence of the smattering of freckles. "There's *no way* I'm going to an all-girls school."

I stared at my twin, surprised at her outburst but proud of her for speaking up. Because of her leadership on the cheer squad, Jenny had become more forceful in offering opinions. I opened my mouth to back up my twin, but Mom glowered at Jenny.

"Excuse me, young lady. Watch who you're speaking to."

Dad sighed. "I guess that leaves Benet. It's further away. A bus or train ride, but it's coed. Let's tour the school and learn when the entrance exam will be held."

All of us were impressed by the school's lush green campus, rich history and traditions, and motto: *Work and pray*. In January, Jenny and I scored high enough to be admitted to Benet. And that is how our high school selection was made. It hinged on Catholicism, a strong education, a safe environment, and boys.

A squeal I recognized broke my reverie. I looked back at my family. Susie's tiny little feet bounced on the wooden pew seat as she craned her head to study the streaks of colored light filtering through the alcove's stained-glass windows. Due to my sister's cataract surgeries, her vision was limited to less than five feet. As a result, she had developed a curious habit. To focus on something outside her scope, she bobbed her head and rolled her eyes repetitively. Often her eyes did not track in the same direction. While our family had grown accustomed to this strange behavior, the reactions from those outside our inner circle ranged from curiosity to alarm. While we never got used to strangers' prolonged stares, we learned to ignore their prying looks—most of the time, that is.

I giggled as I studied Skeeter. He was still stuck between Grandma and Dad, a sullen pout plastered to his face. Slow-moving activities or events with repetition crazed my brother. He had a need to move, to act, to do. But when it came to anything regarding Susie, he had the patience of a god. He was always her champion.

A few weeks earlier, Mom had Skeeter and Susie together with her in the A&P grocery. Mom had stepped away to look for an item on her grocery list and asked my brother to stay with Susie, who was strapped in the cart. Susie was mesmerized by the display of fluorescent lights in the ceiling. Her head bobbed this way and that as she attempted to focus on the strange lights and the landscape they highlighted. Some poor ignorant soul strolling down the same aisle made the mistake of ogling my sister's bizarre mannerisms. Skeeter picked up on their nosiness faster than a line drive.

As Mom returned to the aisle she spotted my brother, his hands clenched in tight fists, blue eyes glaring at the shopper. His deepening voice boomed, "What're you looking at?"

Before the startled offender sidled off, Skeeter edged closer, shouting. "That's my sister. She's not hurtin' anybody. She sure doesn't need some idiot like you staring at her. Get lost!"

Susie's disability, and her quiet, sweet nature molded my family in ways I could not have foreseen. As soon as Susie crawled and walked, Mom didn't have to remind us to keep the floor clear of objects that might harm her. Each of us became cognizant of her favorite traffic patterns in and around the furniture layout.

When Mom asked one of us to "keep an eye on Susie," the responsibility was one we did not take lightly. None of us wanted her to get cut or bruised under our watch. Receiving a tongue lashing from Mom because of negligence was one thing, but witnessing Susie suffer due to our inattentiveness produced unbearable guilt.

The care and concern we naturally afforded Susie morphed into an expansion of our awareness toward others less fortunate. My siblings and I grew to recognize when people we encountered— individuals with Down's syndrome, the physically disabled, the poor, or the elderly—needed extra time or special assistance. Without urging from adults, we opened doors, stepped side, and readily offered an arm. Susie was our change agent; she made us better human beings.

Beside me, Jenny muttered, "Finally. Time for diplomas. And the awards."

I smiled broadly at my twin. *Right. Diplomas. Awards.*

As I focused on the teachers lining up on the altar alongside the priests, crisp vanilla parchment certificates stacked neatly in their hands, my heart quickened. Perhaps it was nerves or the thought of walking in front of the entire congregation to receive my diploma, or maybe it was anticipating the activities scheduled after our ceremony. Mom had planned an open house honoring Jenny and me;

she'd invited relatives, neighbors, and close family friends. That morning we'd helped Mom string streamers, blow balloons, and prepare food and snack trays. The large sheet cake emblazoned with *Congratulations, Julie and Jenny* looked scrumptious.

Certainly, some of the emotions swirling inside my body had to do with my graduation gift: a new puppy to replace our old dog, Gigi. While the new dog would be the family pet, I would care for it and train it. As a family, we'd decided on a fluffy, white male Samoyed. I'd researched the breed and planned to name him Nikki, which meant victory. I promised Mom I'd spend the summer housebreaking and leash-training him before I started at Benet in the fall.

Despite my scattered thoughts and nervous energy, I managed to make it to the altar, offer a smile, shake hands with Father McGinnity, and return to my seat without stumbling or dropping my diploma. As I smoothed out my white gown, and straightened the cap on my head, I stifled tears. In the pews in front of Jenny and me, our friends held tissues to their faces. We all felt it, the strange cocktail composed of unlike ingredients: elation, sorrow, nostalgia, gratitude, relief, and anxiety about what the future held for us.

I was caught up in that strange swirl of emotion; it had sucked me in, slowing down time, forcing me to savor the precious moment with my peers. As if she were a character in a movie, I watched as Mrs. Murphy stepped up to the microphone. She signaled to Father Gallagher. He nodded stiffly, strode from the altar—his elaborate priestly gown swishing and brushing the marble tiles—and came to a jerky stop next to her at the podium. Mrs. Murphy handed him two certificates. I'm sure I was not the only one who wished it was Father McGinnity, not Father Gallagher, tasked with handing out the coveted class awards.

Our teacher tapped the microphone, and once the crackles and sputters had settled, her confident voice sifted through the church's tight air. As the congregation shushed, I heard the intake of my own labored breath. *The awards.*

I had convinced myself it didn't matter if the popular crowd garnered the honors. But as I waited for the announcement, I knew I had only been fooling myself. I cared. I wanted to be recognized by my peers. I wanted to be acknowledged for my excellent grades, my contributions to the cheer squad and volleyball teams, for the support and kindness I had shown my teachers and classmates over the years. Receiving one of the awards would mean validation, acknowledgment, and belonging. It would mean all the striving to be perfect had been worth something: I was enough. While I dared not hope for the recognition, it would mean the world to me if it happened. I stared at my folded hands and concentrated on breathing. Beside me Jenny did the same.

"And now, it's my distinct pleasure to announce the Good Citizen Award recipients for the St. Cletus graduating class of 1973."

I waved my program booklet in front of my face as Mrs. Murphy explained to the audience that our class had voted on the awards. They were being presented to "one boy and one girl who had demonstrated leadership, academic prowess, a strong work ethic, and who exemplified the Catholic values taught at St. Cletus."

She cleared her throat and continued, "The class of 1973 believes that these individuals are most likely to continue their academic studies, to pursue excellence, and to make a profound difference in the world."

When Mrs. Murphy paused, looking down at the paper in front of her, time stood still for me. My body said one thing: *Sit back, rest, breathe, enjoy this moment, applaud your winning classmates.* But my heart shouted something else: *Get ready, it's your time to soar.*

Breath filled up in my chest as Mrs. Murphy announced Jamie's name, a boy I respected. As my classmate made his way up to Father

Gallagher to receive his award, I rose to my feet along with my classmates, who whistled and clapped.

Once Jamie had left the altar, another stifling pause settled over the crowd. I wiped my palms along the sides of my pristine white gown.

"And the winner of our second award, goes to . . ."

My mouth froze, mid-breath, when I heard my name. For the smallest fraction of time, I sunk into myself, gratitude and relief and surprise rooting me in place, but then Jenny patted my knee, her face a thousand smiles. She pushed me out of my seat. My legs felt mushy, barely able to support me. Heart bursting and face glowing, I crept out of the pew. I strode up the center aisle, genuflecting in the direction of the large cross as I had been taught to do, and my inner voice sung to me: *Bring your hopes, bring your dreams, mercy flows and love redeems, all are welcome, all belong.*

17

In a Moment

Fall 1973

I was feeling lucky.

Instead of the usual five o'clock shuttle from Benet to the Lisle train station and a four-block walk home, I caught a ride. My teammate's older brother Jim offered to drive me all the way home. When he pulled the Ford Pinto up to the curb, I disentangled myself from the back seat. For thirty minutes, I'd been scrunched up there with my friend Karen talking doubles tennis strategy.

Wriggling my bags out of the Pinto's hatchback, I shouted, "Thanks for the ride!"

I heaved my overstuffed book bag onto my back and slung the tote containing my tennis clothes and coveted Chrissy Evert wooden racquet over a shoulder. As I watched Karen's brother edge the car out into rush-hour traffic, I held my breath. Within the year, Jenny and I would start driver's ed. While I craved the independence of driving, I dreaded learning to navigate the busy intersection by our house. I couldn't imagine getting behind the wheel of Mom's station wagon and backing out of our garage into four lanes of traffic. The thought of it terrified me.

Jenny and I were slowly getting used to our high school routine. Before seven o'clock each morning, Dad drove us to St. Cletus, where we met our school bus. Each day at Benet was dizzying, ripe with newness. The only thing that wasn't novel was the familiar act of sitting next to my twin in the cafeteria and eating the brown bag lunches we brought from home.

When the school day ended and I headed to tennis, Jenny rode the bus home. My sister had made the Benet girls JV volleyball team, but her team practices hadn't started yet. Because Jen and I were not in any classes together or playing the same sports, the only time we saw one another was at our lockers during class changeovers or in the twenty-five-minute homeroom and lunch periods. If we spotted one another in a jammed corridor, we shared a brief, knowing smile. Those chance glimpses of my twin sister were welcome blessings. They served to ease my angst over the day's little frustrations and reminded me I was not alone. Jenny and I were in *it*—this strange, new, far-off coed Catholic high school world—together. As we strove to make new friends, and to fit in at Benet, we were secure, safe within our own brand of belonging: our twindom.

The knowing glances shared in Benet's hallways meant something else, too. They were promises. I knew when I returned home after tennis each evening, Jenny and I would adjourn to our spiffy redecorated shared room and shut the door. There, we would whisper and giggle and groan and whine as we rehashed our separate versions of the day's ups and downs. The unique and unfaltering bond I enjoyed with my sister was the coping mechanism that allowed me to navigate the strangeness of freshmen year.

"Hey, *Julieee*!"

When I heard my name, I whipped my head around and scanned the many fields and trails at The Park. On the basketball court, I caught the crazy waves of two Benet classmates, guys who had attended St. Cletus and rode the morning bus to Benet with Jenny and me.

"Hey!" I yelled, waving at the boys.

As Mike picked up the basketball and passed it to a friend for a layup, I remembered the many summer days I'd run into these boys at The Park while I leash-trained my Samoyed puppy, Nikki. Whenever they spotted Nikki and me, the boys shouted for us to wander over. They loved running their hands through Nikki's thick white coat, and he lapped up the attention.

I was proud of my beautiful dog, his gentle nature and playfulness, and my efforts in training him. By the time classes had started at Benet, Nikki was fully housebroken. I'd taught him to heel and take commands like sit, stay, and give paw. He'd become the family's prized pet, too. It warmed everyone's heart to see Susie lie down with him on the family room floor. She loved resting her head on his chest, listening to his beating heart, and stroking his soft fur. Another puppy might have nipped, growled, or scampered off, but Nikki welcomed Susie's delicate touch.

Laden with all my bags, I lumbered up the front walk to the main door of our house. As soon as I got inside, I planned to whistle for Nikki, snap on his leash, and venture over to The Park to chat with the guys. I expected to find Mom at the kitchen sink drying dishes and the dinner she had saved for me warming on the stove. Dad was probably stationed by the family room TV while my brothers worked on homework at the kitchen table. No doubt Jenny was in the dining room or upstairs in our room with schoolbooks, colored folders, and spiral notebooks fanned out around her.

The closer I got to the house, though, the cacophony of my siblings in our fenced-in back yard blasted around the side of the house like a band playing at full volume.

Wonder why Mom is letting them play so close to the younger girls' bedtimes.

Then I noticed that the heavy black front door was propped open. *That's odd, too.*

Normally, I rung the front doorbell a couple of times before someone came to unlock it. Since Alan Fredian's murder, locking the doors had become my family's strict habit. If no one answered the doorbell, then I gathered my things and walked around the perimeter of the house, navigating a series of latched gates leading to the patio and back entrance. The elaborate fence system had been installed years ago, but with Susie's vision issues, it had gained importance. All of us were careful to shut the gates for fear that our sight-challenged sister would escape and wander into traffic at the busy street corner.

As I reached for the door handle, I noticed the day's mail and Nikki's brown leather leash dangling like a loose thread from the hall table. Nikki was also absent from his favorite napping spot by the front door. He must be out back with the other kids, I thought. I hoped someone had thought to bring his water dish outside—it was such a warm fall evening!

I passed with my bags through the ornery storm door and into the foyer. In the dining room to my left, my twin sister's homework was nowhere in sight. The smile that had lit up my face a moment ago vanished when I glanced in the direction of the front room. Both of my parents were perched primly in the pair of flocked olive club chairs flanking the fireplace. They weren't talking. Just staring. Staring past one another into space as if they'd used up their allotment of words for the day. A box of Kleenex cozied up to Mom's collection of green glass knickknacks on the filigreed coffee table. The adjacent cream loveseat and its coordinating olive and rust velvet pillows were perfect, like a furniture ad in a decorating magazine. The sofa was empty. I swallowed hard.

What was going on?

I slipped off my mahogany-colored school loafers and met my parents' stares.

"Hey, Mom. Hi, Dad." My voice took on the hushed mood in the room. "Where's Jenny? Is Nikki out back with the kids?"

Because my parents didn't answer right away, my eyes flicked between them like a child awaiting a reprimand. Mom sat with her knees knit together, her hands clasped as if in prayer. The woeful way she looked at my dad sent waves of chilly prickles racing up my naked arms. Dad's dimples were a memory, and the serious jut to his jaw meant he was not going to vanquish the room's awkward air with a tease or joke.

Another sip of air did nothing to quell the frantic thrumming of my heart.

"Hi, honey," Mom gestured to me. "C'mon in."

Clad in my white knee-high socks, I tiptoed into the stiff, formal front room. When my mother gave Dad a stern nod, my stomach flipped like it did whenever Brother Charles announced a pop algebra quiz. I looked wide-eyed, pleadingly, at my father. I desperately wanted him to say something, anything, just one word that would ease the panic creeping up from my belly and nestling under my breastbone.

Why wasn't Jenny in here with me for this serious talk?

Dad's craggy eyebrows hiked up to his graying temples. He cleared his throat. "We have something to tell you."

When I plunked down on the cream loveseat—a place where I'd parked myself more than a few times for the infamous "adoption chats"—the starched pleats of my gray and maroon plaid uniform skirt flopped heavily against the delicate damask. I straightened my skirt, wiping my palms against its pleats. I didn't like this setup one bit.

The *boom-boom* of my heart echoed into my ears. Somehow, I managed to squeak out the worry consuming my entire physical being.

"Where's Jenny? Is she okay?"

Mom's dark eyebrows drew closer together. She looked from Dad to me, and her lips parted as if puzzled by my question. By the time it took for my heart to beat again, it dawned on her that I feared something awful had happened to my twin.

Mom's features softened. "Oh, your sister's fine," she reached out and patted my hand. "Jenny's out back with the other kids."

As soon as I heard those words, "Oh, your sister's fine," I collapsed into the back of the sofa, squashing the artistically fluffed pillows. Then, just as dramatically as I had fallen into the sofa's cushions, I bolted upright.

My heart rate resumed a frantic pace. If my twin sister was okay, then . . .

I wanted to shout at my parents, but I knew better.

"Then what *is* going on?"

Mom shook her head sadly and handed me the tissue box from the coffee table. Part of me wanted to storm out of the room and race Nikki over to The Park; the other part felt like charging into the backyard to see what my siblings were up to. But I didn't. I waited. And that fraction of time felt like forever.

"It's Nikki." Mom gestured at the busy street beyond the front window. "Patrick tried to take him for a walk after school. He pulled away. Ran off into the traffic on Forty-Seventh Street." Her solemn brown eyes filled with tears. "He got hit by a car. He didn't suffer, honey."

My mother joined me on the sofa and pulled me into a hug. "I'm so sorry. He was such a good dog. You did such a nice job training him." She stroked my head and then let a warm palm linger on my freckled cheek. "We can look for another dog when you're ready. Maybe next spring?"

I squirmed out of my mother's too-tight hug. Waves of shock and relief battled for first place in my fourteen-year-old brain.

Jenny was safe! The sweet, fluffy puppy I'd spent all summer training was gone.

The magnitude of the loss I'd been spared juxtaposed sharply with the news of Nikki's accident, causing my emotions to get locked up somewhere between my heart and my eyes. Tears did not come. Grief stalled due to the realization that a bigger loss had been averted. My lookalike—the sister with whom I had shared a room for fourteen years and who had occupied my other mother's womb with me before that—was healthy and just yards away.

I sat frozen in the corner of the loveseat like one of the mannequins in Slocum's department store front window.

"It's okay, Mom," I whispered. "I won't be ready to replace Nikki for a while."

I got up and trudged over to where Nikki's leash hung on the hall console. Attached to the leash's clip was the cobalt-blue dog collar I'd picked out for him in June. I lifted the familiar bundle, pressing it against the placket of buttons at the center of my white uniform blouse.

"You said he died right away?" I glanced at Mom, who had followed Dad and me into the foyer. "You're sure he didn't suffer?"

Mom shuffled in close, her face inches from mine. "The lady who hit him was quite upset. She said she never saw Nikki dart into traffic. Just felt the impact." A sad look consumed Mom's pretty features. "Patrick came barreling into the house, screaming like a banshee. By the time I made it out to the street, Nikki wasn't breathing."

As Mom massaged the sweet spot between my shoulder blades, the three of us heard the back door crash open. A high-pitched squeal from my sister Susie followed. "Potty, Jen-Jen," she repeated. "Potty, potty."

When Susie's wails escalated, Mom dropped her hand from my back and darted off down the short center hallway. My father was one step behind her as Jenny's rushed footsteps and soothing words, "It'll be all right, Suz. We're almost there," echoed from the family room.

Only I remained rooted in the foyer near the front door. My eyes lingered on the dog leash in my hands, while my aching heart rejoiced at the sound of my twin sister's voice. *Nikki was gone, but Jenny was fine.* While I recognized that I had lost something precious that day, the most devastating outcome I could ever imagine had not transpired.

As I stood alone and stroked Nikki's collar, I recognized the turmoil in which my heart had landed. Nikki had not just been a graduation gift, he'd been a steady, loyal, and loving companion to me. All summer long, I'd dedicated myself to his training, just as I had promised. I would dearly miss Nikki's comforting presence as he slept at the foot of my bed, our routine walks in The Park, and the sight of him nuzzling with Susie. But he was a pet, not a person. Four months ago, Nikki had replaced our beloved Gigi. Once the sting of his sudden death faded, I knew our family would welcome another dog.

With the dog collar and leash clutched to me, I watched my mother meet Jenny and Susie as they burst into the back hallway. On a different day, this morning even, Nikki would have chased them and barked playfully, adding to the household's normal chaos.

"I've got her, Jen." Mom sighed. "I'll take it from here."

As Jenny released Susie into my mother's arms, her eyes locked on mine. She glanced at the dog items in my hands and cocked her head, studying my demeanor. As if in sympathy, her lower lip expanded into a pout.

You okay? her eyes seemed to ask.

I nodded. I knew we would talk about this later in our room. And she would share what Mom and Dad had discussed at the dinner table before I got home from tennis practice.

Later that evening, Jenny's face grew serious as she sat on the edge of her bed and observed me stuff Nikki's collar into my desk drawer.

My twin's face wrinkled with thought. "Because of what happened to Nikki, Mom said she wants to start looking for a new house."

I lay down on my bed and threw my elbow over my face. "Yeah, they've been saying that for a very long time, though."

Jenny's voice rose. "But this time it was different. Both of them looked right at Susie. All of us know Nikki's getting hit by a car could have easily happened to her."

I rolled over on my side and stared at my twin.

Jenny leaned in close. "Dad said, 'Business is stronger every day. Let's give it a few more months, Jeanne. In the springtime, we'll get serious about looking, okay?' And then Mom said—get this, Jules—'All right, Jack. Spring it is. In the meantime, I'm going to start cleaning closets and organizing the storage area.'"

Jenny paused, waiting for me to react, but I was too numb, too tired to offer much but ask a question. "How did the other kids react?"

"They didn't go crazy like you'd expect. Skeeter said he was fine with moving if the new house was close to The Park. After Patrick and Lizzie echoed him, Dad changed the subject to the baseball playoffs. And then Mom got up, I cleared the table, and the boys and Dad went to the family room while we waited for you to come home. You know the rest."

I stifled a yawn. "If we do end up moving—finally—maybe some of us will get our own rooms. It's crazy to think that Nikki's death is what will finally make this happen."

Jenny and I gossiped more about the nuances of moving out of "501," —the nickname we had for our house on Waiola—the events of our day at Benet, and my sadness over what happened to Nikki. As the silence of nighttime crept into our room, I let tears soak my pillow. I recalled and drew comfort from—as I have come to do so often in my life—my mother's words, "Life is a fragile gift. We're not in charge of how long we live."

As I lay across from my sister, soothed by the familiar soft breaths of her slumber, I thought about how life can change in a moment. A single incident—a car striking a family pet, a plane crash, a chance exposure to disease—sets in motion a whole trajectory of unforeseen consequences affecting the lives of countless souls. Nikki's death was not the first time I had experienced a life-altering moment in our family, and it would not be the last.

18

The Queen's Court

Winter 1975

The knock at the door pierced the silent tension floating around our bedroom. I knew by the rapid-fire three-knock pattern that it was Mom. Behind me, Jenny's groan was almost a growl.

For most of the afternoon, Jenny had sat cross-legged on the vibrant-hued Peter Maxx-style comforter covering her trundle bed. An *Intro to Geometry* textbook, study guide, and class notes spread out in an arc in front of her. Instead of studying across from my sister on our single beds, I worked at the white Formica-topped desk area Dad had installed the summer before our freshman year at Benet. Even though we liked the layout of our room, we were anxious for our parents to settle on a new house. Finding a house big enough to fit our family of eight, one that was close to The Park and within Dad's budget, had proved problematic. I was beginning to think Jenny and I would be in college before Mom found the perfect home.

Jenny's moan did not surprise me. I knew my sister. She hated interruptions about as much as she hated geometry. Studying for Father Anthony's first-semester geometry final would plague her until the exam was finally over. Unlike me, my twin sister suffered from test anxiety, which sometimes got in the way of proving her abilities.

"Come in," I called out.

While I had sympathy for my sister's plight—her performance on the geometry test meant the difference between a *B* and a *C* for a semester grade—I was grateful for the distraction of someone at the door. I'd had my fill of iambic pentameter, European poets, and the cryptic sonnets assigned in my sophomore English class.

Mom padded into our bedroom, her short brown hair neatly teased and sprayed with Final Net, courtesy of her standing Friday-morning appointment with Mr. Van. Mom's glance took in both of us in less than a heartbeat.

"Sorry to interrupt, girls. I know you're prepping for finals, but I thought you might want to see this. It's from Aunt Ginger. She popped it into the mail after her conversation with Jenny at the holiday party. It's a couple of applications for the Chicago St. Patrick's Day Parade queen contest."

Jenny bounced off her bed, her long legs lean but muscled from hours of JV volleyball practice.

She tugged the application from Mom's hand. "Thanks," she mumbled.

Jenny returned to the warm, cluttered corner of her vibrant bedspread without so much as a peek in Mom's direction. She leaned into the pile of pink, blue, and yellow decorative pillows she and I had crafted together a few summers before.

"Dinner's in an hour." Mom winked before pulling the door shut.

For as long as I could remember, my sister and I had been devoted to the network airings of beauty pageants. It didn't matter if it was Miss USA, Miss America, or Miss Universe, we watched them all. The two of us would ensconce ourselves in the lower-level rec room with a bowl of Jiffy Pop, which we cooked atop Mom's ancient gas range. Once the program began, we sat cross-legged on the thick shag rug fixated on the large vacuum-tube TV set into the rec room's paneled walls. As the show progressed, Jen and I bantered and bickered about which gorgeous gals would make it to the next round. We cheered the answers to the host's interview questions and panned some of the swimsuit selections. If one of our favorites made it to the top two, Jenny and I hopped around the rec room hooting with glee. It felt good to pick a winner.

Once Jenny digested the St. Patty's Day contest application, she hopped up from her cluttered bed and smacked the form down on the countertop next to me.

"Jules," she said, thrusting her freckled face close to mine. "We should do this!"

I eyeballed the paperwork and considered my sister's demand. While I was glad Jenny's mood had shifted from anxious student to enthusiastic contender, I was lukewarm about the contest. Watching a beauty pageant on TV was one thing; entering a contest was entirely different.

Turning back to the list of English poets in my spiral notebook, I muttered, "You do it. I'll be in the audience with Mom and Dad cheering you on!"

Jenny's face morphed into a pleading glare.

"C'mon. We gotta do this. Together. It'll be fun. One of us will win. I just know it. We look *sooo* Irish with our freckles and green eyes. We've got a great Irish name, too."

I smiled benignly at my twin. It was true. We did look like a set of genuine Irish lasses who hailed straight from the old sod. Yet, because of our closed adoption and missing family history, our true ethnic background was anyone's guess.

My twin must've read my mind. "Dad's family, the Ryans, are from counties Galway and Roscommon. We more than qualify."

Jenny was right. Legally, we were Ryans, as decreed by a family court judge from the Circuit Court of Chicago in 1959. But because we didn't know our true biological background, I felt more like an Irish wannabe. Maybe even an imposter.

I pushed the application along the smooth white countertop toward my twin. "Let's wait till semester finals are over to decide. Okay?"

"Deal!"

Jenny strutted back to her cluttered study corner, proclaiming, "Applications must be postmarked by February 15. If we pass preliminary selections, we'll be called for interviews on March 1."

I shook my head, smiling to myself. Jenny had latched on to the notion of entering the St. Patrick's Day Parade queen contest. I knew she would continue pressuring me until I caved in. It was what the two of us had been doing for almost sixteen years. As twins, one of us was always in the passenger seat while the other one drove. For us, swapping roles was as simple as taking another breath of air, but sometimes the results were not what either one of us expected.

Jenny's tendency to freeze up when important outcomes hinged on performance spoiled not just her first-semester geometry grade. Four days before the St. Patty's Day Parade queen and court applications were due, we turned sixteen. Dad drove Jenny and me to the DMV to get our driver's licenses. We stood in line together, clutching our Social Security cards, birth certificates, and learner's permits. Neither of us spoke as we shuttled between the vision and written test stations, acing those.

"Whew. Almost done," Jenny mumbled as we took seats next to one another in the waiting area designated for the "behind the wheel" exam.

"I feel like I should have practiced parallel parking more with Dad," she said.

I patted my sister's knee. "You've got this. And remember, it all depends on the tester. He might not have you do it."

Jenny looked down at her hands, her cuticles had not yet healed from the picking and nibbling she'd done during semester finals.

"Yeah, but I heard they like to trip you up. Ask you to do things, like make a turn into an area marked *Do Not Enter*."

When my name was called, I offered Jen a weak smile and followed the man with a clipboard out the back door. I walked to the car and climbed into the driver's seat, wishing once more that neither my twin nor I would have to parallel park. I prayed that both of us received the driver's licenses we coveted. I got half my wish.

Each of us escaped parallel parking, but Jenny had failed to slow down in a school zone. The examiner refused to pass her. My tester, a kindly older man who reminded me of Father McGinnity, authorized my license without issue.

It was a long and quiet ride home. Even Dad, who dished out some of his best corny jokes, couldn't get Jenny to smile, much less laugh. Mute, she stared out the car window, her expression closed and distant. Her failure to pass the test the first time was a huge disappointment, made worse by my success. I knew not to bug her. She wanted to be alone with her thoughts.

My twin would open up when she was ready. If the situation was reversed, I expected the same courtesy in return. Disappointments such as these were ones we had navigated many times before; they didn't generally cause a rift between us. Our arguments, ones which involved screaming or door slamming or throwing out unkind words, centered around the pitfalls of sharing a small room, negotiating our shared and limited wardrobe, or who would take on which household chore.

When Dad pulled his sedan into the garage, Mom greeted us at the family room door, her eyes bright. "How'd it go?" she asked.

"Bad!" Jenny yelled. She charged past Mom, pounded up the stairs, and slammed the door to our room.

Dad nodded at me. "Well. We're halfway there."

Mom shooed me into the kitchen. The two of us huddled at the kitchen table where I pulled out my new driver's license and she oohed and aahed over it. My photo had come out nicely despite the braces I had finally needed. Dad filled Mom in about Jenny's tough luck, vowing to take my sister out driving every night after dinner to restore her confidence. As proud as I was to have earned my driver's license, my heart ached for my sister. It was our birthday, a cause for celebration, but only one of us felt joyful. The outcome felt cruel, like opening a longed-for gift but finding that it lacked a necessary piece.

The week after we turned sixteen, Jenny passed the driver's test. Her ID photo looked much better than mine; mostly because her smile was perfect and uncluttered thanks to the braces she'd worn for nearly three years. We had one more challenge ahead, one which would test our relationship even more than the driver's license exam.

Dad dropped our St. Patrick's Day applications off at the post office by the due date. Over the previous weeks, Jenny and I had spent hours fine-tuning them. Before we slid the paperwork into separate envelopes, we attached a school portrait. I had to admit, with our shiny light brown hair, bright eyes, freckles, and glittering smiles, we really did look like Irish lasses.

From all the Irish events and parades we'd attended with our family and their wide circle of friends, I knew the competition would be fierce. Chicago vied with New York and Boston as the biggest Irish city centers in the United States, with San Francisco close behind. Our fate was in the hands of the judges. If they were to select finalists to interview, I hoped Jenny and I both made it. Or that neither of us did. We didn't have to wait too long to find out.

The call from a member of the contest committee came as we gathered for dinner in the kitchen. Mom sat next to Susie spooning food onto the tray of her highchair, and my two younger brothers traded elbows and rib jabs while Dad issued the usual warning.

"Knock it off, or else!"

As the rotary phone on the kitchen pass-through jangled, Mom groaned, "Who could be calling during the dinner hour?" Without looking at my father, she said, "Would you get it, dear?"

Dad grabbed the receiver on the fourth ring. "Ryan household," he said, listening. "Really? Well, thank you. That's wonderful news. I'll have Julie and Jenny there on March 1."

We'd made it! Jenny and I had both been invited to attend the final selection process for the 1975 Chicago St. Patrick's Day Parade queen contest. I sent off a quick thank-you to Saint Thérèse that our applications had not gone the same way as the driver's exams.

The evening of March 1 was a blur. Mom got a babysitter for the younger kids, and she and Dad drove us to the hotel where the contest was held. Dad dropped us off at the door, and Mom walked us into the lobby where we found the check-in table. Jenny and I were given timeslots for our twenty-minute interviews with the panel of judges. We learned that the contestant field had been narrowed to twenty-five girls, all aged between sixteen and twenty-one. The queen and her court of four attendants would be announced sometime around 9:00 p.m.

Everywhere we looked, mothers were primping their daughters' sleek curls while older sisters coached them on how to answer questions like: *If selected, what talents could you share? What does your Irish heritage mean to you? How many times have you been to Ireland? Have you participated in other Irish festival contests? And does your schedule allow you to attend mandatory events for several months going forward?*

I looked at Jenny. She was as pale as the character from Susie's favorite cartoon, *Casper the Friendly Ghost*. Mom led us to a corner of the lobby where she found three empty chairs. When Dad joined us, I gave up my seat. I didn't feel like sitting. All I wanted to do was pace so I could go over my prepared responses to the questions we'd been given. Jenny slumped in the seat across from Mom, who whispered things like, "You'll be fine honey, just breathe," and "You're just as pretty as the girls you see here," and, "Once you get talking to the judges, your nervousness will fade."

Of course, my mother was right. I, too, soaked up her stellar advice, but the real question was whether Jenny could control her nerves enough to let her answers shine. When Jenny's name was called, she returned from the interview just as pale as she went in.

"I think I messed up the question about our Irish heritage," she said. Brimming tears made her hazel eyes glow like emeralds.

I swallowed hard and gave my sister a grim look of support. I continued pacing. One of the ideas jiggling for attention was how irritated I was with myself for allowing Jenny to talk me into this silly contest. The other rising notion was, *Did we really belong here?* Even though we looked Irish and had a Gaelic-sounding last name, did that erase the fact that our biological background was unknown?

When I was summoned for my interview, I put aside those mental battles and tried quelling my rising panic. Seated in front of the panel, I tried masking my jitters when I looked each judge in the eye. My smile was bright as I delivered my answers in a clear, calm voice. The twenty minutes flew by. At the end of my interview, I joked with one of the male judges, who reminded me of my favorite uncle.

I said, "It would be my honor to represent the city of Chicago on March 17. I've been practicing my queen wave."

When I tilted my wrist just so, like I'd seen Queen Elizabeth do on the news, the panel chuckled. In retrospect, I don't know where the jest came from, but it must have stuck with the judges.

At 9:00 p.m., we were ushered into the ballroom. Jenny and Mom and I found seats together, while Dad hung out at the back of the hall with several other dads. The head of the selection committee took the stage, thanking the judges, the contestants, and their families for participating.

In her thick Irish brogue, the chairperson said, "We've had a record turnout this year, making the judges' decisions extremely difficult." She paused, her bright blue eyes scanning the full ballroom. "Whether you're a winner here today or not, the committee encourages every *colleen* to enter the Chicago Rose of Tralee contest, which will be held over the summer. This is another wonderful chance for one of our very own Irish lovelies to represent the city of Chicago. The international competition is held each year in Tralee, county Kerry, Ireland, in late August. Information is available at the desk in the lobby. And now, judges, may I have your decision, please?"

When a short, bald man, resembling a leprechaun, strutted to the stage and handed the chairperson a slip of paper, Jenny twisted in her seat and gave me a pained look.

I whispered in her ear, "Please don't talk me into the Rose of Tralee contest, too."

My sister gave me a half smile. "I dunno. Maybe some year we'll have to try that one, too."

Much like the national and international beauty pageants that had glued Jenny and me to the TV set over the years, the host began by announcing the four court attendants. The queen would be named last.

"These young lasses will assist the St. Patrick's Day queen with her duties and fill in as needed. Young ladies, when I call your name, please come up and join me here on the stage."

One after another Jenny and I watched, open-mouthed as three beautiful Irish-looking girls marched onto the stage. One had thick dark hair and the other two were strawberry blondes. All had clear complexions and glistening blue eyes. With only two spots left to fill, that of the queen and her final attendant, beside me Jenny's chest lifted in a sigh. She looked over at Mom and me, flashed a tiny grin, and held up crossed fingers in the air, a sign of good luck.

"And our final attendant rounding out the queen's court is Julie Anne Ryan, who resides in La Grange. Her ancestors hail from Roscommon and Galway counties. Julie is a sophomore at Benet Academy High School in Lisle and plans to study psychology in college."

When I heard my name, my hand flew up to my mouth. Looking over at my twin, I was relieved to see a pleased smile spread across her face.

"I told you one of us would win, didn't I?" she said.

I rose from my seat as if in a trance. Mom squeezed my hand, whispering, "I'm so proud of you, honey."

When I scurried out of the row of seats, Dad was there at my side, hugging me hard and kissing my cheek. "Congrats, Jules."

With each step I took toward the stage, my heart blared like the brassy notes of a trumpet. I found myself thinking about Graduation Day when I received the class award at St. Cletus. Unlike today's recognition, that honor had been much longed for and unexpected. Years of striving and hard work had gone into earning that acknowledgment. It occurred to me that back then my peers had chosen me after years of knowing one another. Today's honor was a result of a twenty-minute interview by a panel of strangers.

As I shook hands with the chairperson, I couldn't help but think back to six weeks prior, to our sixteenth birthday. On that day, Jenny had not shared in my success either; she'd had to wait a little longer to receive her driver's license. The outcome had pained me. Just as I had done then, I wondered, *Why couldn't we both have come out winners?*

Later, my family joined me for pictures on the stage. Jenny's grin took in Mom, Dad, and me, as she repeated her earlier comment, "I told you one of us would win."

I was glad my twin was taking credit for part of my success; she deserved it. If there was jealousy in my sister's heart, I didn't sense it.

"Yeah, well, I wouldn't have been up here if you hadn't made me do it," I said.

"Aren't you glad I did?"

I smiled at my twin. "I guess. What I really wish is that both of us had won."

Jenny closed her eyes as Mom and Dad rubbed her back. I had pulled out the truth in each of our hearts and named it.

Two weeks later, on March 17, 1975, my parents, Jenny, and I attended Mass at Old St. Patrick's Cathedral with Chicago's Irish dignitaries, Mayor Richard J. Daley, the St. Patrick's Day Parade queen, and the rest of the queen's court and their families. It was a chilly spring day and not one cloud dared mar the morning skies. After Mass, my parents, Jenny, and I gathered on the steps of Old St. Pat's for a slew of pictures. Dad's rosy cheeks, dimples, and clear blue eyes mirrored the Irish-looking faces in the crowd. Mom teared up when she and my sister left me with the Parade Committee, who assigned me to a convertible for the parade.

Jenny hugged me. "Have fun today!"

"I will. I've got my queen wave down. See?" We both giggled.

Again, if there was any lingering jealousy on my twin's part, I did not sense it in her smile or her goodbye hug. I'd entered the contest only because she'd wanted a co-conspirator. We both realized that my success had nothing to do with who was prettier or more engaging, it had hinged on conquering nerves.

With one of the biggest grins I've ever worn, I climbed into a convertible with the other girls, making certain my green silk blouse poked through the collar of my warm coat. The car snaked down the infamous St. Patty's Day Parade route, across the green-dyed Chicago River, and along the length of State Street. The crowd on both sides of the cordoned-off route was thick and deep. The mood was electric.

The moment was so exhilarating that I never once thought about whether my genetics meant that I deserved to be there. That concern was for another day. As I waved to the crowds, my heart was full. I had everything that a young girl of sixteen could hope for: a family who was proud and supportive, a sister who was thrilled that I got to live out the plan we had set in motion, and an honor that connected me to Chicago's Irish culture, the city where Jenny and I had been born.

19

꩜

The Compromise

Spring 1975

Once the excitement over Chicago's St. Patty's Day festivities were over, Mom began perusing the real estate sections of our local newspapers in earnest. When the circulars landed at the end of our front walk, Mom ran out, scooped them up, and adjourned to her tiny desk wedged between the kitchen cabinets. With a grave face, she scoured listings and announcements for open houses that met our family's unique criteria: five or six bedrooms, four baths, a large fenced-in yard, a quiet street, and a basement with ample storage and play space. Sometimes the properties that caught Mom's eye were located just a few blocks away from our beloved Waiola Park, but often the listings were across town or in the neighboring villages of Western Springs and Hinsdale.

Dad's reaction to my mother's efforts was always the same. As soon as he came home from work, he kissed Mom on the forehead and offered her a tired but agreeable smile. Once he draped his suit jacket over the back of a chair, he gave her his full attention. Mom's unlined face gleamed with the thrill of discovery as she smoothed out the creased newsprint with the flat of her hand.

"Jack, the market is popping. I think we're finally going to find something that suits our needs." She pointed to a stucco four-square on a neighboring street. "What do you think of this one?"

Whenever Jenny and I overheard these exchanges, we rolled our eyes. *Here we go again* was the unspoken message between us.

For the last year and a half—ever since the day Nikki was hit by a car—Mom had been dragging Dad out to drive by homes or attend showings and open houses. If Mom came home excited about a property they'd viewed, Dad would say something like, "It seems like not enough house for the money." And if Dad thought a place merited going back for a second look, Mom picked it apart like a turkey carcass. We kids read between the lines: our parents were eager to find a more spacious home, but the houses Mom liked didn't fit Dad's family budget.

There was another problem. If the property of interest was outside a two- or three-block radius from Waiola Park, my siblings and I ganged up on our parents. We argued that to take us away from The Park—our home away from home—as well as possibly change schools was cruel and unfair. Where would we ice-skate in the winter? Practice basketball and baseball with neighbors and teammates? Hang out with friends in the summer months? And where would Susie run, slide, and swing, if not at the playground across the street?

Skeeter was the most vocal advocate against moving outside our neighborhood, and he thought nothing of butting into our parents' discussions. With his hands balled up and his face the color of strawberry jam, he bellowed, "I'm tellin' ya, Nikki gettin' loose and being hit by a car was a fluke." He jabbed his finger first at my parents and then in the direction of The Park. "*You'd* better not take *us* away from *there*."

Mom met his brave glare and shook her head sadly. In a calm voice, she silenced further protestations. "What if it had been Susie that day, honey, instead of Nikki?"

One rainy April evening when Dad walked in from work, Mom blindsided him. She met him in the family room by the door to the garage, where her face erupted into a childish grin.

"Before you sit down, dear, and watch the evening news"—she tugged at Dad's coat sleeve—"I have to show you what came on the market today."

Towing him over to the family room table, Mom withdrew the pen she'd stuffed into her apron pocket. She hovered it over the real estate section, much like a child does when crafting a Christmas list. As she gloated over each detail in the home's description, she underlined the highlights.

"And it even has an in-ground pool." She gazed up into my father's blue eyes, smiling. "Just think. You wouldn't have to go to the YMCA so early in the morning to swim." She studied my dad's face for his reaction. "It's perfect, right? Even the price?"

Dad gave her a warm but tentative smile. "Seems like it. Let's drive by after dinner." He squeezed my mother's shoulders. "I know you're excited. But the kids aren't going to want to leave this neighborhood."

My mother's hands slid to her hips. "Let's cross that bridge when we come to it, okay?"

Dad answered her with a wink.

After a hurried dinner of grilled cheese sandwiches and tomato soup, our parents corralled us into Mom's station wagon. Dad had to wait several long minutes for traffic to pass before backing out onto Forty-Seventh Street.

He glanced over at Mom, muttering, "I look forward to the day when we won't have to do that anymore."

Mom sighed. "Me, too, dear. Me, too."

The farther my dad drove away from La Grange and The Park, the more my brothers grumbled from "the way back," the station wagon's rear-facing third row of seats.

"Where are we going? Mom, this new house of yours is too far away."

My mom waved away their comments with a swish of a hand. "We can talk about that more *after* you see the house."

She cuddled up with Susie, who sat between her and Dad in the front seat. Mom cooed to her. "Mommy's found the perfect house, Susie girl."

Smiling, my mother brushed a few dark wisps off Susie's high forehead. Even though she raised her voice loud enough for my brothers to hear, Mom spoke in that annoying singsong tone she always used with our nearly three-year-old sister.

"The house we're gonna drive by, Suz, has plenty of bedrooms. If we like it, everyone— including you—can have their own room." Mom swiveled in her seat and smiled over her shoulder at Jenny and Lizzie and me. "Girls, you won't have to share a bathroom with your brothers anymore. This place has four bathrooms *and* a powder room." Mom shifted in her seat and glanced at Dad. "I bet it's under the staircase just like the old house in Oak Park where I grew up."

"All that sounds great, Mom," Jenny said.

Without acknowledging Jen's comment, Mom huddled with Susie and read aloud from the ad in the *Suburban Life*.

My mother's obvious excitement was contagious. Like the delicious aroma of homemade brownies, her enthusiasm wafted over the front seat, sending waves of yummy energy to my siblings and me. I stared out the window, imagining what it would feel like to have my own room. I could stay up as late as I wanted either finishing a good book or studying for a test without Jenny's griping at me to turn out the light.

Seated next to Jenny, seven-year-old Lizzie squirmed, her blue eyes huge behind the wire-rim glasses perched on her pert little nose.

Lizzie's voice squeaked as she asked, "Mom, this is a new neighborhood. Would we have to leave St. Cletus?"

"Yes, we would, honey," Dad said, his voice tender. "But since Skeeter is already starting at Benet in the fall, only *you* and Patrick would have to switch schools."

Mom turned to look at Lizzie, her face serious. "Moving to Hinsdale means our entire family would have to leave St. Cletus Parish and join a new one. Those are the church's rules. Nothing we can do about it."

Jenny put her arm around Lizzie and gave her a quick squeeze. "Since Julie and I started at Benet last year, we've made lots of new friends." When Lizzie grinned up at her, Jenny added, "It'll be okay. You're good at making friends, too."

For the next few minutes, no one had anything to say. I suppose we were all in our heads, digesting the changes that leaving our neighborhood would bring, which contrasted with the inconveniences we already bore. Dad turned up the radio and smiled at Mom as Frankie Valli's hit "My Eyes Adored You" came on the air.

Once Dad turned the car onto County Line Road and entered the historic section of Hinsdale, I looked at Jenny. She raised her eyebrows and edged closer to my seat by the window. As Dad maneuvered the station wagon around the humps and over the waves of First Street's ancient brick road, we gawked at the large homes on either side of the street. Suddenly, our little house at the edge of Waiola Park looked as if it were from a different planet, a much smaller one at that.

Behind us, Patrick's whistle pierced the awed silence in the car. "Jeez, look at the size of those lawns. I wonder who mows them? I bet it takes forever."

Skeeter chuckled. "Guess if we moved here, Pat, it'd be me and you mowing our lawn. Look at that one over there. I think we could fit two 501 houses in the front yard."

Patrick snorted at the jest. "Yeah, and big enough to have two new Samoyed puppies."

"Jack, that's the house up there," Mom said. "In the middle of the next block."

When Dad slowed the car down and parked in front of an impressive, sprawling English Tudor, excitement churned in my belly.

"Stay put, everyone. No one's getting out. We're only here to look," Dad warned.

While Mom's station wagon idled in park, we sat still as statues as my mother read the description of the house out loud again and again. Each time she came to the part about a two-story staircase with leaded glass windows, every Nancy Drew book I'd ever read came flooding back to me. I longed to rush up the brick-lined walk, throw open the front door nestled in its turret, and chase lickety-split to the upstairs landing. At that moment, I made a secret pact with myself. Even if my parents didn't buy that house, someday I would own a house just like it for my own family.

"It's so beautiful." Lizzie's whisper held the awe we were all feeling. "Mom and Dad, are you going to buy it?"

I noticed Dad's dimpled grin in the rear-view mirror as he gazed back at Lizzie. "Well, first our Realtor will schedule a time for Mom and me to go through the house. If we like it, then we'll bring you kids back to see it."

That is exactly what came to pass.

Mom and Dad fell in love with the Tudor-style home on First

Street and brought all of us back to see it for ourselves. For more than an hour, we roamed the property inside and out, up the front staircase and down the back one, shouting to one another with joy and wonder. We explored the nuances of the attic and every nook and cranny in the cavernous basement. To our clan, delving into the secrets of the potential new residence was like a grand adventure, one that seemed more sport than real.

By mid-May, our family celebrated Mother's Day, Susie turned three years old, and my parents signed a purchase contract on the Hinsdale property. Our collective glee over moving to a big new house—with enough bedrooms for each of us and room to spread out—dwarfed some of the angst we felt about leaving the familiarity of our old neighborhood. On occasion, when one of us grew nostalgic and teary-eyed about relocating, our parents would reason with us, pointing out how the pros far outweighed the cons.

Yet, as quickly as each of us shifted and accepted our family's newly agreed-upon plan, a serious snag materialized.

On the day of the inspection, Dad arrived home with a stack of paperwork and went straight to his makeshift office in the lower level. When Mom sent me down to tell him dinner was ready, I found him at his desk running the adding machine and scribbling numbers in a column on a notepad. His blue eyes held a startled, almost frightened expression.

He threaded his fingers through his short wavy hair and said, "Tell your mother I'll be up in a minute. I need to finish something."

We were all seated around the kitchen table saying our mealtime grace when my dad appeared. Without a word, he took his seat at the table and bowed his head. Mom passed him the bowl of spaghetti, and his face was nearly as red as the sauce.

"What's wrong, honey?" Mom's mouth puckered with concern. "Are you feeling alright?"

Dad draped his napkin over the mound of his belly and cleared his throat. "I'm fine."

Mom pulled her chair in close to the table, and the screeching sound the legs made had us holding our hands to our ears.

"I can tell you're not fine, dear." Mom's voice crackled with concern. "What is it?" As she studied Dad, a wave of understanding whitewashed her face. "Is it the house inspection?"

He nodded at my mother, the flush on his face deepening. "There's a lot of hidden maintenance in old houses." He paused, his voice low and gruff. "I think perhaps a newer home would suit us better."

From my parents' cryptic exchange, we all gleaned that the inspection had highlighted a list of issues adding up to more money than Dad had budgeted. None of us said a word as we realized the deal was off. We were not moving to Hinsdale any time soon. While in our hearts, my siblings and I harbored deep disappointment— our dreams all at once fulfilled and then summarily dashed—it was hard to be mad at our father. Pulling out of the contract and knowing he had let us all down in the process appeared to be a very uncomfortable moment for him.

I'm not sure which devastated my mother most—not being able to afford the house her family had fallen in love with or going back to the drawing board. Everything that came on the market later that spring failed to come close to fulfilling our family's wish list. The experience with the historic Hinsdale house had served to whet our appetites for what was possible, as well as loosen the vise-like grip The Park had held over us for so many years. Instead of arguing with our folks about what we thought our hearts desired, we gave in to trusting them to make the right decision. We all needed time. Time to mourn the house we had fallen for and didn't buy, and time to ready our minds so we might appreciate the merits of the next property.

By midsummer, our parents had extended their search radius to include a few suburbs further from La Grange but closer to Benet. A newer home, just down the street from one of my mother's dearest friends, came on the market. Located in a new subdivision near Oak Brook's shopping mall, the two-story country ranch-style residence was located on an acre of land on a quiet cul-de-sac; it possessed the right layout of bedrooms, bathrooms, and entertaining spaces to appease us all. Susie could have a playground right in our own backyard, and the buses to Benet and local schools for Patrick and Lizzie stopped within sight of the house. All this meant less driving back and forth to Benet for our folks, Jenny, and me.

The Oak Brook house quickly became the perfect compromise. While it was not all that the Hinsdale residence represented—a rich history of ownership, unparalleled materials and craftsmanship, and located in a village known for its character and traditions—we transferred our excitement, hopes, and dreams over to it. Of all of us, Mom was the most excited. Her stack of *Better Homes & Gardens* magazines accumulated as she contemplated numerous ideas to make the new house just right.

In mid-August, when the moving van showed up at 501, each of us felt a strange, stilted joy. At odd moments—like when Mom's rocking chair and the red leather eagle-crested sofa got loaded on the truck—emotions plummeted from cheery nostalgia to deep sorrow. Jenny and I stepped into our completely cleared-out room and exchanged mournful looks. *Was this really what we wanted?* our hazel eyes seemed to say.

Yet, when we peered into the tiny hall bathroom, one we'd shared with our four younger brothers and sisters for too many years, we felt like cheering at the top of our lungs. Leaving our family home, one that we'd memorized, exalted, and criticized, was a strange sensation.

On that bittersweet day when our old belongings made their

way to an exciting future, none of us anticipated the changes in store for us. Did any of us expect that from moving day forward nothing would ever be the same? No, we were blinded by ambition, by promise, by opportunity, by the American dream of rising into the middle class. Mom and Dad had joined that circle by earning it the old-fashioned way. They had wished and planned, strived, and prayed, as hard as they possibly could.

With most grandiose schemes, there is an unforeseen event that derails or sidetracks the main objective. We didn't have to wait long for one to present itself.

20

Any One of Us

Fall 1975

Three months into my junior year, I hunched over a gray metal desk in the back of a classroom on the top floor of Benet Hall. I labored over my Accounting 1 mid-term, cognizant that several classmates—two of them senior hotties on the football team—zeroed in on my answer key. Noisy radiators provided the ideal smokescreen for a coughing scheme that enabled the guy behind me to feed my answers to the other two.

Mr. Weimer, our short, chubby-faced instructor, was so engrossed in grading papers that when a knock came at the door, he jostled his coffee mug, soiling his blue striped necktie. The boys behind me snickered. Our teacher dabbed at his tie with a white handkerchief and rushed to the door, where he shared whispers with a student. When he turned back to the class, he scanned the tight rows of our desks and motioned me forward. As I flipped over my half-finished test, the hasty breakfast I'd grabbed at home roiled in my belly.

Oh boy, I thought, *I'm in trouble. Shouldn't have made it so easy for the guys to cheat off me.*

I bumbled through the maze of desks, straightening my white uniform blouse and tucking a billowing corner into the high

174

waistband of my gray and maroon plaid skirt. I hadn't rolled the waistband that morning. My hem remained the prescribed two fingers above the knees. In my first two years at Benet Academy, my conduct grade was perfect, unblemished by honor code violations or uniform transgressions. As my sixteen-year-old brain obsessed over those facts, I hurried to the front of the classroom with cheeks as red as an August sunburn.

Mr. Weimer pulled me aside, his face puckered with concern. "You're wanted in the dean's office," he said. "We'll figure out later how to finish the exam."

"Oh, okay," I whispered back, too frazzled to ask why the dean of students couldn't wait until the break between class periods.

I rushed back to my desk, shoved my #2 pencils into my book bag, and handed my incomplete midterm to the teacher. I shrugged at the football team—they would have to manage on their own.

The squeak of my loafers reverberated in the deserted corridors. As I neared the deans' corner offices, the worries in my head multiplied. *What could possibly have happened to summon me to the office during a test? Did Skeeter pick a fight during PE or forget his lunch money again? How will I get word to Jenny about what was happening? When will I finish my accounting exam?* I wasn't thinking about home. I was thinking only about myself and my high school world.

I approached the dreaded set of deans' offices at the end of St. Martin's Hall. Through the wall of windows, I spied Jenny's profile. *That's weird. Is she in trouble, too?* Her back to me, Jenny sat stiffly on the "naughty bench"—a row of tightly placed stools where sinners stewed in silent purgatory before being summoned in front of one of the deans. Skeeter paced in front of Jenny like a second-string athlete ready to enter a game. When I saw both of my siblings, it dawned on me something serious was in the offing. Suddenly, it felt as if I couldn't catch my breath.

I slid in next to Jenny. "What's happening?"

She shrugged. "I dunno. No one has said anything except 'Wait here!'"

I followed Jenny's gaze to the high countertop in front of us. The school secretary, Mrs. Purley, held the phone receiver tight to one ear and scribbled on a pink message pad. Beyond her, the doors to both deans' offices were wide open. I figured Sister Mary Ellen and Mr. Shields were prowling the halls examining lockers or in the teacher's lounge grabbing lunch. Skeeter ceased his manic pacing and stopped in front of us, his cornflower-blue eyes bulged like a bullfrog's, pleading, *Why had the three of us been called out of class?*

Mrs. Purley cradled the phone and nodded, ever so slightly, as if acknowledging the cluster of Ryans attending Benet had now been collected. She placed three hall passes on the counter.

In a weary voice, she said, "Go to your lockers. Gather your things. Head straight home." She added, "Be careful driving."

Instead of leaping to our feet and seizing the passes, the three of us stayed rooted in our places. Fear, or maybe it was dread, made our mouths gape wide like children who have just heard a rustle in the closet. None of us had the wherewithal to ask Mrs. Purley why we were being sent home. In that pre-cellphone era, we were dependent on the adults at school for the relay of information from home.

As we filed out of the office, I glanced back over my shoulder at Mrs. Purley. Her shoulders sagged, making her pilled blue cardigan appear two sizes too large. One hand cradled a flushed cheek, the other snatched a Kleenex. Within the hour, I would find people I loved and revered in that same position.

In the school parking lot, I tossed Jenny the keys to the Fiat, the used navy sedan that Dad had purchased over the summer to accommodate two additional drivers. To avoid the usual argument, I offered Skeeter the front seat and climbed into the back. As the Fiat merged onto Maple Avenue toward our new home in Ginger Creek, my brother repeated the tale he'd begun in the school office.

"I got pulled out of an algebra exam. Brother Charles was not cool with it. I thought he was going to whack the knuckles of the kid the dean sent to get me. Wonder what's going on?"

As he rambled on, Skeeter's fingers rifled through his wavy blond hair. I reached forward and patted the sleeve of my brother's buttoned-down blue oxford.

"I know," I said "I had the same thing happen in accounting class."

Jen's eyes met mine in the rear-view mirror. She didn't say it aloud, but I could read her thoughts: *If the three of us are okay, something has happened to Mom, Dad, or Grandma Mimi. Possibly one of our three younger siblings.*

Jenny sped through the yellow light at Route 53. "I bet something happened to Grandma Mimi. She's old."

Skeeter loosened his gray necktie and stuffed it into his jacket pocket. "Yeah, you're probably right. She's a big lady. Doesn't move around much."

Jenny drove as fast as she dared. She cruised through another yellow at Ogden Avenue but stopped obediently at the red light on Highland Avenue in Downers Grove. Mostly, we zoomed along in silence, lost in our own anxieties.

The Fiat's tires squealed as soon as they hit the asphalt driveway circling our house. Again, it was Skeeter's voice that pierced the prickly silence in the sedan.

"Well, here we go. Here we go," he said.

Fifty years later, I still hear him muttering those words.

Jenny screeched to a stop on the pad under the basketball hoop, and we all stared at Dad's white Monte Carlo. He had parked askew, blocking the open two-car garage where Mom's dusty station wagon stood. The angle of his car was odd. Unnerving. It was neither inside nor outside the garage. For a second, I wondered if he'd left any of the car doors ajar, like what happens in crime shows when the cops are in hot pursuit of a criminal. Jenny turned and froze me with a look that said, *This is gonna be bad, and I'm scared.* The three of us scrambled to escape the Fiat, bumped through the double garage thick with bikes and sports equipment, and spilled into the laundry room that doubled as a mudroom.

As we tore into the kitchen, Dad clambered toward us from the family room, his starched blue shirt ballooning over belted suit slacks, his fair cheeks the color of a nectarine. Tears slid past the spot where dimples normally punctuated his beloved teasing grin.

The four of us converged at the kitchen island where Cheerios and Frosted Flakes boxes, bowls with milky spoons, and half-nibbled buttered toast had sat for hours. Dad yanked the three of us into a hug so suffocating that it felt like a wrestling match.

Locked in the terrifying squeeze, Dad kissed the crowns of our heads, over and over, muttering, "Oh, kids. It's bad . . . a really bad day."

His choking sobs drowned out our refrain. "Dad, what's going on?"

In the mayhem of the moment, I groped for Jenny's hand, squeezing it like I had in our younger years when we played hide-and-seek after dark with the neighbor kids. A thought flared and became a beacon. If Dad was here engulfing the three of us, sobbing and babbling about a bad day, and the breakfast dishes were in the sink, where was Mom?

I had last seen my mother at 7:10 that morning. In her nubby pink bathrobe, she had shooed Skeeter, Jenny, and me out the garage door with our sack lunches. "Good luck on your exams," she'd said.

"Dad, what's going on?" I pleaded. My question was too shrill for my own ears.

In a voice husky from emotion, he slipped a horrifying truth into our huddle. "Your sister. Susie. She's gone. Stopped breathing. More than a bad cold. ER docs couldn't save her."

The three of us gawked at Dad, our collective gasp sounding like the choked groans of a cornered animal. Jenny and I stared at one another blankly, our minds incapable of making sense of Dad's words. Our three-and-a-half-year-old sister had been suffering from a bad cold for over a week. None of us had any idea it was anything more than that.

When Dad tried pulling us into him again, Skeeter stiff-armed him and backed away. "Where's Mom?"

Dad gestured behind us into the family room. Through the wide-framed entry, we spied our mother. She slumped like a discarded doll against a spray of decorative pillows on the sectional sofa. She supported her head with an open palm, much like Mrs. Purley had done when we exited the school office. Only Mrs. Purley's face had held a healthy flush, and Mom's cheeks were pale and gray like weathered wood. In her left hand, with its sparkling set of wedding rings, my mother clutched a wad of crumpled tissues.

At the sound of the three of us charging toward her and moaning her name, my mother pried her cheek loose from a trembling hand. She peered at us as if it had been weeks since we'd seen her, and she struggled to sit upright. Her body was so slack that her limbs appeared to be held in place by the clothes she had thrown on that morning. Instead of pulsing with vitality, Mom was a broken mannequin.

Skeeter, Jenny, and I fanned out around the edges of my mother, peppering her with questions like "Do Patrick and Liz know yet?" and "When will they be home?" Throughout this exchange, Mom remained dry-eyed. She accepted our smothering hugs and responded to our quizzing, but the comfort she offered in return felt stiff and distant, lacking the usual warmth. She did not pull us into a group hug, as Dad had done. And not once did my mother say, "There, there, honey. This'll be all right. I promise," or "This is for the best. You'll see," as she'd uttered so many other times when one of us suffered a setback or disappointment.

No, since our early-morning send-off, my mother had become someone else. Gone was the confident parent capable of brown-bagging six lunches daily, stocking the fridge with family favorites like chocolate pudding and ice cream, and serving up a hot supper as soon as Dad's car squeezed into the garage. In her sunken dark brown eyes, I glimpsed a soul that had emptied out. The vision sucker-punched me. Not only had I lost a sister, but I feared I had lost my mother, too.

I lay my head on my mother's shoulder, scooting in as close to her warm torso as the sofa's faux-suede fabric allowed. But as I leaned into her for comfort, nothing came back. At that moment, I had no way of knowing that the misery and emotional detachment I was witnessing in my mother would become a pattern, that her depressive state would cripple her and jeopardize the tight weave of our family fabric. Nonetheless, I found solace in my mother's nearness, the familiar scent of the Dove soap lingering on her skin, and the warmth emanating through her dark cardigan. Huddled with her like that, I squeezed my eyes shut, banishing all thoughts of an incomplete midterm, a perfect conduct grade, and the football team whom I had allowed to glimpse an answer sheet.

Once those teenage concerns left me, guilt stormed in, strong and loud, confident like a drum major leading a marching band. Guilt in the form of an inner critic who scolded me for being a negligent sister and self-absorbed teenager. Susie's battle with a chest cold had not been a passing thought that morning as Jenny, Skeeter, and I grabbed our lunches and peeled out of the driveway. We were more preoccupied with midterms and nabbing a prime parking spot before Benet's first bell rang.

At first, I fought back against the accusing internal voice. *I couldn't have known she was so sick as to be knocking at death's door.*

I defended my position by bringing up other points, such as with each new sibling who joined our family, Jenny and I assumed more and more responsibility. Our parents expected us to babysit, care for, and fill in for them when they were occupied with other tasks. Often, Jenny and I shelved or deferred the pursuit of hobbies and friendships to satisfy our parents' demands.

Yet, the inner faultfinder was unrelenting. *You resented and complained about your chores and family duties. Your burden was not too heavy. Nor was it unusual. Your friends—who also belong to large families—have parents with similar expectations.*

I told myself, *I always treated Susie with love and care*, but the critic countered.

You could've been more aware. When you kissed Susie good night last night, was her breathing labored? Her complexion gray? Her lips blue and energy low? If you had paid closer attention, you might have alerted your busy and exhausted mother.

Yes, I could have. Any one of us could have done that. But no one did.

In our defense, we—particularly my mother—had been relentless in caring and advocating for my sister. My family lavished Susie with attention, accommodated her special needs. We rearranged furniture so she wouldn't harm herself and took the time to explain in graphic detail about scenes and objects that her limited vision prevented her from experiencing. Yet, this time, this one time, when Susie's life depended on our hypervigilance, all of us failed to meet her needs.

I scanned the faces of my family, wondering if their thoughts had ventured down the same guilty path as mine. Were we all beating ourselves up with *if-only-I-had*? How would we navigate this searing, sudden loss, and how would it change our family?

As I brooded over those questions, I picked up on some unspoken dialogue between my parents. Dad offered my mom a sad, quizzical stare that was part *Are you managing?* and *I know this is hard, but I'm here for you.* She glanced at him, returned a sad half smile, then looked off into the adjacent sunroom, a place where Susie loved to dance and move to the changing light. Dad frowned as my mother twisted her wrists this way and that, shaking them willy-nilly as one does when a joint catches or a limb falls asleep.

I shifted to the edge of the sofa to gauge whether Jenny had also tuned in to our parents' nonverbal exchange, but she was busy rubbing Skeeter's back while he cried into his hands. When my dad left his chair at the corner game table and skirted around the sofa to hold Mom's hand, I studied my parents. Their eyes were yawning caverns of sadness, their demeanors anguished and beaten. None of that surprised me, but the worry lines on their fortysomething faces had multiplied, making them look older than their years.

I wondered what else they were concerned about, and whether they were keeping something from my siblings and me.

21

Accused

Fall 1975

"Mom, tell us what happened," I whispered.

My simple question was uttered in a soft, gentle voice, but it echoed across the dark wooden floors of our cluttered family room and swirled around the five of us like a tempest.

Mom gave me a skittish sideways look. Like a spring, her gaze bounced to each of my siblings' faces and then up at Dad. When he nodded at her, she slipped her palm out of his grip. She shook out her wrists and hands, intertwined her fingers as if she intended to pray, and then dropped them into her lap. Jenny stopped rubbing Skeeter's back. My brother rested his forearms on his thighs, his eyes glued on Mom.

Dad patted my mother's shoulder. "Are you up to telling the story, or would you rather I fill everyone in?"

Mom swallowed hard, her face pale, expressionless. "I think, Jack, the kids should hear it from me."

Mom's sorrowful gaze folded us all in. "Right after you left for school, I went upstairs to make sure Pat and Liz were up and moving. When I went into Susie's room, she was snuggled deep under her coverlet. I sat on the side of her bed and touched her cheek. It was clammy. I said to her, 'You don't feel well do you, honey?' She said, 'No, Mommy. Suz sick.'"

We all smiled at this. Susie always talked about herself in the third person. It was one of her many precious quirks.

"Ma?" Skeeter said. "I gotta interrupt. Last night Susie came into my room. You know how she does that sometimes?"

The way my brother's eyes begged for acknowledgment, it reminded me of that moment in the dean's office when he'd paced back and forth in front of Jenny and me near the naughty bench.

"Ma, Susie was cold. Ice cold. I let her climb in bed with me. Got her warmed up and then carried her back to her room. I tucked her in, and she said what she always did, 'I lubba you, Skeetah. I lubba you.'" Skeeter offered a crooked smile and swiped at the corners of his eyes with a tail of his uniform shirt. "I shoulda told you that before heading out this morning."

My mother bolted upright and wagged her finger at my brother. "Listen to me! Don't do that to yourself. This is not your fault. You didn't know how sick she was. None of us knew."

I know my mom's words were not just meant for Skeeter. They were meant for all of us, to assuage the guilt building up in our minds. Her caution made me feel slightly better, but . . . I doubted I would ever completely let myself off the hook. I was already convinced that any one of us could have intervened to prevent the morning's dire outcome.

Mom looked up at Dad, who still hovered behind her, his hand resting on her shoulder. "Maybe the experts at Children's Hospital were right back then. Perhaps the rubella did damage Susie's heart as well as her eyes," Mom said. "Remember they suggested that?"

Dad closed his eyes, nodding. Looking at my parents together made my heart hurt. *Haven't they been through enough?* They'd handled Susie's impairment as best as they knew how—taking her to a gazillion appointments, enrolling her in special education programs, and moving our family to a neighborhood with quiet streets where she could play safely. *Why this, now?* I wondered what good could possibly come out of my sister's death.

"Sorry, Ma! Go on with the story. Tell us the rest," Skeeter pleaded.

Mom inhaled a quick deep breath. "So, I said to Susie, 'Mommy's going to get you in to the doctor. Let's get you up and dressed, sweetie.' I put her in her favorite jumper, you know the blue plaid one with the matching blue cardigan."

My mother's sad smile flickered as she pointed to her own blue sweater. I had a pretty good idea what she was going to say next. We all did. We watched Mom's sweet, sad smile when she told us, "Susie said, 'Wear your blue sweater, too, Mommy.' I said, 'Sure, honey. I will.' So, I brushed her hair into the two high ponytails she liked and carried her downstairs where she nibbled on a piece of toast with jelly. As soon as Dr. Welford's office opened, I called to say I was bringing her in right away."

Mom looked away from us and nodded in my father's direction. "Your dad dropped Pat and Liz off at the bus stop. I threw on some clothes and got the car ready."

Mom stared at her folded hands and whispered, "I nestled Susie into a warm blanket, carried her into the garage, laid her down in the back seat of the station wagon." Mom paused as if retracing those steps in her mind. "And then I went back to the family room to grab her a pillow."

These were familiar images to me. I saw the scene unfolding just as my mother described it. Whenever one of us was home sick from school, my mom doted on us. She bundled us in blankets, fluffed up a pillow or two, and situated us in the family room or her first-floor bedroom with the TV remote, a tray of scrambled eggs, buttered toast, and OJ. Sometimes, she put a little bell on the tray so we could ring for her.

After detailing the scene in the car, Mom paused, nestling her chin at the neckline of the blue cardigan. When she was ready to continue, she glanced at my father. I wondered why she kept checking with him as if she needed his permission to go on. When she began again, her voice was flat, but as she got into the narrative, her delivery sped up as if she couldn't wait to get out the words, the story, the truth.

"As we drove along to the doctor's office, I sang with Susie. Like we always did when we were in the car together. We sang, 'You Are My Sunshine,' and 'Love Will Keep Us Together,' and some old nursery rhymes she loved. I could hear her little voice piping in from the backseat, following along with me. But then as we crossed the tracks into Western Springs . . ." Mom buried her face in her hands. "I couldn't hear her singing anymore."

The room became so quiet we heard the whooshing highway traffic a half mile away. Skeeter hung his head. Jenny and I stared at one another. None of us wanted to ask the obvious question. Had Susie stopped breathing in the car as Mom drove along? I sniffled hard, trying to suck back in a huge sob. I didn't want to let it all out just yet. I desperately needed to hear the end of the story. The part about the hospital. I wanted the truth. All of it. Even if it hurt. Because hurting hard all at once is so much better than hurting in little dribs and drabs.

I swiped at the tears soaking my cheeks and edged closer to my mother. "Mom?"

She lifted her head from her hands and shook them out. *Why did she keep doing that?*

"I was yelling at her," Mom said. 'Susie! Susie! Say something. Anything!' but she was so quiet. I ran a red light. Kept checking in the rear-view mirror to see if she was moving. Several times, I reached back to jiggle her arm, her leg, anything. But she had rolled too far away." Mom's voice was a whisper now. "Instead of going to

Dr. Welford's office I turned off and sped to La Grange Hospital." Mom folded into herself. Her shoulders shook but her sobs were quiet, muted, like the mewing of baby kittens. "I ran into the ER screaming for help."

I rested my head on Mom's shoulder. *This is never, ever going to be okay.*

I don't know how my dad summoned the courage to speak, but he did. He cleared his throat and stood up straight, his hand still on my mom's shoulder.

"The nurses rushed Susie into the ER," Dad said. "They worked on her for quite some time."

My siblings and I sat there and stared at our folks, our mouths open with no sounds coming out. We could have been at the movies watching a horror flick because it felt like that—the racing of my heart, the need for the scene to play out but not wanting to witness all the gory details. Except this was not a made-up plot we'd forget in a week. This was real. This was today. This was our family's story. A nightmare.

Susie died in the car while Mom drove. Susie died in the car. Susie died.

When Mom murmured something about the "authorities," Dad gave her a sharp look. When he squeezed her shoulder, she winced. For the briefest of moments, I wondered what my mother meant about the "authorities," but when Dad interrupted, my question faded away.

He patted Mom's shoulder. "Sorry, hon. I didn't mean to squeeze you so hard." Then he looked at my siblings and me, his long, pale face struggling to contain his sorrow. "Your mother called me from a pay phone at the hospital. I was already at the office. Before I rushed home, I called Benet and Grandma Mimi." He looked at his watch. "She should be here soon with Patrick and Lizzie."

When Dad went to the hallway to check for Grandma's car,

my mother continued the story. She'd gone to a secluded corner of the emergency room waiting area and pulled out her rosary beads. I closed my eyes and imagined how hard she must have prayed to Blessed Mother to intercede. Mom told us that while she worked the beads, her eyes darted to every person who walked in and out of the triage doors. She feared what she already knew in her heart.

A doctor in blue scrubs emerged, blinked, spotted my mother off in the corner, and took a seat beside her. His blue eyes held sympathy, not hope. "I'm sorry, Mrs. Ryan. We tried everything we could, but we could not save her. Her heart gave out. It just couldn't fight the virus she'd contracted."

My mother buried her head in her hands, her anguished sobs resonating throughout the waiting area. "No. No. No . . ." she mumbled.

The doctor leaned in close. "Is there someone you can call?"

Mom choked back a sob, reaching for a wad of tissue in her purse. "Yes. My husband, Jack." She blew her nose into the tissue. "He should be at his office." Mom glanced over at the doctor. "You tried everything?"

He nodded solemnly. "She was already gone when you brought her in. I'm sorry for your loss," he said, patting her arm. "The nurses will be back out to explain what happens next." He stood up, studied her for a moment, adding, "Take care, Mrs. Ryan."

I imagined a chill washed over my mother as she threaded her arms into her black wool coat and pulled it close. As she watched the doctor trudge toward the triage doors, she dabbed at more tears, murmuring over and over, "My sweet little Susie. How can you be gone?"

Mom was not certain how long she sat there alone in the nearly deserted room. She remembered fiddling with her handbag. As she struggled to find her change purse, a hospital staff member came around the desk area with two men in shiny dark suits. The staffer pointed at my mother. As she counted out change in her hand to call my father, Mom saw the two men stride over in her direction.

"Mrs. Ryan?" one of the men asked in a hushed voice.

Mom blinked up at the two men. They had come to stand like a wall in front of her. "Yes?" She wondered why the men didn't sit in one of the many empty seats around her as the doctor had done.

"We're detectives with the La Grange Police Department. We heard about your daughter's death. Can we ask you a few questions?"

Mom blinked up at the men again. "Okay."

She puzzled why two detectives would be interested in talking to her. She'd already explained over and over to the nurses and doctors how Susie had been suffering from a chest cold all week. How that morning Susie's condition had worsened, and she had called Dr. Welford's office first thing for an appointment.

The tall, thin detective spoke first. "Mrs. Ryan, your daughter was obviously well cared for. But you know how this looks, right?" He cleared his throat and took a step closer to her. "All of sudden you storm into the ER claiming your daughter is ill, but when medical professionals examine her, she's already dead."

Mom stared at the two men. A confused look clouded her eyes.

The second detective, the heavyset guy, interrupted his partner. "How did you do it?" he barked.

"Excuse me?" Mom's hands shook as she clenched the loose change in her palm. "What're you saying?"

"Your daughter, Susie. How did you kill her?"

Mom's hand flew up to her mouth. Her retort was charged with fury. "How can you accuse me of such a thing? She was sick, I tell you. Sicker than I knew."

The tall detective shook his head, frowning down at her. "C'mon, Mrs. Ryan. Did you kill her first? Then clean her up and drive to the ER?"

The heavyset cop interjected again. "Did you smother her? Use a pillow?"

"I can't believe this . . ." Mom's hands trembled. "I didn't know how sick she was. I tried to get her help. I was just too late. Too late . . ."

My mother looked up at the detectives, a river of tears pooling at the edges of her anguished brown eyes. She whispered, almost as if she were talking to herself, "Did you know she was handicapped? Legally blind? From the rubella I contracted during my pregnancy. I loved and cared for my daughter every day of her short little life . . . I can't believe anyone would think I'd harm her."

My mother slumped back into her seat and pulled her warm coat tight to her neck. She stared at the detectives, waiting. They shared a look between them that she took to mean, *Looks like we're not going to get anything out of her.*

The tall detective met her gaze, his face stern. "The doctor has ordered an autopsy, Mrs. Ryan. When those results come in, expect to hear from us."

The investigator's words froze my mother in place. As she watched them strut off to the desk area, my mother puzzled why the doctor hadn't mentioned the autopsy. She also wondered if the autopsy meant Susie's burial would be delayed. Mom didn't know how long she sat there alone, trembling and weeping. Somehow, she summoned enough energy to wander over to the pay phone and shove enough coins in the slot to reach my father.

After she went through the horrific details surrounding Susie's death, she assured my dad. "No, dear. I really think I can drive. I'll meet you at home."

Choking back another onslaught of grief, my mother picked up her handbag, made certain she had the car keys, and straggled out to the parking lot. She found her station wagon where she had left it, sticking out into the aisle and straddling two spots. At first the idea of getting in the station wagon without Susie—knowing it was the place where she had breathed her last breath—caused Mom to reconsider my father's offer to come get her. But as she looked through the window into the back seat at the nest she had created for Susie, her heart flooded with emotion.

The car was the last place she and Susie had been together. Suddenly, there was no other place my mother wanted to be.

As Mom finished telling the story, she looked at all of us. "I know it sounds crazy, but I felt your sister's spirit lingering there. In the car with me. It soothed me to remember all the times the two of us sang together there. Those memories buoyed me. I knew I could get myself home."

My mother gave us another weak smile and smoothed down the placket of buttons on her blue cardigan. I wondered if Mom would ever take the sweater off. Or maybe she would bury it in the back of her closet because it would always remind her of this terrible day. The day Susie died. The day our family died a little, too.

As I think back now to the events of November 18, 1975, I wonder what crossed my mother's mind as she sat alone in the ER, grief-stricken and accused of murder. Did she think of Alan Fredian's murder and the nearly three years it took for the suspect, Karl Rettger, to come to trial? Did she for one second think that she might be subjected to the same ordeal, or that our family would become so demoralized by a murder trial that it would force us to move out of state like Karl Rettger's family following his acquittal?

I didn't learn about the detectives and that part of the story until recently. While I don't fault my parents for keeping the detective's accusation a secret—such information would indeed have troubled my younger siblings—I wish they would have shared it with Jenny and me. We were mature almost seventeen-year-olds. Our folks had always relied heavily on us and exposed us to experiences and responsibilities far beyond our years. I think we could have handled the delicate information.

I also believe that if I had known the full extent of what my mother experienced that morning, it would have softened my heart, steeling me enough to cope with her behavior in the difficult months ahead.

22

Where's the Milk?

Fall 1976

I glanced at the alarm clock on the nightstand. "*Arrgh*! It can't be four thirty already," I muttered.

Outside my bedroom window, darkness poured into the flat gray clouds consuming the late-November skies. Groaning aloud again, I slammed my English composition notebook shut and tossed it across the bed. I stretched out my lanky frame until my fingers and toes grazed the ends of the antique walnut bed Grandma Mimi gave me when we moved into the Oak Brook house. Scrunching my eyes shut, I contemplated whether I would follow through with the plan I'd been toying with, one that would put me at odds with my parents. At that instant, it felt right.

Since the meager Sunday brunch Mom had served that morning, I'd been sequestered in my room, alone, where I struggled to prepare for upcoming midterm exams. I frowned, thinking about how Jenny had been off at volleyball practice all afternoon. Without my twin's steadying presence, my brain kept skipping away from my studies, reminding me of the year before: the day my siblings and I learned Susie had died.

I flipped my legs over the side of the full-sized bed and yanked my Benet Redwings sweatshirt down over my favorite faded blue jeans. Despite the worn knees and straggly bell bottoms, I wasn't about to slip into a nicer pair of pants. Sauntering over to the cheval-style mirror that coordinated with Grandma's old bedroom set, I raked through my Dorothy Hamill–style haircut.

I smiled wryly at my reflection. "Your time is your business. You don't have to tell your parents everything," I whispered.

Earlier in the day, at brunch, when Patrick passed the platter of overcooked scrambled eggs, I'd avoided Mom's gaze, announcing, "I think I'll go to five o'clock Mass instead of noon with all of you. I'm in the thick of studying for modern lit."

Mom nodded and didn't put up a fuss about my staying back. I hadn't expected her to. Since Susie died, the only things my mother pressured any of us kids about were picking up our rooms and setting our dishes near the kitchen sink. Beyond that, Mom didn't show much interest in anything.

For the last year, my mother had missed most of Skeeter's high school baseball and football games. It was too bad, because his coaches were grooming him for varsity as the starting shortstop and quarterback. But he wasn't the only one Mom neglected. Lizzie was either down the street playing at the neighbor's or in front of the TV, while Patrick roamed the local streets on his bike without any accountability. So far, my mom hadn't shown up at Jenny's volleyball matches, even though she was on course to receive a college scholarship. And despite my undefeated four-year conference record at first doubles, Dad was the only one who had appeared in the stands during my entire senior season. Deep down, all of us knew our mother's inattention and negligence were not because she didn't care. Nonetheless, her indifference was demoralizing; it made me feel unimportant, rejected, abandoned even.

Those behaviors were not the only changes we witnessed in our mother. My forty-three-year-old mom acted so listless, distracted, and melancholy that I often wondered if she knew what day it was.

Her complexion had become sallow, and her clothes flapped around her thin frame like a flag on a windy day. She seemed so miserable in her own skin that I found it painful to look in her direction. And since my mother didn't drive any of us anywhere—thanks to school buses and our family's third car—I questioned what she did with her time. Did laundry and grocery shopping consume her day? Or did she spend a good portion of it staring out the sunroom windows, blaming herself for Susie's death?

Of course, all of us kids had empathy for our mother, but we were all limping along in our own brands of grief. Our only coping strategies were to put our feet on the floor, go to school, play our sports, and stay on top of our studies. Perhaps cry a little when our heads hit the pillow. Because talk therapy wasn't a thing back then, the guiding wisdom in our household was "just learn to deal with it." Privately, that is.

When my senior tennis season ended, I'd started riding the Benet bus home so Jenny and Skeeter could keep the car for their afterschool sports. When I'd slip in through the back door and holler, "Hello, anybody home?" I'd either discover Mom taking a nap in her room or a note on the counter that read, "Down at the neighbors. Be home soon. Mom."

It didn't take me long to figure out what those frequent meetups with Mom's local friends were all about. When the front door clicked open, Mom strolled into the house, her gait wobbly and her words muffled or slurred.

"Oh, hi, honey," she'd say to me. "I'm gonna lie down for a while. Would you mind getting Lizzie at Christie's around 5:00 p.m.? And set the table for dinner, please."

I'm not sure what irritated me the most, my mother's tipsy behavior, her overreliance on me, or the fact that I had to deal with all of this, alone, without Jenny around to complain with.

On one of those wine-with-the-neighbor-ladies afternoons, I'd been studying at the kitchen table when Dad came home from the office.

"Where's your mother?" he asked in his usual cheery voice.

Instead of dishing out a snarky comment like *She got trashed with her friends again*, I scowled and jabbed my thumb toward their first-floor bedroom. A flush crept up my dad's broad neck, filling his handsome face. With his trench coat still bunched around his shoulders, he stormed through the family room, muttering a weak, "Hello, kids" to Patrick and Lizzie, who were glued to the *Scooby-Doo* show on television.

Even with the TV blasting and my parents' bedroom door closed, Lizzie and Patrick and I heard enough to get the gist of my folks' argument. Dad insisted Mom slow down on the drinking and see a doctor for treatment for her prolonged dark moods as well as the frequent numbness in her hands. That malady had started the day Susie died, and it persisted. To get the blood flowing and restore normal feeling, Mom had developed odd behaviors like shaking out her wrists and wringing her hands. We all wondered what was wrong with her and if it could be cured.

When my dad emerged from the bedroom that day, he avoided our curious stares, turned sharply down the hall, and shut the doors to his office with an echoing clatter. Moments later, Mom wobbled out of their bedroom, her dark hair in disarray, and her eyes dull and distant.

She wandered in front of Patrick and Lizzie, straightening her disheveled blouse and sweater. "What would you like for dinner tonight? Leftover meatloaf or McDonald's?"

Mom must have followed through with Dad's demand to see a specialist. I'm not sure what the doctor prescribed for her moods, or if talk therapy was part of her treatment, but things improved. The odd hand-wringing behavior seemed less frequent. She appeared more alert and attentive, especially with Patrick and Lizzie. Instead of asking me, she started retrieving Lizzie from her playdates. I noticed her quizzing Patrick about his after-school whereabouts and with whom he was hanging out. These were motherly tasks that had consumed her before Susie died but to which she hadn't paid much mind in the months since.

Sighing, I banished the year's dark memories, straightened the bangs of my perky haircut, and stepped away from the large bedroom mirror. I grabbed the Art Institute tote bag from the closet, stuffed my economics book, journal, and a few spiral notebooks inside, and plucked my leather-fringed shoulder bag off the doorknob. Still uncertain about whether I'd follow through with my rebellious little plan, I figured I didn't have to decide until I hit the stoplight at the main road. Maybe I'd proceed directly to the Ascension church and attend five-o'clock Mass. Then again, perhaps I'd drive to McDonald's, order an iced tea or TaB diet soda, and hunker down in one of the cozy back booths to rack up more precious study time.

As I descended the front stairs and strutted into the family room—my eyes on the key rack in the kitchen and two-car garage beyond—my heart did a little stutter step. In a culture where adolescents were rebelling with drugs, gangs, sex, protest marches, and dropping out of school, my skipping church might have seemed like a small infraction. But it was a big deal in our household. If I got caught at it, I'd be grounded for weeks. I also wondered if I'd get sent back to my room to change out of my shabby jeans.

My parents sat side by side on the tan faux-suede sectional with their feet up on the coffee table, their eyes dreamy from zoning in and out of a TV program.

Dad's eyes flicked in my direction. "Off to Mass?"

"*Mm-hmm,*" I grunted.

I hated lying to my parents, but somehow my teenage brain had me convinced that I wasn't really being deceitful. Mumbling was a noncommittal noise; it wasn't speech. So, technically I wasn't fibbing to them.

From the kitchen, Patrick shouted out. "Hey, Mom. Where's the milk?"

Dad poked Mom, she shrugged sleepily, and then her eyes shot over in my direction. Dad never missed a beat.

"Jules, pick up a gallon of skim milk on your way home from church, will ya?"

Inside, I grimaced at the errand, one I had fielded far too often. "Okay."

That exchange was indicative of how the year following my sister's death had played out. Occasionally, we would run out of something—such as butter, milk, or eggs—and one of our parents would send Jenny, Skeeter, or me to the store. But often, the reason our pantry or refrigerator shelves were insufficiently stocked was because of my mother. She had either not felt like making the supermarket run, or she had gone to the grocery store and left her list on the kitchen counter. Other times, she had scribbled down the items we asked her to purchase but neglected to pick up basic staples like skim milk.

I don't know if it was because of my father's all-too-familiar-and-annoying request to go to the store, the stress of impending midterms, or the growing unease I felt over the first anniversary of Susie's death, but something inside me sparked. And then it blazed. All at once, I had had enough. I was so consumed with resentment and anger and discontent that I thought my chest would heave open. Why I experienced that visceral reaction on a Sunday as I headed off to Catholic Mass, I cannot say. Yet, somehow Dad's harmless, repetitive chore became the impetus for a dramatic shift in my psyche.

I was fed up, exasperated with life as I knew it.

I was disgusted with my mother's absenteeism, disinterest,

forgetfulness, and day drinking. Every time my parents asked me to step in and care for my younger siblings or our household, I longed to blast them with, *They're your kids. It's your house. Not mine. You take care of them/it.* But instead, I suffered in silence, ripped about it to Jenny, and wrote scathing passages in my journal.

That wasn't all of it. A gloomy tone had permeated every floorboard and ceiling tile in our new home, which made me not want to be there at all. I wished I could get in the car and just take off. The other thing that incensed me was the expectation that my siblings and I would blindly follow our parents' way of doing things, heed their rules to the letter of the law, as well as those of our schools and church. My need and willingness to be compliant and to please others were garments I wanted to rip off and throw in the nearest trash can.

During the previous year, I had grown more outwardly contrary, defiant, and rebellious. Whenever Dad brought up college choices or college majors over dinner, I glared at him.

"I told you already. I'm going to major in psych, not business," I huffed.

"Careful," Mom warned. "Look who you're talking to."

I had stared her down. "All I'm saying is, if I have to take out student loans, I should be able to study whatever I want."

Over the last months, I had become weary of being controlled. All I wanted to do, short of slapping someone, was to argue and challenge the status quo. I knew I had to figure out how to get through the remaining months before my sister and I left for college without exploding. So, while internally I seethed over bigger issues beyond fetching a gallon of milk, I stuffed the cash my dad handed me into my fringed purse.

His eyes followed me as I cruised out of the family room. "Be careful. Make sure there's an ice scraper in the car. It was icy when we were out at noon."

I flipped him a hasty backhanded wave. "Got it, Dad," I grumbled.

Charging through the kitchen, I nabbed the keys to Dad's Monte Carlo and streaked out of the driveway confident of what I was and wasn't going to do next.

At the McDonald's drive-through, I ordered a large TaB and slid the Monte Carlo back onto the main road. It was slick just as my dad had predicted. A half mile down, I edged the white sedan into the back row of the church parking lot. The spot was perfect; it allowed me an easy exit once the Mass let out. I unbuckled my seat belt and eyed the tote bag bulging with study materials.

"Nope. Not going in," I said aloud.

There was something liberating about verbally affirming my intentions. My wily and argumentative teenage brain came up with reasons to justify the deliberate disobedience.

You told your parents you would go to church. And you're here. No one's going to ask whether you went in or not. Besides, you need more time to study.

I knew that the best college psych programs, the ones I had my sights on, took only the top students. In my journal, I wrote often about my itch to understand why people developed certain personality traits and behaviors, why they reacted in particular ways, and what led them to make certain choices. Certainly, my adoption had made me conscious of the "nature versus nurture" debate, but the college courses I planned on taking were more influenced by the faulty family dynamics that erupted following Susie's death. Subliminally, I may even have been on a quest to understand how our first mother could give up not just one but two healthy newborns to strangers to raise as their own daughters.

Pushing the driver's seat back, I kept the motor running and pulled out my economics textbook. Instead of concentrating on the business terms I needed to memorize, my mind tapped in to the events of the previous November. Circumstances that led to where I sat at that moment: doubtful, angry, and alone in a dark, cold church parking lot chewing on traumas and concepts far outside the scope of what my high school peers seemed to be consuming.

I tossed aside my econ book and grabbed my journal.

"What kind of priest would have denied my parents?" I wrote. "What kind of church would refuse to let us grieve in the space where we felt comfortable? What kind of God would allow all this to happen to my family?"

Once our family moved from La Grange into a different diocese, we were required to register at the parish servicing our area. Leaving St. Cletus, a strong, faithful community made up of long-time friends and neighbors, had become more painful than any of us could have imagined. We had belonged to St. Cletus since Jenny and I were two years old. My family's involvement predated our joining the congregation. My mother was teaching third grade at St. Cletus when she got the call from Catholic Charities in February 1959 that my sister and I were waiting for them at St. Vincent's orphanage in Chicago. So, even though my family had followed church guidance and dutifully joined Ascension parish in Oak Brook three months prior to Susie's death, one of the first calls my parents had made the day she died was to Father Gallagher, the pastor at St. Cletus.

I can still hear my dad's voice saying, "Father Gallagher, it's Jack Ryan calling. I'm phoning with sad news. Our youngest child, Susie—the three-year-old with vison issues, who you yourself baptized—died suddenly this morning from a virus." Dad's face was mottled with various shades of red and pink, his eyes puffy from tears, yet he winked at Mom as the conversation progressed. "Thank you, Father, your prayers mean a lot to Jeanne and me."

Dad cleared his throat. "Father, we have a request." He paused, staring at my mother, who gawked at her hands, then shook them willy-nilly. "As you know, we recently moved. But because of our long-standing ties with St. Cletus, we'd feel more supported if Susie's funeral Mass could be held at St. Cletus."

As Dad listened to Father Gallagher rattle on, his eyes closed. I thought my dad might be praying, but when his chin found his broad chest and his shoulders caved in, I knew Father Gallagher had disappointed him. He'd rejected our family in a crucial time of need. As I watched the call play out, I hoped my dad wasn't going to break down on the phone with that crotchety old pastor.

He didn't disappoint me.

No, Dad straightened up to his full height of six foot three, and as he pressed his ear into the receiver, his face turned the rich fiery red of hot embers. I don't think I have ever seen him so angry. Yet, Dad was always the ultimate gentleman. He would never do anything disrespectful or deliberately unkind, much less yell at a priest.

"But, Father, why can't you make an allowance?"

With each word he spoke, Dad's voice dropped deeper, like thunder. When it settled in that unfamiliar territory, all of us in the room were set on high alert.

"Especially after my family's many years of involvement, of service to St. Cletus." Just short of a threat, Dad let his meaning settle. "I implore you to reconsider, Father. Many of our family and friends are still your parishioners."

When Dad hung up, he stared at my mother, shaking his head dejectedly. Our puzzled gazes roamed between our parents. My father collapsed onto the family room sofa beside my mother, grasping her hands between his and silencing her tremors. Love and hurt and disbelief and fury flickered like a movie reel in his blue eyes.

"I'm sorry, Jeanne."

Mom's eyes were as dark as coal. I sensed the anger building in them. "What did he say exactly? Tell me."

Jenny and I shared startled expressions. Our parents were like two volcanoes ready to explode. Their reactions triggered our own indignation.

"Father Gallagher said, 'No! St. Cletus is no longer your parish. If I make an exception for you, it will set a precedent. The funeral Mass for your daughter should be at Ascension.'"

Our old pastor's response to my parents' request fulfilled my expectation of him, and it was instrumental in fueling the anger compelling me to question my faith. I knew from my religious studies that the church is not the building in which we worship. The church is made up of people. People are human. They're prone to error in judgment and often lose sight of their mission and purpose. Father Gallagher erred that day. While I have never forgotten his lack of compassion, it was easier to comprehend than the larger issue I grappled with in Ascension's dreary parking lot.

What kind of God allows so many tragedies to happen to such well-meaning souls like my folks?

In my journal, I wrote out the growing list of God's failings: Mom's many years of miscarriages and infertility, Mark's stillborn death, Susie's cataracts and visual disability, her sudden death. As I slurped down the last sip of my diet drink, my thoughts went to a more troubling place.

Are we all fooling ourselves? Is there really a supreme being?

After dashing to the gas station for milk, I rounded the curve toward the Oak Brook house and spied the navy Fiat Jenny had driven to volleyball practice. My sister had parked the small sedan on the pad under the basketball net, just as she had done on that fateful day when Susie had died. I was glad Jen was home. After dinner we would chat in her room or mine, and I would probably confess to her about skipping five-o'clock Mass.

I pulled Dad's car into the garage and snatched the sweaty gallon of skim milk from the floor. Inside, the kitchen was a hubbub of activity. I plopped the milk down on the counter. Mom was at the stove spooning Ragú meat sauce onto a platter of steaming ravioli. Lizzie and Jenny were setting the table together, and at its center was the leafy green Advent wreath with its four candles, three purple and one pink. Had it been there all day, or had Mom resurrected it in time for dinner? Could it mean she was healing, and our family life would soon get back to normal?

When Susie died, it felt as if the mother-daughter bond my mom had forged for sixteen years had suddenly been revoked. While I could not articulate it at the time, my mother's emotional abandonment compounded the already deep primal wound of rejection imposed by my closed adoption. At some level, my teen-age brain had processed the situation and declared, *Your first mother discarded you, and now the second one is turning away, too.* On the flip side, my mother's withdrawal intensified the unique connection I already enjoyed with my twin sister. Our tight relationship provided the healing salve for the darkest moment in our adoptive family's history.

Of course, I couldn't have known it then—despite being an intelligent, responsible, and mature-beyond-my-almost-eighteen-years teenager—but Susie's death and my parents' difficulties in building their big American family showcased an important truth. Each of us, regardless of who we are and where we come from, carries within us our own brand of brokenness. What we do with our brokenness, and how we handle other vulnerabilities, faults, traumas, and failures, determines the people we become and the course of our lives. The folks who help us champion those struggles—the ones who listen and support and teach us about acceptance and forgiveness—coax us into developing a blueprint for identity and belonging.

Mom turned from the stove. "Julie, pour the milk in the pitcher there on the table. Lizzie, call your dad and brothers for dinner."

Once we were all settled in our places, Mom's eyes traveled around the table. When she spoke, the corners of her mouth lifted in a pleasant smile.

"In honor of Advent, the Christmas season, and the beginning of the liturgical year, let's bow our heads and thank the Lord for our many blessings." Mom caught Dad's eye. "Jack, please light the first purple candle on the Advent wreath."

As the flame strengthened, I felt a warmth, a sense of hope I hadn't felt in a very long time.

23

Apron Strings

Summer 1977

"Finishing up some packing, Mom. Be down in a sec," Jen yelled. "Okay," Mom hollered back.

I rolled my eyes at my lookalike. We both figured our mom had an errand for us to run or a sibling to fetch from the Oak Brook Bath & Tennis Club. In a few days, Jenny and I were to drive to Bloomington, Indiana, with our parents for freshmen orientation. When we left for college, Mom would lose her two best errand girls. I chuckled to myself, thinking how it was Skeeter's turn to step up.

All morning long, Jenny and I had tramped back and forth across the hallway separating our second-floor bedrooms. We chattered about how thrilled we were to be assigned to Willkie, a coed dorm versus the all-girl dormitory Mom had preferred. Jenny and I hadn't requested to room together, so we felt doubly fortunate to have been designated rooms on the same wing of Willkie's eleventh floor.

As we raked through our wardrobes, packing for our fall semester at Indiana University, we bantered about how different Big Ten college life was going to be compared to Catholic high school. For the first time in eighteen years, Jenny and I would attend classes wearing whatever we wanted. No more knee-highs and loafers. No more stiff, white button-down blouses and plaid uniform skirts.

"You know what else I won't miss about high school?" I asked.

My sister looked up at me from the floor where she stuffed T-shirts and shorts into an oversized duffel.

"Getting a detention for my skirt being too short," I said.

Jenny giggled. "Yeah! And if we miss class at IU, Mom and Dad don't have to phone in an excuse." Her eyes glinted. "We can even chew gum in class if we want to. Think about that."

As I watched Jen layer colorful tanks on top of shorts, I fingered the frayed edge of my favorite white cut-offs and thought about the previous March when both of us decided to attend IU. I had already settled on Miami University, where I planned to study psychology and room with a Benet classmate. Jenny wanted to study business. She was considering Eastern Illinois University if they offered her a volleyball scholarship. The only college to which we'd both applied and been accepted was IU.

So, toward the end of March, our parents drove us down to visit Bloomington. Not only were we impressed by the business and psychology programs, but we also fell in love with the sprawling green campus, the stately fraternity and sorority houses, and all the amenities a big school offered. Something else became obvious that weekend. Two young women who'd been inseparable since before they were born needed more time together before charting futures that would push them in different directions.

Jenny peeled herself up from the carpet, rubbing her stiff knees. "Almost done," she said.

I locked eyes with her.

"Are you ready to leave all this?" I asked, sweeping my arms wide to take in our two rooms, the long hallway that linked the other three upstairs bedrooms, and the sleepy street beyond.

Jenny pursed her lips. Her hazel eyes drifted toward the bank of large windows behind her frilly canopied bed. So much had happened since our family moved to the Oak Brook house before our junior year at Benet. There was the heartbreak of our sister Susie's sudden death and then mom's debilitating grief, depression, and emotional withdrawal from family life. While my anger surrounding Father Gallagher and the church's rigidity had softened some, I still grappled with whether my god was fearsome, righteous, or loving. In the meantime, our family had pressed through those big issues in a home ensnared in the continued chaos of remodeling projects, a physical reflection of the turmoil in our family dynamics.

While I waited for my twin to answer me, I considered my own question.

Despite having my own room for the past two years—something I had dreamed of for as long as I could remember—I had never bonded with the Oak Brook house. Despite its many shortcomings, 501—our home across from Waiola Park—was special. I had lived there since I was two years old. Those sixteen years of growing and becoming had transformed 501 from a mere dwelling place into a dear old friend. Our house on The Park had etched itself into my bones, refusing to be supplanted by something newer and bigger and swankier.

The lack of attachment to our new home was more than prolonged homesickness. The move out of 501 had ushered in an era of loss and misery for me and my family. I sighed, realizing perhaps for the first time that I couldn't wait to leave the Oak Brook house. I needed to set aside its dark history, as well as to escape my strict Catholic upbringing. I craved freedom and power. Freedom from the duties and chores of a big family, and the power to make my own decisions without my parents' constant oversight.

As freshmen orientation week neared, imagining the fresh challenges and new experiences that college would bring prevented me from falling asleep at night. I was excited but not apprehensive. Probably because my twin sister would be at IU, too. Right down the hall from me. Close, like she had always been.

Jenny turned away from the window, her perfect teeth bright within a winning smile. "Yeah. I'm more than ready. You?"

I nodded, matching her grin. "Let's go see what Mom wants."

The two of us descended the large staircase in the two-story foyer. We chattered about the things we needed to pick up from Venture, the Oak Brook superstore that carried everything from hair dryers and laundry soap to apparel and small furniture. At the landing, Jenny patted the back pocket of her jean shorts.

"I've got my list. Whatever it is Mom needs, we can pick it up when we're out," she said.

We heard clattering in the kitchen and found Mom behind the kitchen island, the back of her dark head framed under the over-sized pot rack where tarnished copper pans dangled like fish on a line. Next to her at the sink, a couple of overturned frying pans dried on a rack. Below those, the dishwasher splashed and hummed. The only thing that remained from breakfast were the loaf of hearty wheat bread and butter dish propped by the toaster.

Jenny and I came to a standstill, elbow to elbow, on the outside of the narrow island. Mom spotted us and turned, edging close to the wooden countertop separating her from Jenny and me. The morning sun hurled a stream of bright light through the window above the sink, caught the assortment of pots on the rack above the island, and cast a hodgepodge of shadow and brilliance around the three of us.

"How's the packing coming along, girls?" Mom asked, a pleasant grin warming her face.

"Just a few more things to pick up from Venture," I said, "and a bit of last-minute laundry to stick in the suitcase."

I kept my face neutral, not wanting to appear too eager about leaving home, even though my heart bounced with anticipation.

Jenny squinted at my mother through the peculiar ribbons of light. "Do you need anything while we're out?"

Rooted next to my sister, I shifted from one flip-flop to the other. As I struggled to view my mother through the shadows and sunbeams, I spied two white gift boxes tied with an abundance of curled, colorful ribbon. My mother's smile widened as she slid them across the walnut-colored countertop toward Jenny and me. The numbness in Mom's hands that had incapacitated her in the months following Susie's death was now almost nonexistent.

I caught my twin's quizzical glance and telegraphed my own curiosity. We had a family farewell dinner planned for the night before our trip to IU. I couldn't imagine why my mother was giving us these packages now.

"Open them at the same time," Mom said.

I slid one end of the tightly tied ribbon off the small white box and glanced at Mom. Her palms pressed against the countertop. Her pretty face assumed that pensive look that gift givers hold, a mixture of expectancy over how a present will be received and the pleasure of having selected something deemed right for the occasion. Wonder lit a fire in my belly. I peeked at Jenny to make sure I was on track with her, tugged the remaining ribbon free, and tore into the box.

I unfolded a flap of white tissue and stared at the wrinkled and sheared ends of fabric layered there. A startled "*Ohhh*" slipped from my lips.

As quick as lightning, Jenny's foot nudged my instep. I clenched my jaw and tried harnessing the giggle chomping to get loose. Within the white tissue, I recognized the scattered scraps as the tail ends of the aprons my mother wore every evening as she cooked our family's supper.

Mom rubbed away tears at the corners of her eyes, murmuring, "The gifts are symbolic, of course. I just wanted you girls to know that since you're heading off to college, I'm letting go. I've cut my aprons' strings. From here on out, you're free to make your own choices."

Mom's show of emotion sent Jenny and me scuffling around the island, where we encircled her in a hug. Our mother's excitement about giving us the clever gift and her obvious sadness in sending us off to college tore into my heart. I suspected that our absence was even a bigger loss, magnified because of Susie's so recent death.

"I'll miss you girls," Mom repeated as she melted into our hold.

Jenny and I assured her we would miss her, too, and that we would call every Sunday night. We reminded her for the hundredth time that we'd be home in a few short months for fall break.

"I know. I know." Mom reached for the boxes, closed them, and stacked them neatly on the counter.

As I watched her do this, I wondered if she expected us to take them with us to college or if she would reattach them to the old aprons. Or were they ours to take up to our rooms to hide under a bed or at the back of a closet, only to rediscover in the future?

Jenny winked at me and grabbed the Monte Carlo keys from the key rack on the wall. "Let's go, Jules. We've got stuff to do."

"See ya later, Mom," I said, waving.

As I traipsed after my sister toward the garage, part of me felt sorry for my mother and guilty about leaving her behind, but an inner voice rumbled into action, reminding me how hard I had worked to earn the opportunity to go off to college.

Go and do, the voice thundered. *Figure out who you are, what you want, and where you belong. You owe it to yourself. It's time.*

Part Three

BECOMING

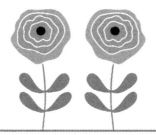

24

College Coeds

Fall 1977

D ad edged Mom's green station wagon into the long line of cars waiting to access the drop-off zone at our dorm, Willkie North.

In front of us, Mom's shoulders seemed to ease as she said, "Look, Jack! There's a greeting committee helping unload the cars."

The old tremble in Mom's hand was negligible as she pointed at the throng of students sporting matching white T-shirts emblazoned with the red IU logo. From a distance, the big *U*, superimposed over an even larger *I*, looked like the Greek god Poseidon's powerful trident. Its resemblance to our school's symbol had never dawned on me before. I considered whether it was an omen, a sign that the college experience Jenny and I were about to have at IU would prove impactful and worthy.

I wanted to believe that. The thought of it, the hope of it, made my whole body tingle.

Jenny and I scooted forward in the jam-packed second row of seats in the car, our heads nearly touching as we squinted through the windshield. The sight of the army of volunteers teaming up with families to unload vehicles, stack possessions on wheeled carts, and escort everything and everyone into Willkie North's lobby was mesmerizing. It felt like watching a movie progress in real time.

Within minutes, our scene—Jenny's and mine and our parents—and our bits as naïve freshmen coeds in a college adventure flick would roll into action.

We're finally here. Jen and me at our Big Ten college. Freedom. Independence, at last.

I reached across our nest of pillows and belongings and pinched the back of my sister's arm. Laughing, she swatted my hand away. Jenny's perfect smile was like a neon sign lighting up the crammed car, but our shenanigans did little to release the bottleneck of nerves and excitement electrifying our insides. We couldn't wait to get out of the car, meet our roommates, and settle into our assigned residence hall rooms. Once we kissed our parents a tearful goodbye, I knew my sister and I would set off on foot and explore IU's gorgeous sprawling campus together.

Dad whistled. "They sure have got the unloading process organized." He looked at Mom, his face erupting into a pleased grin. "At this rate, we should be able to get the girls settled and be back on the road in a few of hours."

Instead of answering, Mom adjusted her sunglasses and turned her attention to the scene outside. Jenny and I saw her mouth pucker into a slight pout. I expected that saying goodbye was going to be harder on our parents than on Jenny and me. In a few hours, our folks would climb back into an empty car and arrive home to find fewer voices clamoring about the house and two less faces around the kitchen table. In turn, Jenny and I would be together at IU, in dorm rooms located right next to one another, whispering and plotting as always, about everything from roommates to classes, boys, and a future stretching out as far as our hazel eyes could see.

The four of us had risen at dawn. While Mom packed up snacks and issued instructions to the babysitter left in charge of our younger siblings, Dad, Jen, and I had wedged all the stuff we thought we'd need until fall break into Mom's station wagon. With Dad at the wheel and Mom in the passenger seat with her stockpile of *Better Homes & Gardens* and *Good Housekeeping* magazines, we hopped on the interstate for the four-hour drive to Southern Indiana.

Within minutes of leaving our Oak Brook home, Jenny and I had spread out the pillows we'd nabbed from home across the stuff between us. We dozed until Dad stopped for gas somewhere outside Indianapolis. Once we exited the interstate for good and pulled onto the main road leading into Bloomington, I jerked upright and rolled down my window. I scanned the downtown grid of roads, memorizing the streetscape's fascinating mix of retail stores, bars, bookstores, and sandwich and pizza shops. On her side of the car, Jenny was busy doing the same. Occasionally, she grabbed my hand and gestured to a place she wanted to check out later.

As we neared IU's campus, awe consumed Jen and me. Even though we had spent our June orientation weekend in Bloomington, I marveled again at the university's impressive grounds and imposing structures. Located at the edge of the bustling downtown area, the school held a commanding, sturdy presence. I loved how its careful blend of architectural styles bisected the many parks, paths, and streams trickling through the academic quads. *My school.*

It seemed like forever until the army of sweaty but cheerful, rosy-cheeked students in matching shirts encircled Mom's tightly packed station wagon, chanting, "Welcome to Indiana University, home of the Hoosiers."

The process of unloading Jen's and my belongings, collecting our room keys, IDs, and meal cards from the lobby check-in points, and then commandeering the elevator to ride up to our side-by-side rooms at the southernmost end of Willkie-11 was a nightmarish blur. Outside, the humid air was well into the nineties, but inside the temp rose exponentially because of Willkie's non-air-conditioned spaces.

Our shirt backs dampening, my parents and Jenny and I traipsed after our assigned team of volunteers, trudging down the long hallway ridiculously laden with suitcases, boxes, crates, and overflowing garbage bags stuffed with necessities. As stifling as it already was in our residence hall, suddenly there were too many things and too many people in our rooms, obstructing the airflow. Sweat caked my feathered bangs against my forehead.

Next door, I heard Jenny meeting her roommate, Linda, and her parents at the same time my roommate, Camille, introduced her parents to me and mine. The odd cocktail of fatigue, pent-up nerves, excitement, awkwardness—combined with the unbearable heat—threatened to push me to a breaking point. Within minutes of stepping into my strange room, I felt overwhelmingly irritable, crabby as when one's last meal was too far in the distant past. As I stood smashed against the wall of closets in the tiny space I'd soon consider my home—suffering through small talk with strangers— all I could think about was how I desperately wanted all the parents to hug, kiss, wave, and be gone so that I could put my things away, get to know Camille, and meet the other girls on my floor.

While Dad and Camille's boyfriend assembled our box fans and stuffed them in the windows, another reprieve appeared in the form of our resident advisor (RA).

"Welcome to Willkie-11, Camille and Julie. I'm Mariel, a graduate student. I live across the hall from you."

Within seconds of Mariel introducing herself to my mother, Mom stopped nagging me with "What can I do to help?" "Shall I make up your bed, honey?" and "Where would you like me to put your shoes?" Upon meeting our RA, my mother brightened. It was like watching the sun appear after several days of serious downpours. Mesmerized, I watched Mom lean in close to Mariel in the hallway, chatting away like old friends would do.

My impending meltdown faded into oblivion.

Like a whoosh of cool air, Jenny appeared in my doorway. I fielded her nod and caught her brief glance at Mom and Mariel. When her gaze returned to me, my twin and I shared the knowing smile of the relieved. Without so much as speaking a word, we telegraphed an important message: *Mom's mood has shifted, and our imminent goodbyes will go much better than expected.* We knew that when our mother met Mariel and discerned her role as keeper of order on Willkie-11, all would be well. We were also cognizant that Mom would make something abundantly clear to our RA. She, our mother, would entrust Mariel the RA with an incredible responsibility: the oversight and care of two of her most important treasures, Jenny and me.

At the curb, Mom's lingering goodbye hug was tight and heartfelt. Neither Jenny nor I attempted to hold back our tears. As our parents climbed into the empty car, Dad pulled out his handkerchief, mopped his forehead, dabbed his eyes, and then handed the soggy cloth over to our mother. On the sidewalk, I moved within an inch of my twin. Her nearness was everything, enough to help me sort and settle the turmoil of my conflicting emotions.

How can I be happy and sad at the same time?

Dad made us laugh by tooting the horn four times as he pulled out of Willkie's circle. Her window rolled down, Mom waved, shouting, "We'll call you tonight when we get home."

Jen and I stood there, eyes aglitter, stomachs in knots, as the old green wagon made a right turn onto Third Street and was gone.

As it turned out, I got luckier with my roommate assignment than Jenny did. Hailing from Colorado, Camille was a freshman just like me. She was kind and considerate and quiet and reflective. The only things Camille and Jenny's roommate Linda had in common were their dark hair, blue eyes, and steady boyfriends. Linda was one of the rare dormitory sophomores. After he helped with the move-in,

Camille's boyfriend returned to Colorado, but Linda's boyfriend, a resident in a nearby dorm, continued spending more time in Jenny's room than he did in his own.

It turned out to be a glorious thing for all of us that Jenny was right next door to Camille and me. Over the ensuing weeks, the three of us spent more and more time together. We hit the campus stores for supplies, hiked to the library for study time, and met between classes at the Memorial Union for snacks. We ventured out to the same "Little Sister" fraternity parties and looked out for one another at dorm social exchanges, taking extra care that none of us walked back to Willkie alone in the dark. Another reminder about the strength in numbers was what transpired at the Sugar Bowl when two strange boys threatened Jenny, Lori, and me.

Our tight little trio held the elevator until everyone was on board and rode it down to the cafeteria connecting the girls' wing of Willkie North to the boys' building. In the central area near the buffet line, we grabbed a large table, and as our dorm friends strolled in, we hollered for them to join us. Most evenings, we stayed there, munching and sharing stories until the janitors shooed us out. It felt grand to be settled into Willkie and to have found our group.

As our fall semester classes and dorm activities kicked into a routine, Jenny and I set about learning more about sorority life at IU. Ever since that August day when our parents drove us to campus, we'd harbored a curiosity about Greek life. As Dad steered the station wagon down Third Street with Mom directing him from the atlas in her lap, we had cruised past the long string of sorority and fraternity chapter houses.

Jenny and I had our windows rolled down as far they would go. I had to remind myself not to gawk and appear like the dumbfounded teenagers we were. But it was hard not stare. To my eye, each sorority was like a singular bead in an exquisite strand of pearls. Each house was different—bigger, older, traditional, modern, and constructed of brick, limestone, or wooden shingles—but combined, they stood in perfect harmony. The girls streaming out of the front doors and strolling down the front walks looked just like our friends back home: clean hair, a smattering of makeup, and coordinated contemporary outfits. Jean shorts and tank tops appeared everywhere due to the late-summer heat, but we also saw thin cotton dresses and short skirts in bright colors and bold patterns.

Mom had turned in her seat, a dreamy look settling across her features. "Girls, are you thinking about signing up to rush the sororities? We didn't have sororities where I went." She inched her fingers along the seat back until they rested on Dad's arm. "The idea of living in a beautiful house with your friends sounds amazing, don't you think, Jack?"

Dad had turned down the radio. "*Mm-hmm.* I guess. If the twins want to investigate sorority life—and the costs aren't too high—it's okay with me."

Jenny's expression had grown serious. "Well, we want to see what dorm life is like first before deciding, don't we, Jules?"

I nodded quickly at my twin. "For sure. I don't think it'll hurt to sign up for the sororities' Fall Open House weekend though." The corners of my mouth turned up as I added, "That way we can check out whether sorority girls are fun or stuck-up."

Jenny chuckled as her hand swept wide. "Well, it would be cool to see what the insides of those houses look like."

I brushed Mom's hand to get her attention. "We learned at orientation that the sororities have strict grade cutoffs. First-semester grades are really important. That's why rush doesn't officially begin until after Christmas break."

Jenny butted in. "Yep, and if your grades are bad, you don't get invited to attend the second round of parties in January."

In the rear-view mirror, Dad's blue eyes had flashed. "Scholarship first. I like the sound of that."

So, one steamy September day, Camille, Jenny, and I met between classes at the student union and searched out the office for the Panhellenic Association, the governing board of the sororities in charge of rush.

The Panhel rush chairman, a perky full-faced junior named Jane, who was careful to hide her own Greek affiliation, handed us booklets and interest forms to fill out. Back at Willkie, we devoured the information. With more girls registering for sorority rush than there were spots in the chapter houses, Indiana was one of the most competitive Greek systems in the United States. For years, Greek fraternity and sorority life had been under scrutiny across the country because of its reputation for attracting members of privilege, raucous and irresponsible partying, and lack of concern for academic achievement. But at IU, Greek life was not just making a comeback, it was thriving.

For Jenny and me, part of the allure was the privilege of living in the beautiful, stately chapter houses situated along the campus's main avenues. Their proximity to the psychology building, for me, and business school, for Jen, were big pluses. In contrast, after about a month of living in a residence hall, we had found the physical structure to be cold and sterile, offering limited amenities like cozy gathering areas and quiet rooms for study. The transitory nature of the dorm system was also unappealing. Very few sophomores returned to the residence halls, preferring instead to rent off-campus apartments, which meant commuting to campus on buses or having a car on campus and purchasing a parking permit.

So on a beautiful October weekend, Jenny and I, along with most of our dorm friends, gathered outside the sororities in assigned rush groups. We toured each of the sorority houses for twenty minutes. At the lightning-fast parties, we learned the chapters had academic and social standards that were enforced by a house mother, sorority leadership, and local and national governing bodies. Besides a resident house mother, each sorority hosted family-style sit-down dinners during the week, and there existed strict rules about alcohol on the premises and guest visitation hours. Unlike the dorm standards, men could be entertained only in the first-floor formal areas.

After the open houses, Jenny and I compared notes with Camille in our dorm room. For the sixty to eighty girls living in the chapter houses, there seemed to be a rich environment of leadership and networking opportunities. The living situations ranged from two-girl rooms to six- and eight-girl suites. Because room assignments switched up each semester, the opportunity to get to know more girls in each class year meant more friendships could thrive in a cohesive environment.

From the outside, the Greek system may have looked as if it restricted entry, but it was established for those who wanted the structure and familiarity of family life. Because it resembled the situation that Jenny and I experienced at home, we were eager to take our chances at rushing. Hanging out with like-minded women was one appeal to pledging, but so was taking advantage of the extensive social and extracurricular calendars they provided. For me, joining a sorority also meant narrowing the huge size of our Big Ten school, so that belonging felt achievable.

But first, Jenny, Camille, and I had to get through the first semester and keep our grades up.

On a rainy October day, shortly after the exhausting round of sorority open houses, Jenny stormed into my room, her face nearly as red as the IU logo on her sweatshirt.

"Jules, I'm sick of coming home from class to find a *Do Not Disturb* tag hanging on my doorknob. Jeez, it's not even the weekend." My sister tore out the rubber band holding her ponytail. She raked her nails, ones she had carefully polished a shimmery pink, through her long brown hair. "The exact same thing happened on

Tuesday. Can't Linda and her boyfriend do *it* in his dorm room once in a while?"

Scowling in sympathy at my twin's predicament, I pointed at Camille's desk. "She's in class till five. Just hang out here."

Jenny slammed the door, hung her corduroy jacket on the corner of my bed, and dragged her backpack over to Camille's study desk. Much like an unhappy four-year-old, she huffed and banged her stuff around until I shut my *Intro to Psych* textbook and gave her my full attention.

Hands bunched up in her lap, my twin glared.

"I've had it. I like Linda well enough, but getting kicked out of my room all the time isn't fair." Jenny pointed at Camille's bed, bunked a few feet below mine. "If she didn't go home most weekends to see her own boyfriend, I'd be stuck sleeping in the lounge or on your floor in a sleeping bag."

Eyeing my sister, I handed her a stick of gum. "I heard at lunch today that Tasha's roommate is transferring out at semester. Maybe you could ditch Linda and room with her."

Jenny's face brightened. Jenny and I knew Tasha from Willkie-10. A short, spunky blonde who we knew to be friendly and honest, she was also carefree and adventurous. Fun either found Tasha, or she sought it out.

Jen grew contemplative. "I think Tasha and I would get along. But how do I explain the switch to Mom and Dad without getting into details?"

Frowning, I nodded my head. I knew what my sister was getting at. Neither of us wanted to let on how rampant sex was on Willkie-11 or across campus. And our resident counselor, Mariel, whom Mom had befriended in August on move in day, was worthless. She did little to enforce the university's dorm policies, which stated that out of courtesy to others, all male guests should be entertained in the student lounge. We all knew the reason Mariel wasn't a stickler on that point—she spent a lot of time at her boyfriend's off-campus apartment. I smirked. At least she told everyone on the floor to keep the noise down during the evening quiet hours.

As Jenny and I talked more, we agreed. We would have to lie. If our mother got wind of the truth, she'd phone the dean's office and demand an immediate transfer for both of us to Forest, the all-girls dorm. We were both vehemently opposed to Forest and to switching dorms at this point in the semester. We preferred Willkie-11. We had established strong friendships and created set routines, such as grabbing big tables in the cafe, riding the bus, and walking to class with girls whose schedules matched ours.

But the roommate situation had to change.

As if in a stupor, Jen stared out the east-facing bank of windows. I wondered if she even saw the scene stretching out beyond the edge of campus—the incredible golden-brown and reddish wave of trees changing color. I suspected she was close to tears, and I hated seeing her so miserable.

"What if you told our folks you have nothing in common with Linda? Say you want to switch because she's a sophomore."

When she turned back to me, her face was pale, and her voice was soft. "You mean, just say I'd rather room with a freshman? Nothing else." Her mouth eased into a weak smile. "That happens to be true, too."

Neither of us liked lying to our folks. My mind flicked back to the day I sat in the church parking lot instead of going into Mass. Reminiscent of Jenny's current dilemma, back then, withholding information from my folks and offering them partial truths had felt liberating and somewhat empowering. I had rationalized my little lie, believing that it was important to make my own choices and take control over the course of my life.

"Mom and Dad don't need to know everything that happens here at IU. I'm just saying that you need to do what's right for you."

My sister nodded, stood, and stretched. There was attitude and confidence in her stance. "I'm going down to Tasha's room," she said, "to see if she's back from class. See you back here in a bit."

Jenny's roommate dilemma was one of the first exposures she and I had to morals and values that differed from our upbringing. What we discovered about life on a college campus hadn't surprised or upended us. One of the reasons we had gravitated to a Big Ten school in the first place was to experience life beyond the sheltered world of our Catholic high school and home life. We figured how other people went about living their lives was their business. Not ours. Our unspoken goal was to follow our own inner compass and try not to judge those around us.

Little did we know those goals would soon face a major test.

25

Bid Time

Winter 1978

"Jules, our rush counselor just got off the elevator. She's headed to the lounge."

I looked up to see Jenny skid through the open door of the dorm room I shared with Camille. My twin tugged at her crimson IU sweatshirt, pulling it down over the gray baggy sweatpants we'd both taken to wearing when we studied or hung out with friends on Willkie-11.

My sister's hazel eyes bore into mine. "C'mon! Let's go. It's bid time."

Jenny's words had the same effect on me as if someone yanked the fire alarm. My heart rate skyrocketed, and the muscles in my legs and back felt tight, twitchy. As I jerked out of my desk in the corner of the room, the notebooks and folders I'd been labeling dropped with a smack on the desktop. I shoved them aside.

Behind me, Camille scooted her chair away from her desk where she'd been reading a new poli-sci textbook. When we returned to campus after New Year's to begin rush week, Camille had dropped out of rush after receiving only a handful of bids. Her first-semester report card hadn't met some of the sororities' strict GPA requirements.

"It's my own fault," she'd confided to me. "I should've spent more time studying and less time visiting my boyfriend back home." She reached for a pair of hair clips, tamed the frizzy tendrils of dark hair escaping her ponytail, and gave me a limp smile. "Maybe I'll rush as a sophomore," she mumbled.

While I had attended the five rounds of rush parties during the previous week, Camille had gotten a head start on material for her second-semester classes. I hated that rush had turned out the way it had for my roommate, but I knew she and I would remain buddies whether I became a sorority girl or not.

"Good luck, you guys." Camille's thick glasses, which she often wore at the end of the day, obscured her deep blue eyes.

When she said, "I hope you both get the houses you want," I knew she meant it, but the grin I returned to Camille was as shaky as the one on Jenny's face.

Since waking that morning, my sister and I, along with a handful of our friends who were still rushing, had been overcome by debilitating nerves. The rigorous pace of rush week—its crazy cycle of worry, anticipation, doubt, adrenaline, letdown, and fatigue—had left us overwrought. Our faces held the glazed stupor of overstimulation, as our bodies melted into the cozy comfort of sweatpants and sweatshirts—much preferred over the previous week's wardrobe of heels, pantyhose, jewelry, and fancy outfits.

Jenny beamed at Camille, quipping, "Thanks, Chameleon."

The three of us erupted in giggles.

Since that steamy August day when Jenny and I had met my easygoing roommate, Camille, the three of us had grown close, calling each other by pet nicknames and chuckling at silly inside jokes.

"Hey, you guys!" Annie, the vivacious blonde from across the hall, shouted into my open doorway. "Bid time. I'm headed to the lounge."

Jenny yanked my arm to follow Annie. I gave Camille a sheepish wave.

Annie linked arms with Jenny and me in the hallway. Her silky voice boomed, "I'm so nervous I haven't been able to eat a thing all day. How 'bout you guys?"

I snickered. "Well, that bowl of popcorn we snarfed down last night sure had my belly grumbling all night."

The previous evening had been Two-Party or Final Night, the last round of rush when rushees received invitations to return to just two sororities. After attending the evening activities at each chapter house, we had returned to our dorm floors, ranked our final selections on a preference card, and then turned those over to our Panhellenic Association rush counselor. Our rush counselor had coached us well about the risks surrounding the last round of rush. If a girl was lucky enough to make it all the way to the final night, picking between two sororities might prove difficult. Also, in the end, a rushee might not receive a bid at all. That notion caused many of us to have fitful nights of sleep.

On the other side of the Greek system, Final Night for the sororities meant drafting a list of preferred pledges and submitting those to the Panhellenic Association. In turn, the Panhellenic rush committee fed the rushee preference cards and sorority pledge class lists into a computer program that sorted and matched them. Twenty-four hours later, the resulting bids for the 1978 pledge classes were to be delivered to rushees in their dorms via rush counselors. At the same time this unfolded, the sorority rush chairmen at each chapter house received and read aloud the list of their new pledge class to the membership.

So far, Jenny and I had been fortunate.

We'd made it through all the early rounds of sorority rush parties to Final Night without serious disappointments. Each of us had finished with two strong choices, chapters with girls we liked and where we could see ourselves fitting in. Much like the decision to attend college, my twin and I had only one sorority preference in common. Jenny and I had both attended the party at Delta Gamma (DG), then she finished the night at Pi Beta Phi (Pi Phi) while I went to Kappa Alpha Theta (Theta). If my twin sister and I were to remain as close together physically as we had always been—that is, live in the same house and have similar friends and experiences—then I would have to preference DG, not Theta, as my first choice.

Just thinking about what I had marked on my preference card the night before made my head throb.

Jenny slipped out of Annie's hold and hollered down the hall to a girl with short hair who loitered near the entrance to the student lounge.

"Amy, save us seats together, will ya?"

Jenny charged off ahead of Annie and me to meet up with Amy.

As Annie and I approached the lounge, she moaned. "I'm sure glad this is over." Annie had attended Pi Phi and Theta. The odds were strong she would end up with either Jenny or me in her pledge class.

"Me, too, Annie," I confessed.

In a few minutes, we'll all know. I hope I did the right thing. I sure think I did.

It felt as if my heart were beating as loud as a trombone. I tried settling myself down with the notion that if Jenny and I made it into different pledge classes, it would be nice to have Annie as a sorority sister at Theta.

In the cozy student lounge located at the center of our dorm floor, Annie and I piled onto a sofa next to Jenny and Amy, our expressions cheerless.

"Oh, God. I feel like I'm gonna throw up," Annie blurted out, her voice resonating throughout the space now teeming with too many anxious females.

Everyone cracked up. Annie's flare for drama was one thing, but her honesty and knack for connecting with others by stating the obvious made us adore her. When Marcie, another pal from Willkie-11, handed Annie the metal trash can from beside the sofa, the crowd applauded, shouting, "Woo-hoo. Good one, Marcie."

It felt so good to laugh. But Annie's comment served another purpose. It underscored the importance of the moment. Everyone in that student lounge knew and acknowledged that each of us stood at a crossroad. Whether or not we pledged a sorority determined where we would live for the next three years, whom we would call our friends maybe for a lifetime, and what activities and events we would become involved in. Those distinct paths would form us as students and women, directly influencing our majors and, once we left IU, career choices. The threshold at which we found ourselves was mind-blowing. Some girls were already mopping away tears.

As quickly as the tension in the room had dissipated with laughter, it returned when our rush counselor—a girl we could only know as Sara so as not be influenced by the sorority she belonged to—rose from a study desk where she had been sorting envelopes. When she walked to the center of the lounge, I felt air trap inside my chest.

"Okay, girls. Without further ado, I'm going to start reading names and hand out your bid envelopes. Please wait to open yours until everyone receives theirs. Good luck, everyone."

As I listened to Sara call out names, the armpits of my jean shirt dampened, plastering against my upper ribs. Before turning in our preference cards after Final Night, Jenny and I had whispered together in the hallway outside our dorm rooms. I knew my sister had selected Delta Gamma (DG) over Pi Phi as her top choice. When it was my turn, I ticked off the reasons why I loved the Theta house: the two-story front staircase with its stained-glass windows, the secluded library where I could see myself studying and journaling with a cup of warm tea, and the short two-block walk from the chapter house to the psych building.

During my last party at Theta, one of the conversations influencing my pledge decision had been with Mary, a fellow psych major. She and I sat huddled together in her two-girl room for close to an hour. We discussed why each of us had chosen our majors, as well as our curriculum goals and career ideas post-graduation. Our easy dialogue about courses and teachers made me feel as if I'd found a mentor and a friend. In all the rush events I'd attended at DG, I hadn't had an in-depth conversation like I had enjoyed with Mary.

"I really think I feel more at home at Theta than at DG." My eyes had pleaded with my sister for understanding. "Would you be upset if I put Theta as my first choice?"

Jenny was quick to shake her head no.

She said, "If I get DG, and you get Theta, we'll only be a fifteen-minute walk from one another for the next three years." She reached over and patted my hand, grinning. "Besides, we can study together every night at the Union. And two sororities mean twice as many friends for both of us."

My face lit up as I squeezed her hand. "Okay, then. That's what I'm going to do. I'll put Theta first, but you never know . . ."

I didn't have to finish that sentence. Jenny knew what I meant.

Even though I set Theta as my preference, there was still a chance that Jenny and I would end up in the same pledge class at DG. If the sorority rush gods granted us our wishes, we would be forging new territories on our own. Neither of us dared putting a voice to the other side of the equation. If the Greek rush system at IU failed us, one of us might get our top choice and the other might be cut completely. The chance also existed that we might both be disappointed, forced to live out our college years in a dormitory or an apartment, which was the route Camille was set on for the next year at least.

What had we set in motion? Would living in different sororities, forging unique friendships, and enjoying separate and diverse experiences interfere with our lifelong sisterly bond? Or was the sorority decision we had agreed upon something that was long overdue? Was it an error in judgment or an invitation—the right opportunity presented at the right moment—to explore our individual uniqueness, to blossom as separate beings, and to embark on definitive paths?

The worry in my belly and the excitement in my head were at war with one another. I regretted the cafeteria sloppy joes I'd had for lunch and found myself eyeing the trash can Marcie had jokingly placed in front of Annie and me. At that moment, I doubted everything—whether living apart from my sister was a good idea, and if I'd like living in a sorority at all. I wondered why I'd been swept up in the rush craziness. Was it attaining the status of becoming a member of an elite group, the stately Theta sorority house that reminded me of the Hinsdale home my parents almost bought? Or was it simply the need to cut down the size of a Big Ten school into something more manageable, a place where I felt like I fit in and where the most opportunities existed?

As Sara continued reading off the names and got close to the *R*'s on the list, my brain reverted to what it had been trained to do in times of personal crisis.

I prayed.

Please, Lord! If you are that all-knowing, loving God I was taught to praise, look out for Jenny and me. Don't let one of us get cut and the other receive a bid. Let us both fail, or both succeed.

As Jenny rose to receive her envelope from Sara, she gave me a timid look, her eyebrows arching as if a question was forthcoming. I wiped my hands on my sweats and forced myself to breathe. After I sat down with my envelope, I flipped it this way and that, trying to discern its secret without desecrating the seal.

When Annie, whose last name was at the end of the alphabet, accepted her envelope, Sara said, "Okay, you can all open your bids."

The sounds of paper ripping became dwarfed by sighs and moans and cheers. I unfolded my letter, studied it, and then my eyes went straight to Jenny's face. It was as if we were the only two people in the room. For me to be truly happy, I needed her to be happy, too. My sister's eyes gleamed. Elation filled my being. She gave me a thumbs-up, meaning she was pledging DG. I matched Jen's gesture and mouthed the syllables that filled me with cautious contentment: *Theta*.

On the sofa next to Annie and me, Amy and Jenny hugged. Both had gone DG. Annie peeked over my shoulder and read my letter, squealing, "We're gonna be Thetas together. Wippee!"

I laughed. There were never any secrets when Annie was around. I hugged her. It was comforting to know I had an instant friend with whom to share the same pledge experience.

Amid the chaos, Jenny stood and leaned toward me, whispering, "Jules, let's go tell Camille. I know she's dying to know what happened."

As we ran down the hallway waving our invitations to pledge the sororities we had chosen, I wondered what was in store for my sister and me. But just like that day when Mom gifted us her apron strings, an inner voice reminded me that this was my time. *Go and do. Figure out who you are, what you want, and where you belong.*

For the first time in my eighteen years, I would take those steps completely on my own.

26

Clash

Winter 1978

While my mom had symbolically—and literally—cut the apron strings with Jenny and me, it turned out that truly letting go was not easy for her. By the second semester of our freshman year, events occurred that helped me define my own beliefs and resulted in viewpoints that differed from my family's. I also learned that in establishing independence—both in physical distance and in thought—the bonds of belonging sometimes follow you where you least expect.

On a crisp January afternoon after Christmas break, Camille huffed as she walked into Jenny's new room with a pile of hanging clothes tightly pressed to her chest.

"Where do you want me to put this stuff?" she quizzed Jenny.

My sister glanced up from the standard-issue five-drawer dresser into which she stuffed folded clothes. "Over there, in the closet, Lizard Woman." She pointed to the sliding closet door on the right.

From where I stood tucking in the floral sheets of my sister's twin bed, I saw the frown brushing across Camille's face.

I grimaced at my twin. "Of all the nicknames you have for Camille, that's the worst."

Jenny gave my roomie a hangdog look. "Sorry, Camille."

The three of us had spent the better part of the day helping Jenny and her new roommate, Tasha, settle into a double room at the complete opposite end of Willkie-11. Jenny had made the decision to switch rooms at semester because of her roommate Linda's inconsiderate behavior and frequent overnight visitor. The move turned out to be a good thing for Jenny, but it was just the beginning of the moral issues and challenges she and I would face.

When Tasha moved up to the eleventh floor to room with Jenny, she brought with her an influx of new friends and acquaintances. One was Lena, a short, stocky girl with wild, thick, dark hair and plain features. Her effervescent personality and boisterous laugh endeared her to our crowd. If we gathered in Willkie's eleventh-floor student lounge, Lena found the epicenter. Even though she wasn't part of my inner circle of freshmen friends, she was one of us: a Willkie girl. Which is why when she found herself in trouble one cold and dreary night in late January, we rallied behind her.

Jenny, Camille, and I had emerged from the elevator following another long dinner in the cafeteria and spotted Lena huddled with Tasha in front of us in the student lounge. As she leaned into Tasha, Lena's large chest heaved with shattering sobs. Pointing at the distraught Lena, Tasha signaled to Jenny and me to hurry over.

With a quick wave, Camille peeled off to our room. My sister and I trudged into the lounge. Tasha stroked Lena's dark, unruly hair as she whimpered.

"Calm down, Lena. Here come the twins. The three of us are gonna help you think this through. Okay?"

Jenny snuck me a wide-eyed glare that meant, *Oh boy, what are we walking into?*

I shrugged at my sister and shut the doors to the lounge. Lena slouched against Tasha on one of the sofas, her green eyes brimming with more tears. When she rubbed them away, she dragged her fingers across her cheeks, leaving red streaks so pronounced I was certain she'd end up with welts.

Tasha massaged our friend's shoulders. "*Awww*, Lena. You're making yourself sick, honey. Tell the twins what's up."

Lena peeked at us through the mane of her thick, wavy hair. Her face was so distraught, her hair so disheveled, that it looked like a Halloween mask. "I can't. You tell 'em, Tasha."

Jenny glanced at me, and I figured her mind had gone where mine went. Either Lena was flunking a class, had gotten caught cheating or plagiarizing, or had been dumped by one of the many boys she had been chasing around campus. The truth turned out to be so much worse.

Lena was pregnant.

It was every coed's nightmare. Our breaths heavy, my twin and I stared at Lena. As stunning as the news was, neither of us was surprised. Lena was fun loving and very boy crazy. During our first term at IU, Jenny and I often passed on frat parties or off-campus keggers because of a looming French quiz or a math assignment. Lena had done the opposite. Her coursework took a back seat to partying. Often when she made it back to Willkie after late-night socializing, one of the girls had to peel her out of the elevator, or off the hallway carpeting, and then help unlock her room.

"Oh, Lena," I said, looking at her with profound pity.

Beside me, Jenny sighed and uttered a thought I'd kept to myself. "Are you *sure* you're pregnant?'

During the entire aching reveal, Lena's chubby chin rested in the warm hollow of her neck. When she finally lifted her head to speak, her voice was dull and hoarse from hours of raw emotion.

She squinted at Jen and me. "Yep. Went to the health center today. They did the test."

The magnitude of her words pierced the close space of the lounge. Lena's secret ballooned, pressing against everyone and everything. I found it difficult to breathe, much less offer any comment or suggestion. While I couldn't imagine myself cornered like Lena, my mind played with her options.

What would I do if I were her?

With glazed eyes and a crumpled demeanor, Lena was defiant. "I can't have this baby, you guys. And I can't tell my folks. They'll kill me. I need an abortion. But I'm dead broke." She disintegrated into convulsed sobs, muttering, "What am I going to do? My life is over."

"Don't you worry, now honey," Tasha cooed. "We'll all chip in and help you. Won't we, girls?"

Jenny and I locked eyes. We were blindsided by Lena's news and Tasha's assumption that we would support an abortion. Raised by strict Catholics, I knew what our religion preached about situations like Lena's. Life began at conception, not when a heartbeat was detected by a doctor's stethoscope. Ending a life, whether the soul was living or in utero, was considered a grave sin. My head pounded. Whether we wanted to or not, Jenny and I were drawn into a moral predicament—one that was real, not a hypothetical classroom discussion or a priest's Sunday homily—with serious considerations and consequences.

As I sat there absorbing the magnitude of the circumstances, I heard Mom's voice in my head. *An unborn child is a gift from God.*

In the adoption chats Jenny and I had with our folks over the years, they consistently professed their belief that we were their gifts from God. Mom often reminded us of the facts proving our destiny: our birthday coinciding with the Feast of Our Lady of Lourdes and their pilgrimage to the shrine, and then our baptismal date landing on our mother's birthday. But to Lena, her surprise pregnancy was not a gift. It was a burden, a problem to solve, and she refused to consider carrying her baby to term for an adoption, stating, "Too many issues at home."

That night I tossed and turned in my bunk above Camille's.

What if my birth mom had chosen abortion over adoption for Jen and me?

As I debated the moral dilemmas of abortion and adoption, I vacillated between sympathy for Lena and indecision. If I contributed to Lena's abortion, would the blood be on my hands as well as Lena's?

At around three in the morning, I came to terms with my doubts. Despite my Catholic upbringing, deep down I believed that it is a woman's right to choose what she does with her body. I also concluded that whatever role I played in the situation, full responsibility remained with Lena. Even if I did contribute some of my hard-earned savings—money that was not from my parents but from my summer job as a salesgirl in a shoe department—the abortion would be on her conscience.

I also decided to help Lena because I feared for her mental stability and well-being. I chose between the lesser of two evils: the threat of Lena harming herself versus ending the life of an unborn child. I placated myself with the reasoning that while I would never personally destroy a God-given gift, it was not my place to judge what other women did with their bodies.

When Jenny and I walked to class the next morning, I was relieved to hear my twin had reached the same conclusion during her own fitful night of sleep.

She gripped my arm, a stern look coming over her pretty face. "This is between you and me," she said. "You know, Mom and Dad would be very disappointed in us if they ever found out."

I nodded in agreement at our little pact, but my insides were still in turmoil. Assisting Lena with her plan to abort was a real-life choice, and I made it with less than a hundred percent degree of confidence.

Later that day when Tasha came to my room with an envelope,

I slipped in a few twenties to help Lena. After Tasha trudged out, my head dropped to my chest while my heart whispered a prayer for absolution. *God, forgive me for my role in this.* As I lifted my tear-filled eyes up to the ceiling, I pulled out all stops, beseeching my ace in the hole. *Saint Thérèse, watch over Lena. Keep her safe.* Slogging my way to class, I prayed some more, grateful that it wasn't me who faced Lena's difficult decision.

The problems Jenny and I encountered on Willkie-11 opened our eyes to the "real world out there," something our parents had labored to shelter us from for more than eighteen years. Lena's unplanned pregnancy and her decision to go through with an abortion was a pivotal moment for my sister and me. It helped us define our stance regarding a woman's right to choose, a weighty decision that we came to irrespective of our faith, upbringing, personal inclinations, and adoption.

The sexual promiscuity on campus, our friend's unplanned pregnancy, and contributing to her abortion fund profoundly changed me, but these acts of growing up and establishing my own identity apart from my family were never spoken of again. Lena's abortion and our role in it was not the only information we withheld from our parents that year. It became a conscious decision to be more selective with what we shared with them as we continued to break free and shape our own lives.

While my world kept moving forward, my parents struggled to hang on to how things used to be, sometimes with comic outcomes.

During one of those dinners in the cafeteria that morphed into a gabfest, the subject of spring break took center stage. Once we emerged from the elevator on Willkie-11, our friend Debbie motioned for Jenny and me to follow her into her room.

Curious, we plopped onto her neatly made bed with its vibrant comforter and matching throw pillows. Smiling shyly from her desk chair, Debbie flipped her clean, sleek, dark blond hair behind her shoulders. She glanced at her soft-spoken roommate, Gayle, who nodded.

"Would you guys like to go to Fort Lauderdale on spring break with Gayle and me?"

Later, in our usual Sunday evening phone call home to our folks, Jenny and I worked up the nerve to plead with them to go to Florida for our break. The crux of our appeal was that everyone we knew was going somewhere, and we'd be "losers" if all we did was go home to Oak Brook for the week.

"How will you get there?" Dad asked while Jen and I pressed the receiver between us.

"Debbie! You've met her. The quiet, studious girl with long hair. Her room is right off the elevators near the student lounge."

"*Ahhh*, the young lady with a pretty smile and good manners," Mom said.

"Yeah, that's her." Jenny's eyes glinted at me. "She has a car. Her folks said she could drive it to Florida if we pitched in for gas." I gave Jen a thumbs-up, a signal to continue pouring it on. "We promise to let you know the minute we leave campus, and then call and check in along the way."

My stomach tickled with excitement. I couldn't help myself. I grabbed the phone away from my sister.

"Jen forgot to mention that Debbie's parents have a friend whose condo we can stay in. For a small fee. Please, please. It's all set. Whaddya say?"

There was a pause on the line, and Jenny pressed her cheek so close to mine that the receiver dug into my ear. I grimaced, squeezing my eyes shut.

When Dad said, "What do you think, Jeanne?" my eyes flew open. He hadn't shut down the idea.

Jenny jumped back from the phone and slapped me a high-five.

"How many of you girls are going?" Mom asked.

I rolled my eyes. I could just see my mother's wrinkled brow as she ticked off still more reasons to say no.

"There's four of us." I tapped my fingers on the desk next to the rotary phone, trying to keep my cool even though my heart rate was going lickety-split. "Jenny, me, Debbie, and her roommate Gayle."

Jenny and I passed the receiver back and forth as our folks asked other questions. Things like what kind of car Debbie drove, when we planned to leave campus, what route we'd take, and where we might stop along the way. With each query we handled, the more we felt as if we had closed the deal.

Our faces glowed when our dad said, "I think you've thought this through. It's okay by me. Jeanne?"

"If you say so, dear," Mom mumbled.

Once we hung up, we danced around Jenny's room, chanting, "We're going to Lauderdale. Lauderdale. Wahoo."

The next Sunday night when we called home, Mom answered, her voice dripping with enthusiasm.

"Well, girls, we liked your idea of a trip to Fort Lauderdale so much that we got to thinking. Maybe we should treat your siblings to a vacation, too."

Jenny's eyes grew as big as Frisbees. My stomach lurched.

Oh, please, God, no!

Mom rattled on, her silky-smooth voice thick with excitement. "Your Dad has found a place. It's not far from where you'll be staying. Isn't that great?"

Jenny scowled and stuck her tongue out at the phone receiver.

Mom continued her crowing. "So, if you need anything, we'll be just down the street. And we promise to treat you and your friends to dinner one night."

Were they kidding? They weren't.

After the call, Jenny's voice rose higher than mine as we stormed around the tiny dorm room whining about them tagging along on our trip. What if our family showed up at the condo rental when some of the frat guys we knew were partying with us? What if they caught us sunbathing in the skimpy bikinis we planned to buy at the mall? What if they spotted us having a beer at a local dive they didn't approve of? Why couldn't our parents trust us more and just let go?

Despite our fears, Jenny and I saw Lauderdale as yet another notch in the belt of independence we were eager to wear. There was also something about the vacation we hadn't shared with our parents—a detail that made us feel like we'd gained a power position even though our folks were going to be just down the street.

Debbie's car was a stick shift. Jenny and I had no experience with manual transmission, and even though Deb had tried to teach us a few times in the Willkie parking lot, it hadn't been good for the car. Rather than admit defeat, fess up, or cancel the trip, our foursome hatched a plan.

Whenever it was Jenny's or my turn to take a turn at the wheel, we'd slip into the driver's seat and put both feet on the pedals. From her place in the passenger seat, Debbie coached us through the footwork while she handled the gear shifting. During the first few exchanges, a lot of frayed nerves charged the air in the small red Vega, but thanks to Debbie's patience, we persevered.

After a long night on the road, we pulled into a Publix parking lot in Fort Lauderdale and called our folks from a pay phone. Weary from lack of sleep, the stress of driving through Atlanta with just a road map, as well as navigating the numerous mountain switchbacks, our voices were strained and clipped as we delivered the news.

"We made it to Lauderdale. Nope, no problems. At the grocery store now. See you tomorrow. Bye."

As it turned out, our worst fears were never realized. We saw our family only once for dinner at their hotel. They never saw us in our bikinis, stopped over unannounced, or showed up at any of the bars we hit on the strip. But knowing they were there made us still feel as if they were looking over our shoulders.

Gaining the right to drive to Florida with friends for our first college spring break was a small win. It thrilled us to drive Debbie's stick shift car and experience the joy and freedom that comes with asserting independence. Because of the situation with the car, we felt as if we got away with something.

Attaining independence is not a straight line, and as I soon learned, sometimes we go back and forth, wanting our freedom but craving the belonging we have with those who know us best.

27

Never Far

Spring & Summer 1980

"Look! There's a spot over there."

Jenny pointed to a pair of oversized, worn tan leather chairs in a secluded corner of the crowded room.

"Perfect," I whispered. "Let's grab 'em."

Behind us, students surged off the escalator, peering into one of the student union's most popular lounges with the hopes of finding a place to sit with a coffee or snack, study between classes, or catch up with a friend. As she scuttled to claim the prized seats, Jenny's ponytail swatted the back of her pale blue Delta Gamma sweatshirt.

Two and a half years before—when we had first come to IU's campus as freshmen—the hall we just entered had stolen our hearts. Much like the Theta house where I lived, the room boasted dark traditional furniture, fringed area rugs, and deep ceilings dressed in a crisscross pattern of dark beams. Since moving into separate sorority houses, Jenny and I had met in the Union most evenings. Much like our early years as growing girls, she and I were never far from each other's side.

Our daily meeting spot in the Union was when we hashed over the goings-on in our sororities, whined about boys and the rigors of our chosen majors—me, in honors psychology, and she in the School of Business—and negotiated over who had dibs on the Monte Carlo our dad had given us to keep on campus. Of all the things the two of us bickered over during our twenty-one-year history as siblings, sharing the car, not clothes, proved to be the most divisive. When it was my semester to store the car in the Theta lot, Jenny had to check with me to use it, and vice versa. If one of us had plans with sorority sisters and the other one needed the car, a squabble ensued. The result was that it might be days before we joined up in the Union. Somehow, we always found a way to work through the lingering hard feelings.

But on that day, because we had an upcoming road trip arranged to visit high school friends at the University of Iowa, the mood between us was carefree and agreeable. Plopping down into one of the cushy, deep chairs—a place in which the two of us intended to camp out—my lookalike issued a satisfying yawn.

"Whew. I'm beat," she mumbled.

"Me, too. How about a coffee? A no-bake cookie from the Sweet Shoppe?"

It was impossible to be anywhere in the Indiana Memorial Union (IMU) without catching a whiff of the Sweet Shoppe, a place we frequented with Camille until she transferred after sophomore year. The result of all those sugary treats meant each of us had packed on the "freshmen ten." Jenny and I had whittled away those extra pounds thanks to jogging and intramural sports like racquetball and volleyball. The healthy, well-balanced meals served during our sit-down family-style dinners at the Theta and DG houses also helped.

Jenny nodded. "Yes to the coffee. No to the cookie."

I placed my book bag on the chair beside her. "Okay, two coffees coming up."

There was good reason our energy lagged that day. Besides attending class, keeping our grades up to sustain academic scholarships, and participating in sorority functions, Jenny and I worked two or three days a week as servers in IMU's Tudor Room. The pay was meager, but the hours and location were ideal. IMU was a three-block stroll for Jenny from DG and a hundred yards from the Theta house. The money we earned supplemented our student loans and the stipend our parents gave us.

More than half an hour later, I handed Jen a large coffee. "Two creams just as you like it."

My sister's neatly plucked eyebrows arched into a thin line. "What took so long?"

"I ran into Barb, my Panhellenic advisor, outside the coffee shop." My wide grin equaled that of the Cheshire Cat.

She studied me for a second and then her face lit up. "Did you get it—the nomination?"

"Yep." We high-fived. "Yours truly is next year's candidate for Panhellenic president. All that needs to happen is for me to give a speech. The Panhel reps will vote on the slate at our next meeting."

As Jen held my gaze, I saw the pride there. That's all I needed. She didn't have to spell it out. Despite the grueling lunch-hour work shift, the day was shaping up to be a good one. Settling back into the comfy lounge chair, I sipped the hot brew, reflecting.

Hard to believe only one more year at IU.

After Jenny and I had finished up our freshmen pledge duties and moved into our respective sororities, she and I had gotten involved in campus and sorority activities. Jenny focused on leadership roles at DG. During house elections at the end of sophomore year, she was named the VP for pledge education, which entailed indoctrinating the new pledge class about all things Delta Gamma. As a rising senior, she hoped to be voted VP of chapter relations, a role for which she was well-suited since it meant maintaining harmony among ninety or so busy and strong-willed women.

Because I had become fascinated with the intricacies of the rush process as a freshman, I got involved in the Panhellenic Association.

In the fall of my sophomore year, I was asked to be the assistant Panhel rush chairman, under Jane, the same young woman who registered Camille, Jenny, and me for rush when were on Willkie-11. I found the mechanics behind running the campus-wide rush system more compelling than what my sorority sisters faced during rush parties—meeting and making conversation with a steady stream of girls. When Jane graduated, I succeeded her as the rush chairman. It was a huge position to assume as a junior, but I'd been eager to take it on. It meant getting to know girls in other sororities, like DG, and serving on panels with campus leaders and university administrators.

Jenny tapped my arm. "You look like you're in dreamland, Jules. Let's talk about our trip to Iowa this weekend. And"—she paused— "we need to discuss the brochure Dad sent about student travel programs in Europe."

Back when we were looking at colleges to attend, Jen and I had plotted how we might study abroad our junior year. But between course loads, work schedules, and leadership commitments, it just hadn't made sense. The financial commitment was a factor, too. With three of us in college at the same time, it wasn't in Dad's budget, but "funding a trip to Europe for a few weeks over the summer," he said, "I can handle that." He'd been true to his word and researched affordable, interesting programs. All Jen and I had to do was to decide which one appealed to us most.

"Let's go over the summer travel stuff when we're in the car this weekend." My eyes sparkled at the idea of an adventure with my sister. "I've got a few favorites."

"Okay, good." She leaned toward me. "Listen, I talked to Pete last night. He has a friend he wants you to meet."

My eyebrows raised with curiosity.

"His name is Mike. Pete says he's outgoing and lotsa fun. He's from the Chicago area, too."

"I'm game," I smiled.

As much fun as I'd had at the season's sorority-fraternity keggers and formal dances, there was no one I was serious about dating.

The weekend visit to Iowa was a whirlwind. After the six-hour drive, Jenny and I hung out with high school buddies, hit the bar scene, and then stayed up late talking.

Before we dozed off in sleeping bags on the floor of a friend's apartment, Jenny had quizzed me. "You talked a long time with Pete's buddy Mike. What did you think of him?"

"I liked him a lot. Fun, smart, and a good sense of humor. I gave him my number." I shrugged. "We'll see what happens."

I wasn't as noncommittal as I sounded. Mike had impressed me. I liked his Irish looks, curly brown hair, captivating blue eyes, and generous laugh. As I snuggled into my pillow, I was honest with myself. I wanted to get to know him better.

When we made it back to IU's campus on Sunday, I buzzed around the crowded room I shared with five other Thetas, filling them in about the fun-packed weekend and meeting Mike.

"*Uh-oh*, sounds like this guy has potential," Kate teased.

As I stowed my suitcase under my bunk bed, Kate ran to pick up the phone ringing in the hall outside our room. She pulled the receiver and its long curly cord into our room and handed it to me.

"It's for you," she smirked. "It's a guy."

Mike and I chatted for over an hour. At the end of our call, he voiced what was in my heart.

"In a few weeks when we're home from school, how 'bout we do drinks or catch a movie? I'd like to see you again."

Going back home for the summer wasn't going to be as bad as I thought. A new guy in my life, and a big trip on the horizon.

After pouring over the glossy summer student travel brochure, Jenny and I decided on the United Kingdom trip and Ireland extension package. We liked the ease of travel within English-speaking countries. Because of our family history, Ireland had always topped our wish list.

In mid-June—after a few dates with Mike—Jenny and I boarded a flight to London. We met our tour director and group at a hotel off Piccadilly, and for three weeks we traveled by coach to see top destinations in England, Scotland, and Wales like Liverpool, Stratford-upon-Avon, Cambridge, Oxford, Stonehenge, the Roman Baths, and Edinburgh. A few of our favorite traveling companions had also booked the five-day Ireland trip, so the camaraderie we had enjoyed in the United Kingdom deepened while we tasted Guinness and whiskey and stopped in Dublin, Blarney Castle, Galway, the Ring of Kerry, and Cliffs of Moher.

When Dad picked us up at the airport, he asked, "What was your favorite?"

Jenny and I both yelled at once. "Ireland! We can't wait to go back."

Little did we know that within a few weeks' time, the chance to return to the lush green island that had captivated us with its storied history, enchanting music, and endearing down-to-earth people would present itself.

Jenny's face was rosy with excitement when she stormed into my bedroom and dropped a flyer on my lap. It read, *The Chicago Irish Committee to select its representative for the 1980 International Rose of Tralee Festival in county Kerry, Ireland, is taking applications. Final round of interviews to be held at the Glendora Banquet Hall in Chicago Ridge.*

My sister plunked down on my bed, sprawling across the cream macramé comforter. "What do you think?"

I glanced at the form, chuckling. When my twin had been keen to enter the St. Patrick's Day queen contest as teenagers, I was tentative. But now, I found the idea—squeezing in another travel adventure before my senior year and representing Chicago's Irish in a big way—downright compelling.

"What have we got to lose?" I asked.

And just like before, neither of us had an inkling how the decision would alter our relationship and become a factor in shifting goals and career paths.

28

❧❧

The Big Swerve

Summer 1980

"*Juuuleee*," Jen shouted from the upstairs landing. "Mike's on the phone."

Mom and I were clustered at the kitchen table where we pored over the travel itinerary for the Rose of Tralee Festival. The experience of being named the 1980 Chicago Rose of Tralee still felt as if it had happened to someone else. Much like the St. Patty's Day contest, Jenny and I had made it through the Tralee application process and into the interview round at the Glendora Banquet Hall. Once the interviews and deliberations had taken place, the emcee took the stage to thank the contestants and judges and to announce and crown the winner.

Hearing my name called—rushing to the stage in my strapless pink formal gown where a glittering tiara was set on my head and a lush bouquet of red roses placed in my arms—had been electrifying, magical. Camera flashbulbs popped as I took a triumphant stroll down the runway. It was an extraordinary moment, one to savor and relive over a lifetime. The only pin bursting my celebratory balloon was Jenny's lackluster response to my glory.

She'd pecked my cheek, issued a stiff smile, and given me a stilted hug. "Congrats. I'm sure it'll be the trip of a lifetime."

While she hadn't said so, I imagined she was tired of coming up short on the contests we had entered. Her mediocre response that evening was one thing, but her obvious lack of interest now, in helping me plan my wardrobe—and her tendency to change the subject whenever the Tralee trip surfaced—ate at me. I didn't want to feel guilty about the honor, but I did. I convinced myself that Jen and I would navigate the rough patch as we had countless times before when clothes or the car interfered with our sisterly bond. In the meantime, my parents' overwhelming response had warmed my heart, filling me with necessary support.

On the night after the Chicago contest, when the platters of chicken, rice, and green beans had made their rounds at our family dining table, Dad set his fork down and fixed his lively blue eyes on mine.

"This Tralee contest is quite a big deal." His eyes danced to my mom's and back to mine. "Your mother and I would like to see the festival firsthand and then tour Ireland after you head back to school."

Unlike my reaction to their tagging along on our trip to Fort Lauderdale, I was elated. "I would love to have you there."

I studied Jenny through the fringe of my bangs.

As she cut her chicken, she mumbled, "If I didn't have to be back at IU for the first week of classes, I'd come, too."

I gave her a warm smile, feeling terrible about the ramifications of her statement. Not only would she miss the festival, but she would have to register me for my fall semester, pick me up at the airport, and drive us back to IU. Those bitter consequences were tacked on top of being second best. To her credit, Jenny didn't grumble about the outcome. I assumed this was due to our spending so little time in each other's company. While she hung out with friends, I was on dates with Mike.

"I'm going to run upstairs and take Mike's call." Smiling, I squeezed Mom's shoulder. "When I come back, we can finish planning the trip to Tralee."

My experience representing Chicago at the 1980 Rose of Tralee Festival reminded me of the title character in the *Gidget* movies and TV series. The week's itinerary was a never-ending sequence of exciting, frustrating, funny, uplifting, and exhaustive adventures. My roommate, Grace, who hailed from county Cork, and I shared a row of seats on the official Rose of Tralee motor coach. Emblazoned below our window were the words *Miss Cork and Miss Chicago*. In that bus, twenty-some other Roses and I made frequent publicity stops at dog racetracks, concert halls, nursing homes, and local pubs along the route from the Shannon airport to Killarney and Tralee.

As in the other Irish contests I'd entered, Tralee's panel of judges held several interview sessions. We were also evaluated on our presence and conversation during the public events to which we were escorted by handsome local guys. On the night of the televised finals, Gay Byrne, a popular Irish radio and television host of *The Late Late Show*, conducted his own brand of interviews. During my three-minute stint on camera, Byrne's wit and clever questions disarmed me. It felt more like a cross-examination than a friendly chat. While I didn't stutter or embarrass myself, to my own ears I sounded flat, unimpressive. It was no surprise to learn I had not made the queen's court and that Miss Galway had snagged the 1980 international crown.

I left Tralee grateful to have witnessed my parents' proud faces in the crowd and to have returned to a noble country that had made me feel welcome and special. In one summer, Ireland had worked itself into my heart. She granted me a sense of belonging that I hoped one day to confirm as my genetic genealogy. Despite the impressive and unforgettable experience in Tralee, I was more than eager to return to the States and begin my senior year at IU.

There was a lot in my head as I boarded the flight in Shannon. Fatigued from the late-night post-party celebration, my whole system buzzed. I believed I had honorably represented my city while soaking in the culture. Yet, I was going back to school one week behind in my classes and commitments.

When I landed at O'Hare, Jenny was waiting for me in the Monte Carlo. Besides my sharing about the experience in Tralee, we spent the four-hour drive to IU touching on topics we had in common, like the annual DG-Theta Barn Dance, our work and course loads, sorority rush, spring break plans, and pairings for the Little 500 bike race. In the Theta parking lot, she helped me unload the car and carry my things to the two-girl room I'd been assigned to share with my Theta "little sister," Mary.

One humid afternoon during my first week back on campus, I left the psych building and slogged the two blocks home to the Theta house. I trudged up the magnificent two-story front staircase to my room, set the box fan in the window on high, and lay down on my single bed with its familiar floral print. I threw my arm over my face and let a few tears escape and dampen the pillow sham.

"I don't want to do this anymore," I said to the empty room. "I need to switch gears."

The Tralee experience had broadened my perspective, taught me how limited my worldview had been, cajoled me into having more fun, and begged me to answer some hard questions. Did I really want to be a clinical psychologist? Did I want to assume more student loans to get a PhD? Was there another career path I should consider?

What if . . . I thought.

What if I dropped the honors part of my degree, continued applying to post-graduate psychology programs, but concurrently explored career opportunities through the College of Arts & Sciences (A&S) placement office?

Naming and affirming my doubts that afternoon and my subsequent decision to act and try something different—all of which were influenced in no small way by my summer travels with Jenny and the Rose of Tralee Festival—changed the course of my life.

It was my big swerve.

The very next day, I dropped out of my honors psych class and enrolled in an A&S placement course to practice interview skills and learn how to construct a resume. After that, I checked in with Barb at the Panhellenic office and staked out a spot in the IMU for Jen and me. A month later, I signed up for several interviews with companies coming to IU's campus.

One of the slots I claimed was with Hart Schaffner Marx, a Chicago-based corporation specializing in the fabrication of men's clothing. It also owned and operated a national chain of retail clothing stores. The posted opening was for their Hart Scholar Program, a two-year management training program with an equal focus in retail and manufacturing. But what attracted me most was the additional perk in the form of a fully funded MBA at Northwestern University's Kellogg School of Management in downtown Chicago. It was a job and an MBA rolled into one.

On the day of my interview, I outfitted myself in a navy-blue skirt and blazer I'd borrowed from my sister and a crisply ironed white button-down blouse. I slipped on a pair of navy pumps and walked the two blocks from Theta to the A&S building. As I sat in the lobby waiting to be called into the Hart Schaffner interview—one I hoped would be less intimidating than the chat with Gay Byrne—I reminded myself to breathe, smile, talk slow, and enunciate. I glanced at the clock and stared at my carefully prepared resume. As I had done at so many other definitive junctures in my life, I wondered, *Does all that I have accomplished qualify me? Am I good enough?*

Before I could dwell on those thoughts, the conference room door swung open. A smiling, jovial man, who resembled Mr. Weimer, my high school accounting teacher, introduced himself as Rob Myer. He ushered me in, and I handed him my resume. Pensive, I sat still while he perused the details, which spotlighted my high GPA, leadership roles, and personal goals.

After scanning it, he looked up and smiled, and then the stream of carefully worded questions began: *Can you elaborate on your duties in the Panhellenic Association? Have you ever worked in retail? Do you think you could manage a full-time job while going to school several nights a week?*

Near the end of our thirty minutes together, Rob glanced at the clock. "Do you have time to talk with someone else from our company?"

I nodded.

"Great. Give me a minute," he said, scurrying out the door.

Two back-to-back interviews. That hasn't happened before. Does it mean I nailed it?

When the door reopened, Rob introduced me to his colleague, Carl, and for the next fifteen minutes, the three of us sat around chatting as I would with my parents and their friends. The entire time, my mind interjected its own commentary. *If these men personify the company culture, then take this job, Julie. Take it!*

At one point, Carl gave a slight nod to Rob, who smiled warmly at me. "You're an impressive young lady," he said.

With another glance at the wall clock, Rob closed our time with a comment that sent hope coursing through my system. "The starting pay for this position is $16,800."

I gulped. An MBA from Northwestern, and they're paying me

this much money? It sounded like something I should seriously consider.

Rob and Carl rose from their chairs, and I followed them to the office door.

"We'll be in touch soon about next steps," Rob said, "which will probably be a visit to our corporate headquarters in Chicago."

A few weeks later I received a letter in the mail, congratulating me on my success at IU and inviting me to call Rob Myer and schedule a second wave of interviews before Thanksgiving at the Chicago offices. In January, after my final rush commitments with Panhel were over, I received a call from Rob. The job was mine if I wanted it. I just needed to let them know by March 1.

The timing served me well. By then I'd heard from some of the postgraduate clinical psychology programs to which I'd applied, but I had already formed an opinion. Assuming more student loans in comparison to a free MBA was an imbalanced equation. And if Mike received a job offer from one of the Chicago-based engineering firms with whom he'd interviewed, then the future, *our* future, looked bright and shiny.

29

Turning in the Crown

Summer 1981

B efore we donned our IU crimson and cream graduation caps and gowns, Jenny had snagged a two-bedroom apartment in Indianapolis with a sorority sister. The training program for her position as a marketing representative with Xerox Corporation began right after graduation. So Jen moved out of the Delta Gamma sorority house, where she had lived for three years, and into a spacious two-bedroom apartment. She had launched her postcollege career as a businesswoman.

I had yet to do so.

I'd accepted the job offer in the Hart Scholar Program, but my start date didn't begin until the month after graduation. In the meantime, I moved out of my sorority house and back into my parents' home in Oak Brook.

Skeeter, fresh from his sophomore year at the University of Dayton, greeted me at the door to the garage. "Welcome back home, Jules," he said with a smirk.

I breezed past him, muttering, "Thanks."

The household was as hectic as I remembered, something I found both unnerving and settling. Patrick and Lizzie were more grown up. He would start at Benet in the fall, and Lizzie was a rising middle schooler. As I settled into my old room across the hall from my twin sister's bedroom, it might have been just like the old days. Except Jenny wasn't there. Her bed was made, and her closet had been picked clean.

Jenny's postgraduate social life never missed a beat. Because so many of our IU classmates had also taken jobs in the greater Indianapolis area, she was surrounded by friends. While it felt as if I had taken a step backward instead of forward like Jenny, I consoled myself with the knowledge that my situation was temporary. Once Rob and Carl at Hart Schaffner Marx decided on my first work assignment, then I could rent an apartment and get out from under my parents' relentless oversight.

My living situation was not the only aggravation I faced.

I was used to seeing my twin every day in the Union where we shared our daily lives or wrangled over who had first dibs on the old Monte Carlo. Those days were a memory. My sister was so busy that it was impossible to speak to her, a fact that frustrated me more than my folks. I either left Jen a voicemail at her apartment or gave her roommate, Nancy, a message.

I'd say, "Just let Jen know I called again, will ya? I wanna hear how the training is going. I have stuff to tell her, too."

Sometimes it would be a few days before I heard my twin's voice on the phone.

"Sorry. Xerox is keeping us crazy busy. I have no time to do anything, much less, like, go for a jog, or talk on the phone."

I swallowed my disappointment. "It's okay. I get it."

The inability to connect with the person who knew me best and with whom I had shared ninety-nine percent of life's events frustrated me. Not only was Jen hundreds of physical miles away, but I harbored regret over the ridiculous rift that had formed between us over Tralee and sharing the car. Now that was a moot point. Once my sister and I had graduated and had proof of income, we qualified for car loans. Dad had fixed us up with our car dealer neighbor, and we both purchased new Ford Mustangs. Mine had a bright yellow body, the color of an Easter egg, and sported a black canvas convertible top. Jen selected one in red with a T-top.

As the month of May rolled on, my sister's life continued hitting high notes, while mine was in limbo. I felt like the beauty queen who at the end of her year of glory had to turn in her crown.

Mike—the burly Irish-looking guy I dated my entire senior year at IU—returned home from the University of Iowa and called with news.

"I got an offer letter from Schlumberger. The Houston oil company. Remember I told you I interviewed with them on campus?" His deep voice was serious and hesitant. "They have a solid civil engineering training program."

I choked back my disappointment. I had hoped he'd get an offer in Chicago. Instead of acting downbeat, I chose positivity. "That's so exciting! Let's go out and celebrate!"

After I hung up, I puzzled why Mike had seemed so reserved, almost glum, about his new job. Over the previous year, not only had Mike stolen my heart, but I had also fallen in love with his family. I had clicked with his older sisters, frequently gossiping with them in their kitchen while we snacked on his mom's delicious seven-layer cookie bars. Being with Mike's family was almost as easy as hanging out with mine.

That evening, Mike picked me up from my parents' home, and we drove to TGI Fridays for drinks. In the car, I plied him with questions about his start date and apartment options in New Orleans. I should have known something was up when he answered each query with just a *yes* or *no*. At the restaurant, he asked the hostess to seat us at a high top in the gloomy back corner of the bar.

When our beers arrived, I clinked my mug against his. "Cheers! Here's to your new job!"

But Mike didn't match my cheerful grin. Instead, those crystal-blue eyes that always turned me to mush focused on the beer mug.

Uh-oh, what's going on?

"Jules, when Schlumberger assigned me to their New Orleans office, they said I'd be there at least three years."

"So . . . you'll be home for the occasional weekends and holidays. Whenever I can, I'll visit you," I said with an encouraging smile.

Leaning forward, I slipped my slender hand into Mike's beefy fist. Instead of gripping my hand, he dropped it and scratched at a nick in the highly shellacked tabletop.

"We made it through our senior year apart, Mike. We can figure this out," I said, expressing more confidence than I felt.

Since meeting Mike the previous summer, we had talked nearly every night. When our schools were in session, we saw each other every chance we got. Fall break, the holidays, as well as numerous road trips back and forth between IU and Iowa. It seemed that any time spent apart had only made us crazier about one another. Yet now Mike refused to meet my eyes. We sat like that for only a breath or two, but it felt like forever.

He leaned in, whispering, "Jules, long-distance relationships are just too hard," and then he glanced away, looking off into the swirling bar crowd.

I watched his Adam's apple bobble and held my breath.

"I think it's best if we call it quits. Now. So each of us can make a fresh start," he said.

He can't be serious!

"Wait, what?" I leaned in, trying to get him to look me in the eyes. "Why can't we see how this goes? Why split up?"

Mike's news disoriented me. I had counted on having him home for a while, us growing closer, and making plans. Suddenly the world looked, smelled, and sounded different, muffled, warped, unreal. I wanted the cloud of uncertainty to clear, not descend and consume me.

Once Mike spilled his news, he ordered a second round of beers. No matter what I said or how I said it, he refused to budge. When he drove me back to my parents' house, the interior of his gray Datsun was quiet, charged like the air before a storm hits. The thoughts in my head raged over the hum of the motor. I couldn't believe it. I'd gone into the evening ready to toast the future: his, mine, and ours. Instead of continuing our romance, albeit long distance, my Irish heartthrob had broken things off.

As soon as Mike pulled into the driveway, instead of our usual lingering kisses, I slammed the door of the Datsun without glancing back. Slipping through the laundry room door, I threaded through the kitchen and family rooms and skulked up to my teenage bedroom. The room was as I had left it: the ecru crocheted bedspread spread evenly across the full mattress, the mauve taffeta pillow shams fluffed and stacked against the heavily carved antique walnut bed—the one Grandma Mimi had given me. Whipping the pillows and covers aside, I crawled into bed with my clothes on and let hurt settle into my bones. The comfort of the familiar setting released an avalanche of tears.

I had thought Mike was "the one," that we would have a life full of adventure and deep friendship, marry, and raise a crew of Irish-looking lads and lasses. Had I been propping myself up with delusional thoughts?

All cried out, I flipped off the covers and changed into pj's. As I struggled to fall asleep, my thoughts spun. Summer had barely started, and I had lost my boyfriend and twin sister to out-of-state jobs. I buried my head in the pillow and screamed a familiar refrain from the time after Susie died: "Life is so unfair."

In the days that followed, besides yielding to ugly crying jags, scouring the Northwestern business school course catalog, and shopping for my work wardrobe, I jogged. Each morning, I skirted Mom's pitying gaze and took off running through Oak Brook's many subdivisions. Sometimes, I racked up close to ten miles at a time. On those long-distance jaunts, I convinced myself that life could only get better. But it was hard to deny my circumstances. Life had flip-flopped for me. In a month's time, I'd gone from rising to the top of the heap at IU, graduating with honors, and receiving important leadership accolades only to return to the Oak Brook house and find myself dumped and sidelined.

Yet, my inner cheerleader persevered, consoling me with platitudes. *Once you get your job assignment, it'll be stimulating and important, just like Jenny's. And you'll make loads of new friends—perhaps even meet a cute guy or two—through work and grad school.*

I tried forgetting about Mike and focusing on my forthcoming job placement. On my long runs, I convinced myself that because the bulk of Hart Schaffner Marx's retail and manufacturing operations were based in downtown Chicago, my other dreams would come true. I fantasized about working in Chicago and living in a downtown high-rise apartment.

So, on a warm morning in late May, the day finally came for me to meet my fellow Hart Scholars. When my mother dropped me off at the Clarendon Hills train station, I was as nervous as a kindergartner on the first day of school. Much as I had done whenever I rode the train to and from Benet, I scaled the stairs to the upper deck and nabbed two seats across from one another—one for me and the other for my purse and the mahogany leather briefcase my folks had given to me for graduation. From my roost on the train's upper level, I sat transfixed, staring but not seeing the buildings and villages whiz past as we sped to Union Station. As silly and childish as it sounds, I crossed my fingers, closed my eyes, and sent wishes out into the ether for a plum assignment.

In my khaki business suit, crisp white blouse, and sensible black pumps, I followed the throngs of commuters out of Union Station and onto Wacker Drive. In the swanky lobby of 101 N. Wacker, I punched the elevator button for the twenty-first floor, the home of Hart Schaffner Marx corporate offices. Shyly, I glanced around the lobby at the people coursing through the glass revolving doors at the entrance. Besides me, the company had hired two other Hart Scholars for the 1981 recruiting class: a young man and woman, both of whom had attended the University of Wisconsin. More than anything, I hoped that my new colleagues and I would click. Become friends, too.

Inside the elevator, I moved to the rear. As the doors began closing, an Asian American woman about my age glided in; she was out of breath. She gripped a shiny leather briefcase and wore sleek black pumps. Her soft dimples deepened as she pushed dark feathery bangs to one side of her round face. She looked confident but approachable, like someone I might like to know. On the twenty-first floor, she exited, and I traipsed after her to the reception desk.

"I'm here to see Rob Myer. I'm Vivian, one of the Hart Scholars," she said.

I approached the desk and touched the sleeve of Vivian's dark gray suit jacket. Smiling, I introduced myself. "I'm Julie. A Hart Scholar, too."

The receptionist led us back to the conference room. On the way, Vivian and I whispered confessions about our angst: working full-time, going to business school classes two nights a week, finding time to have fun while excelling in our courses, and securing affordable apartments. In the meeting room, we spilled into adjacent leather chairs, chatting softly, and beaming with pleasure.

Rob, our program director, chuckled. "Vivian and Julie, you two look like you have known each other a long time."

Vivian and I shared a shy grin. The program director was right.

I had felt an instant rapport with my new colleague. It was if we were right where we belonged. We were two fun-loving college graduates who were anxious about leaving home and eager to start their first jobs. My insides warmed. For the first time in weeks, I relaxed, feeling as if my luck was changing.

Soon a tall, studious-looking young man entered the room. Rob rose and introduced us to Kurt. After Kurt shook our hands, he moved to a corner of the conference table, clicked open his hard case briefcase, and pulled out a clean tablet and mechanical pencil. Although I couldn't see from my vantage point, I suspected there was a pocket calculator in there somewhere. He might end up being a friend. Nothing more.

Rob opened the meeting. Looking each of us in the eye, he said, "Over the next two years, each of you will get experience in both the retail and clothing manufacturing sides of Hart Schaffner Marx."

When Rob said, "Now let's get started," my stomach tightened.

He opened his file folder and slid paperwork across the dark tabletop to Kurt. Because of Kurt's interest in engineering, his first role was in the corporation's clothing division. Kurt nodded agreeably when he heard that for the next twelve months he'd work at the Franklin Street production plant, assisting the management team with the installation of new computer-generated cutting software.

Vivian was up next. She nodded enthusiastically as she learned that she'd report to the retail division's corporate floor at 101 N. Wacker, a few floors from where we sat. Her year-long internship meant rotating departments and completing special projects. While I didn't envy Kurt's appointment, I hoped my assignment would mirror Vivian's.

But when Rob turned to me, there was something in his tentative smile that made me suck in a breath and hold it.

"Julie, we've assigned you to Jaymar-Ruby, our men's slack manufacturer based in Michigan City, Indiana. The staff at Jaymar is thrilled to welcome you and will assist in finding an apartment there. Preferably one near the expressway, which will ease the commute from Northwest Indiana twice a week to Northwestern's downtown campus."

I met Rob's eyes but pinched myself under the table to disguise my raging disappointment. I felt as if I'd received a guilty verdict instead of a career opportunity. Moving to Michigan City, an industrial town bordering Lake Michigan, wasn't remotely close to the dreams I'd envisioned.

After dinner that night, my folks and I adjourned to the living room. Over beers, we discussed my placement. While it felt nice to have their undivided attention and relax with an adult drink, it's when the ramifications of my new job—its unappealing location, the long commute to grad school classes, and the logistics of moving away—really sank in.

Not only was I not going to live or work in the city, but I would reside far from the exciting life I had imagined. I was tired of whining and crying to my parents about the downturn my life had taken. When I started sniffling, Mom did what she always did.

"Don't worry, honey," Mom said. "Together, we'll figure out what you need besides your bedroom furniture. And I'll help you get settled there."

Mom was true to her compassionate words. She helped me pack up my teenage bedroom and hire movers. On moving day, she loaded the family station wagon and trailed behind my new yellow mustang. When we arrived in Michigan City an hour or so later, I grabbed us lunch from a local deli while my mother directed the movers. I burst into my second-floor apartment with fresh sandwiches and cold drinks and discovered that my mom had the furniture in the entire one-bedroom apartment arranged perfectly. She'd even managed to locate building maintenance to repair the bifold closet door that had loosened from its track. I oozed gratitude.

Once Bill from maintenance repaired the broken closet, Mom convinced him to set up my new shower rod. Thanking him for his help, she said, "Please keep an on eye on her for me."

Memories of my first day as a freshman at IU and our RA, Mariel, came to mind. My mouth hung open.

Bill glanced at me and shrugged. "Yes, ma'am. Will do," he said.

Flabbergasted, all I could do was hope that Bill had better things to do than stop by my place. I was an adult, twenty-two, and Mom didn't have a clue about who Bill was or what his background held.

The week following my move-in, Bill, whom I had sized up to be in his thirties, appeared at my apartment door all showered and spiffed up. I peeked through the peephole in the door of my apartment. I groaned softly to myself and backed away into the living room.

In my head, I screamed, *Sometimes, I just want to kill you, Mom!*

As soon as I was certain Bill had left, I picked up the wall phone. Jenny's apartment phone just rang and rang, so I dialed Vivian.

"You won't believe what my mother did."

Vivian and I dissolved into outrageous laughter at my mom's expense, and then I laced up my sneakers to go for a run.

The summer may have started off badly, but I was managing with and without the support of my twin sister and boyfriend and despite the annoying consequences of my mother's good intentions. I felt a prick of pride. While I couldn't change my short-term circumstances, I hoped that if I excelled at business school and at Jaymar-Ruby, I might garner a first-rate assignment during my second year as a Hart Scholar.

I clung to what Dad had said on the night I'd received my job assignment.

"Jules, this is one rung in the ladder of a successful career. You gotta put your time in. Show 'em what you're made of, honey."

I planned to do just that and more.

30

Living the Dream

Fall 1982

As I readjusted the crimson floppy bow tied at the collar of my white starched oxford—fretting about whether the snag at the heel of my nylons would explode up my calf—the door to the human resources office eased open.

I sprang out of the upholstered seat and tugged at my navy blazer, so it lay flat against the waistband of my suit's coordinating straight skirt. I coaxed my lips into a benign smile and pressed my palms against the skirt, more to rid my hands of perspiration than to smooth out any wrinkles.

The second phase of my Hart Scholar training program had begun. It had taken fifteen months, two weeks, and three days to get to this point. I smiled inwardly. My new Chicago high-rise studio apartment at McClurg Court, while smaller and more expensive than I'd hoped for, was within walking distance of my new job as a retail stores planning analyst. I'd survived my year at Jaymar in Michigan City, rotating through various departments as I learned the men's clothing manufacturing business and completed special projects. Twice a week I had driven my yellow Mustang back and forth to downtown Chicago for night classes at the Kellogg School.

Despite the mileage I put on my snazzy car, it thrilled me to spill onto Lake Shore Drive and soak in the vibrant city life. With little to do in Michigan City but work, study, and run, most weekends found me returning to Oak Brook or meeting up with Vivian and other classmates to complete group projects. I'd dated a few guys I met in class, but no one interested me as much as my old flame, Mike. Because I hadn't heard from him, I faced reality—the relationship was over.

Now, as I watched the door to HR widen and forced myself to breathe, I was conscious of a few things. First, at twenty-three and a half, how young and fortunate I was to be assigned to the corporate headquarters. Despite my age and career-minded goals, I was nonetheless a female in a male-dominated corporation. Mindful of the issue with my nylons, I shifted my weight from one pump to the other, prompting myself for the hundredth time: *Be professional. Friendly. And, for God's sake, don't spit or stumble over your words.*

Justine, the dark-haired, petite vice president of human resources, strode into the small anteroom first. Her navy pumps were smart and low, like mine, and perhaps in sympathy with my own polyester pantyhose, hers gleamed in the blistering glare of the fluorescent lighting like loose change on pavement. It gave me little comfort to know that Justine's hose probably gripped and pinched her waistline, too, leveling and compressing the wombs to which we dared not draw attention in corporate America. I sighed inwardly, all at once, despising the boring clothing that differentiated us from the secretarial and administrative staff—lucky gals who wore slacks and bold print separates.

Justine, who was about twenty-five years my senior, extended her hand. "Hi, Julie. Welcome! Nice to see you again."

Returning her firm handshake, I looked her in the eye. "Good to see you, Justine. Glad to be here."

Her warm brown eyes zeroed in on mine, and then like a graceful dancer, she slipped aside to make space for the young executive who followed in her wake, the man who would be my supervisor for the next nine months: Stephen C. McGue.

From Vivian, I'd gleaned a few facts about Steve. In his midthirties, he was young to have been promoted to a vice president, but he was considered an up-and-comer, a wunderkind. He had been the deal maker for acquiring Country Miss, a women's clothing manufacturer—a sector that boosted the corporate balance sheet and fulfilled the company's growth plan. From Justine, I knew Steve had attended the US Military Academy at West Point and earned his MBA from the Wharton School. Because Vivian had already interned with Steve, she shared that he was easy to work for, clear on goals and expectations, and generous with praise.

One night after our finance class, over beers and a deep-dish Gino's pizza, Vivian confessed that she found Steve "honest and very, very smart," and then her infectious giggle filled our back booth. "He stands out. Especially compared to the stodgy Old Guard who snooze at their desks."

So, while I knew all those details, nobody had warned me that Steve McGue was handsome, not in a movie-star sort of way, but attractive because his appearance expressed character, confidence, and charisma. As this man—the rising executive and my new boss—moved closer, his hand reaching out to shake mine, I noticed other details.

Steve's dark eyes and hair, which were a striking contrast to his pale complexion and ruddy cheeks—a combination to which I have always been attracted—screamed Irish heritage. Not a soul had suggested that his captivating grin, reminiscent of Jack Nicholson's, implied a willingness for adventure and perhaps alluded to his youth as a hotheaded and cocky high school football star.

As Steve's warm palm confidently folded around mine, that uncanny grin punctuating his face, I discerned that he had a sense humor. When he was just inches from me, I noticed how his soulful eyes, more brown than gold or green, flashed, hinting at a temper that might not tolerate foolishness or lack of forethought or opinions that did not align with his.

"Welcome to the retail stores division, Julie. I'm Steve McGue," he said. "Call me Steve."

After Steve greeted me, the ceiling fixture that had highlighted the shine in Justine's pantyhose now spotlighted something else. On Steve's left hand, a thin gold band gleamed.

Six months later and weeks after my birthday in February, I sat hunched over my desk in the private office I could hardly believe was mine—it came complete with a metallic name plate right outside the door. Out of the corner of my eye, I spied my boss rounding the sea of secretarial desks. Steve came to a standstill and leaned into the doorframe of my office, his dark eyes glinting as he straightened the tails of his red striped necktie. The smoky smell of cigarettes, no doubt the Marlboro Reds he preferred, drifted my way.

"Morning. How're you doing with the New York stores' analysis?"

I returned his pleasant smile. "It's coming." I swallowed hard to tamp down the tension smoldering inside me. "Should have it for you to review by Friday. Unless the printer acts up again." Frowning, I pointed at the computer equipment consuming my desktop. "Willie from RadioShack will be here soon to check out why connectivity is sketchy."

Despite loving every detail about my professional life, I couldn't pinpoint why I felt edgy every day when reporting to work. I tried to discount the feeling, speculating that it was due to the year of pent-up aspirations while stationed in Michigan City, the rarified air at the corporate offices, or just new-job jitters. My early-morning runs along Chicago's lakefront didn't relieve the strain. Juggling school and work contributed to the pressure I felt, but the issue ran deeper. I was striving for perfection at too many new things: how to operate the new TRS-80 Micro Computer, manage its fragile eight-inch floppy discs, master the cumbersome VisiCalc spreadsheet software, navigate our company's diverse reporting systems, and discern my boss's specific needs. All the while shooting for *A*'s in two night-school graduate business courses.

In contrast, during the year I spent at Jaymar-Ruby, I held little responsibility. I often felt under-stimulated and underused. Now, a year and a half later, I was too jazzed up. Everywhere I turned, there were challenges to meet. Pleasing my handsome boss added to that mountain of stress.

My eyes scrunched up. "You leave for New York on Monday, right?"

Steve stepped inside my office and sank into the chair across from my desk. "Yes. Let's talk about that."

My heart did a little stutter step.

Whenever he did this—sat close to me in my office or called me into his—my heart rate climbed like it did on my morning runs. I felt it at that moment, hammering under my ribs. His presence disarmed me. I argued with myself. *That is also the case whenever you meet with other top executives at work.* While I found Steve's intelligence, demeanor, and physical appearance appealing, our relationship had always been professional. On a few occasions, he'd taken me to lunch in the lobby restaurant where we discussed my training program or an analysis he'd assigned. So, while I recognized that I was attracted to his type—smart, funny, honest, and with clean Irish looks—I considered my married older boss off-limits. Besides, I was content. I had begun dating a fellow grad student with similar qualities who was single and closer to my age.

Pushing away from my desk, I escaped the shadow of the clunky TRS-80 and waited for Steve to elaborate on the New York trip. His gaze traveled to the ceiling tiles and then back to me.

"I've been thinking."

I knew what those words meant. They were the prelude to his launching a big idea, a project for me to consider, or research to dive into. I reached for my notepad. While he drummed his fingers on the corner of my desk and that charming smile emerged, I readied my pen.

He leaned back into the chair, considering me. "I think it would benefit you to come with the team to New York. You've done all the analysis." He pointed to the printouts crowding my credenza. "You should see how your work translates into an actual performance review. What do you think? Can you miss class on Tuesday night?"

What an opportunity. Corporate travel. A few days in NYC. Maybe time to see a college buddy.

I blinked several times before my lips moved. "Uh, sure. I can miss class. Vivian will catch me up later."

"Great." Steve stood, repositioning his tie against a crisp white shirt. "I'll have the corporate travel desk set it up." He paused at my door. "We leave Monday afternoon. Return Wednesday. You'll be back in time for the St. Patty's Day parade." When I laughed appreciatively, his grin widened. "Someone with a name like Julie Ryan can't miss that."

He winked and was gone.

Wait, what was that? Was he flirting with me or just being clever?

As I sat there struggling to control the bewilderment flooding my system, my mind skipped to confusing news that had been revealed earlier in the week. Not gossip, but confidential information Steve had instructed an administrative assistant to disseminate within our small department.

Before the ball had dropped on New Year's Eve signaling the start of 1983, Steve McGue and his wife of thirteen years had separated and filed for divorce. The news had frozen me in place. After the assistant left, I stared at the white walls in my office, recalling a time when I had seen Steve with his soon-to-be ex-wife. Vivian and

I had gone to see the movie *An Officer and a Gentleman* at Water Tower Place. We'd run into the couple outside the theater. His wife, a tall, plain-looking blonde, had been pleasant. Later, I had commented to Vivian, "She's not what I expected," and we left it at that.

While I wondered why my boss and his wife were splitting up, it hadn't been my place to ask. To the colleague delivering the news, I'd simply said, "Thanks for letting me know." But all week I'd had to reign in my thoughts. My boss, the man I'd been instantly attracted to in Justine's office on the day we met, was now single. I refused to let my brain dwell too hard on that fact. I had a new boyfriend I liked.

The phone on my desk buzzed, rattling me out of my reverie. "Willie from RadioShack is here to see you."

"Send him back, please."

While waiting for Willie, I flipped the pages on my desk calendar. I wrote "NYC" on Monday, March 14, and backtracked from there. Class on Thursday night. On Friday, Jenny was driving up from Indy for the weekend. My lips parted into a smile. I couldn't wait to show off my sixteenth-floor studio in Streeterville, its southern view of the skyline down Lake Shore Drive, and its prime location just a short walk to Kellogg's downtown campus.

Saturday night, Jenny and I had a night out planned with Vivian and some high school friends at the bars along Rush Street. After that, I figured we'd do what we always did when we were together: stay up late giggling and whispering heart-to-heart confidences. After hearing about her phenomenal success in sales with Xerox, the guy she'd gotten serious with—a fellow IU alum and an Indianapolis cop—I would tell her more about my upcoming trip to New York and the new fella I had started dating. With strong starts to our careers and dating solid guys, we seemed to be on similar paths.

Or were we?

After ordering a round of happy hour drinks at the Hang-ge-Uppe bar, Vivian scooted in close, her dark eyes glistening with curiosity.

"Have you heard any more about Steve McGue's divorce?"

Lifting my beer for a swig, I avoided her eyes. "Nobody's talking about it."

Next to me, Jenny cocked her head. She leaned in, eyeing me. "He sounds like a great guy. From all you've said."

I looked at Vivian. "He is. Right, Viv? You've worked for him, too."

"Yeah, but for only a few months." Giggling, she flicked her dark bangs aside. "Not as long as you have."

Jenny's lips thinned out into a tiny smile. "You sure spend an awful lot of time talking about him, Jules."

When they both squeezed in and gawked at me, my body tensed up. I recognized that same edgy feeling I felt every time I was near Steve at work.

"Look you guys, cut it out. I have a boyfriend. Besides, Steve's my boss. Off-limits. End of story."

31

Sparks Fly

Winter 1983

Steve hailed a yellow cab outside New York's posh Le Parker Meridien Hotel and held an umbrella for me while I clambered inside. Settling my bulging briefcase on the floor beside my black pumps, I scooted over to make room for him. He slammed the door and rattled off the address of our New York offices to the cabbie.

Collapsing into the well-worn seat, he gave me a sardonic look. "Nasty March weather. Lucky to get a cab considering all this sleet." Pulling out a handkerchief from his dark suit jacket, he wiped the rain from his dark-framed glasses. "Typical, miserable New York spring weather."

"Not much better in Chicago today," I said with a brief smile.

Steve pocketed the hankie, pulled out his cigarettes, and cranked the window down before lighting up. "After today's meetings, I'd like to do a recap with you over dinner." He cocked his head, looking at me sidewise. "Unless you already made plans."

When I shook my head, my tight French twist barely budged. "No plans." Despite the knot forming in my gut, I kept my voice neutral. "Last night was when I connected with my friend from college."

Steve took a few hits from his cigarette, inhaled deeply on the last one, and then flicked the glowing stub out the window. "I hope you like French food. I booked a table at the hotel restaurant for seven thirty. Heard it's excellent."

The previous evening—when Steve conferred with Abe, the Chicago-based management consultant traveling with us and advising our team—I'd met up with my IU pal. Erika and I had served on the Panhellenic Board together. My evening with Erika was the perfect antidote to an afternoon of hectic travel. We met at a casual restaurant, toasted to old times, and laughed until our sides ached. Reminiscing with Erika sidelined the uncertainty swirling in my head about my work itinerary.

As our cabbie darted in and around Manhattan gridlocks, Steve glossed over the agenda for the next few days. He would present the stores' financial results and planning goals, while Abe covered the new marketing concepts and proposed advertising campaigns. Steve explained that my role was to listen and absorb—and if asked, explain the details I'd assembled, checked, and rechecked on the VisiCalc printouts.

I nodded. "Got it."

The lightning-fast pace of our meeting agenda, the thrill of the novel experience, and my underlying anxiety about defending my spreadsheet analyses was akin to the wired feeling I got before running a 10K. The only benefit to the whole ordeal was not having time to think about making conversation with Steve over dinner.

Back at the hotel, I changed into a fresh print blouse, slimming black slacks, and flats. I rode the elevator down and spotted Steve chatting with the restaurant's hostess.

She picked up two menus and gestured for us to follow her. "This way, sir, madam. I have a nice table for you here in the center of the atrium." As she set our menus atop folded linen napkins, a smile teased her lips. "The tiny white sparkling lights overhead set quite a nice mood, don't you think?"

I breathed. Perhaps it was my own insecurities about the dinner, but I sensed her sizing us up. It was as if she was discerning whether we were a couple out on the town or two colleagues collaborating over dinner.

My face warmed as Steve slid out my chair before settling into the seat beside me. *What a gentleman.*

His glance took in my outfit change. "You look nice. Is the shirt one of ours?"

I smiled. "Yes. It's from Baskins on State. I interned there over the summer before joining your group."

"*Aha*, I recall that. Here comes our waiter. What'll you have to drink?"

"*Hmm.*" My eyes flicked from Steve's to the server. "I'll have a Dewar's on the rocks with a splash, please."

Steve's eyes twinkled with amusement. He placed his order and turned back to me. "A young woman who likes Scotch. How does that happen?"

Smirking, I placed my napkin on my lap. "When your father is Jack Ryan, and you grow up in a big Irish Catholic family who host frequent parties, Scotch is a staple."

Steve tipped his head back and roared. "Looks like there's a lot I don't know about you, Julie. Let's order. I'm famished. We can talk about your observations from today, and then I wanna hear more about your career goals. Your family, too."

With easy dialogue established, I took a sip of my Scotch and relaxed. *This is okay. He's easy to be with. I like how open and honest he is.* Before our fancy fish entrees arrived, we dissected the meeting. During dinner, we discussed the clothing business, my aspirations to move into store management, and Steve's career history after serving in the army.

Once our plates were cleared, he asked the waitress for matches. "This doesn't bother you, does it?" he asked, tapping a cigarette out of a nearly empty pack of Marlboros.

"No, I don't mind. My parents both smoked for a long time." I turned to study him, noticing for the first time the missing wedding ring, his receding hairline, the absence of any gray, and the proud jut to his jaw. "I just never got in the habit," I said, draining the remnants of amber liquid in my glass.

He signaled for the waiter. "Another round?"

"Sure."

He took a long draw from his cigarette. When he cocked his head again, his dark eyes gleamed with interest.

"So, your family are good Irish Catholics from the western burbs. You enjoy a stiff cocktail. You're a runner. Do you play racquetball?"

"Yes. I played a lot in college. Before that only tennis."

"Were you any good?"

I couldn't stop the flush flooding my neck and cheeks. I lifted my fresh drink and peered at him over its chilly rim. This was a man who appreciated honesty. *Go for it.*

When I said, "Very," I was rewarded with another one of those explosive Jack Nicholson–like grins.

"Good for you," he chuckled. "What else should I know about Julie Ryan?"

After the bantering, which centered mostly on sports, our conversation hopscotched through history. His and mine. I learned more about his army career and his present position in a North Shore reserve unit. I learned that he'd been an army ranger and an officer in the Special Forces, serving ten months in Viet Nam training Cambodians. Steve shared that at the height of the civil rights movement—a time when emotions between Blacks and whites had reached volatile levels in the United States—he had spent ten months in Germany and witnessed conflict among the servicemen on their base. One enlistee had thrown a grenade into the mess hall. He'd had to step in, diffuse the tension, and court-martial the offender.

"The climate there was volatile," he said, his face serious and reflective. For a second or two, his gaze considered the sparkly lights overhead, but when it returned to me, he smirked. "How old would you have been, then?"

I did the mental math, my eyes crinkling. "Probably a freshman in high school."

I sat back, watching him shake his head over the difference in our ages. I decided to play it up.

"Not just any high school. A private Catholic high school. Think, pleated uniform skirts, nuns, and monks. But coed."

His eyes smiled at the picture I painted.

From me, Steve also learned how I morphed from an undergrad psych major with sights on a PhD to a Hart Scholar and Kellogg MBA. He quizzed me about being a twin, my relationship with Jenny, and our blended family of adopted and biological siblings. When I shared the dark times that followed Susie's death, his dark eyes explored my face.

He popped out the last cigarette in his pack. "Don't take this wrong. You seem a lot older than twenty-four."

As I watched him swipe a match and light the tip, I deliberated about my response. When he glanced my way, I met his gaze squarely.

"I've been told that before. Many times. I've also been called 'an old soul,' for whatever that's worth."

I slipped him an easy smile and shifted to a subject that took me out of the limelight: St. Patrick's Day. Before Steve signed the check, we chitchatted about the hoopla surrounding our hometown's very special Irish holiday, the dyeing of the river green, the roadblocks along the parade route, and the overflowing bars serving green ales and Guinness stout.

When I gave him a scaled-down version of my roles as an Irish lass in the pageantry and revelry, he commented. "Impressive. Hart Scholar and an Irish princess."

"Fame is fleeting," I joked.

He chuckled along with me, his dark eyes twinkling. "This has been fun. Shall we call it a night?" He stood, helped pull out my chair, and mumbled, "I'll walk you to your room."

When we hit my floor, Steve held the elevator door for me to exit first. For the few yards it took for us to reach my room, he strolled so close that I thought he might slip his hand around my elbow, guiding me like old married couples do. But he didn't. What we whispered about during that short walk is a good question. My brain was in a fog. It leapfrogged from one scene to the next: the days' meeting, our delicious dinner, and how much I enjoyed getting to know him. Outside my hotel room, he waited while I fumbled in my purse for the key.

Holding it up like a winning raffle ticket, I thanked him for dinner, and "for inviting me to participate in the store review."

He winked. "You earned the opportunity."

As easy as the dialogue had flowed during our fancy meal, all at once, silence was everywhere. It pervaded the long dark hallway, screeched to a halt outside my hotel room, and infiltrated our clothes and hair, ensconcing itself in the foot or so between us. It dared to tickle the back of my throat and thicken my tongue. I stared at Steve. It appeared that silence had taken his words captive, too.

But the brick wall of corporate propriety, the division between boss and intern, had already been breached. Over the course of the evening, our eleven-year age gap had also narrowed. Not only had we found common ground, but it became evident that we were two souls surprised by how much we enjoyed each other's company.

And so there we were. A guy and a gal acutely aware of the wall that had been scaled but also of the thin line drawn between us. As those revelations took hold, we gaped at one another. I looked into his dark brown eyes, noticing the delight and wonder, the questions clouding them. Perhaps he saw the same reactions in mine, but neither of us moved. Barely a second or two had elapsed. It felt so much longer.

Whether it was the Scotch, the French food, or the intimacy shared under twinkling lights in "The City That Never Sleeps," a thought pierced the quiet in my brain.

Is he going to kiss me?

I felt his breath, tinged with nicotine, consume the space between us. His heavy-lidded eyes darted down the empty hallway and back to me. As my room key dug into my palm, and he shifted in those well-shined black leather shoes of his, the air became charged.

"I'm going to be the gentleman here and say good night." I felt his warm eyes memorize my face. He turned to go and then stopped. Over his shoulder, he whispered, "See you in the morning. In the lobby. We'll share a cab with Abe to the wrap-up session and go directly from there to the airport."

"Okay," I muttered, offering him a tight little wave. "Good night."

Inside the room, I pressed the length of my spine into the cold backside of the wooden door. Squeezing my eyes shut, I melted into it, half expecting and half longing to feel the vibration of a knock there. *He had wanted to kiss me, hadn't he?* For what felt like hours but was only a moment, I waited, but a knock never came. Disappointment engulfed me. Tears infiltrated the impregnable fringe of my Maybelline mascara.

What just happened?

As I lay down to let sleep claim me, a parade of emotions galloped across my heart: confusion, pleasure, trepidation, wonder, and desire. In the fog of the moment, it wasn't clear which of those sentiments was hell-bent on overtaking the field and finishing first. One thing was certain, I was smitten, and I was positive that I hadn't imagined the energy between us. The real question in my mind was what tomorrow would bring.

32

Sláinte

Spring 1983

Shortly before 8:00 a.m., I piled into the hotel elevator with my bags and shuffled to the restaurant to coax the hostess into fixing me a strong coffee to go.

"With cream, please," I said.

As she hustled toward the kitchen, I scanned the scene. It hit me how the mood in the restaurant had changed overnight. The atmosphere the previous evening had felt light, soft, romantic even. Now the place reverberated with a crisp professionalism mindful of meetings to attend and planes to catch. Like a sucker punch, the transformation threw me off-balance.

Perhaps it was the early hour, the double pour of Scotch, or a scattered night's sleep, but the scene's mood shift filled me with uncertainty. Had the dinner Steve and I shared been one of intimacy or just another work meal on the road? What about the walk to my hotel room, the impregnable silence full of promise at my door, the kiss that seemed as if it was in the offing?

I tried shaking off my unease as I thanked the hostess and trudged with my bulky bags to the lobby. At the front of the long checkout line, I spotted Steve in a sharp blue suit and gold necktie, his hanging suit bag and briefcase flanking his polished shoes. Next to him, the ever-jovial Abe jabbered away while Steve half listened, a lit cigarette in one hand and a new pack of Marlboro Reds in the other. Within seconds, the pair waved for me to join them.

From there, the moment became unruly for me. All at once, the receptionist motioned Steve forward, he stubbed out his cigarette, and Abe strode back to help me with my bags. During my brief procession to the head of the line, an inner furnace flamed, tinting my face and neck the color of Steve's pack of Marlboros. It wasn't just that I was jumping the line that flummoxed me. It was the uncertainty of how Steve and I would greet one another.

I needn't have worried.

As I approached the counter and laid down my room key, the corners of his full lips edged up. Behind his dark eyeglass frames, his brown eyes found mine and held them.

"Morning," he whispered. "How'd you sleep?"

He could have said anything else, like "Ready for the day?" or "All set for the trip home?" Or he could have remarked about the much-improved New York weather. That simple question, "How'd you sleep?" and the way he said it, the concern evident in his face, was to me a clear, albeit subtle, inference to the time we had spent together. It buoyed me.

"Maybe one less Scotch would have improved the situation," I joked.

He rewarded me with a quiet chuckle.

I held up my Styrofoam coffee cup. "This will certainly help."

The rest of the morning blurred with the business of our final work session. After a catered in lunch, Abe, Steve, and I climbed into a taxi that snaked through late-afternoon traffic to La Guardia, where we boarded a full flight to Chicago O'Hare.

Because of their frequent flyer status, Abe and Steve garnered adjacent seats near the front of the plane about ten rows ahead of me in the smoking section. From my middle seat near the back, I spotted the tops of their heads—Steve's dark hair, straight and fine, a contrast to Abe's thick, almost matted curls—as they huddled in conversation and jotted down notes on yellow legal pads. After take-off, I thought I heard Steve's good-natured laugh rise above the seats and drift in my direction along with the haze of cigarette smoke.

"Is Chicago home for you or is New York?" asked the heavyset man next to me.

His build, ruddy complexion and thick, curly salt-and-pepper hair reminded me of my dad. I set down the magazine I had bought in the airport shop and smiled pleasantly.

"Chicago is home. New York was business. How 'bout you?" I noticed how his blue eyes and craggy silver eyebrows also reminded me of my father. I figured if I couldn't be sitting up front with Steve and Abe listening to their dialogue about the NY visit, this was okay.

"Me, too. I'm Joe. Joe O'Donnell." He gave me a sweet little nod, almost like a curtsy. "You're heading back home in time for the big parade tomorrow."

Joe's statement was more like a question. I had grown used to people sizing me up, assuming my lightly freckled complexion, greenish eyes, and light brown hair meant I hailed from one of Chicago's many Irish communities. One of these days, I would figure out if my looks really did qualify me for membership, but that day was a long way off.

"Yes. Yes, I am." My smile ramped up into a full-out Irish grin. "I haven't missed one in a while. I'm Julie Ryan."

"Wonderful. Sitting next to a pretty Irish gal is just the way I like to fly. Nice to meet you."

When the attendant rolled her drink cart to our row, Joe nodded at me. "Ladies first. What will you have? My treat."

"A beer please."

"The same," Joe said to the attendant.

When she served us, I held mine up in salute. "*Sláinte* (slawn-che) to you," I said.

"*Sláinte is Táinte* (slawn-cha iss toin-che)." Joe's eyes twinkled. "May health and wealth come your way. A true Irish blessing."

Throughout the hot meal service and our second round of drinks, Joe and I reminisced about Chicago's Irish festivities. He was a Sunday regular at Old St. Pat's, the church where my family, and I, and some of Chicago's Irish dignities had gathered when I was sixteen, before I climbed aboard a convertible to wave at the crowds along State Street. I shared that memory and the story of the 1980 Rose of Tralee Festival. He confided how he and his wife were praying rosaries over their oldest daughter Maureen being accepted at Notre Dame. As we finished our second beer, our flight was on its final approach to O'Hare.

"Well, you've made my night, Julie. Not everyone gets to sit next to an old Rose on the eve of St. Patty's Day. I feel like I should either go to church in the morning or buy a lottery ticket."

"I enjoyed it, too, Joe. I'm hoping for the best for your daughter Maureen. I've got a feeling Notre Dame will work out. She sounds like a star."

As Joe and I deplaned, and I came through the arrival gate, Steve and Abe were waiting for me, their khaki trench coats on but unbelted.

Joe lingered for a moment as I thanked him again for the drinks.

"Don't forget your green tomorrow," he chuckled as he walked off.

I stepped closer to where Abe and Steve lingered, and Steve's eyes glittered. "Who the heck was that?"

I laughed. "Just an Irish guy who reminded me of my father and needed a drinking buddy on the eve of St. Patty's Day."

Abe cracked up and picked up his briefcase. "I forgot that tomorrow is St. Patty's Day. The city's gonna be nuts." He considered Steve and me. "Shall we all share a taxi into the city?"

Since Abe lived on the north end of Lake Shore Drive, the taxi stopped at his building first. Steve got out, shook Abe's hand, and made a date for our team to meet with him the following week. For the thirty-minute cab ride to Abe's place, I'd been smooshed between the two guys in the back seat. It had been nearly impossible to keep my skirt from riding up or my thigh from pressing against Steve's pants leg. Because the situation felt inappropriate and unprofessional, it washed me with embarrassment. Crossing my legs hadn't worked either. It had just made me more unsteady, and several times I'd careened against Steve's shoulder.

He'd smiled gently when I whispered, "Oops, sorry 'bout that."

"Take a right here and then left on Astor," Steve said to the cabbie. To me, he explained, "I used to live in Northbrook, but because of my divorce, I'm staying at a friend's place until next month. Then I take a longer lease on Division."

The cabbie cruised down Astor looking for the address.

"Nice street," I said, admiring the elegant homes and low-rise condo buildings.

"This is it," Steve said. He pulled out his wallet to pay for the ride. "Let me take care of this," he said to me. "How much farther do you have to go?"

"Not far. I'm in Streeterville. I could probably walk from here."

"Well, why don't you get out with me here then? Come up for a drink. I can share Abe's feedback and then you can be on your way."

I looked into his eyes. They looked so warm, sincere. My heart melted. I wanted the chance to talk with him again, just the two of us, as we had the night before at Le Meridien. But going up to his apartment? I swallowed. My mind tossed the idea around like a salad. *Why not?* I trusted him and had no reason not to. He'd always been the perfect gentleman.

Steve unlocked the apartment door and hit the lights. The

two-bedroom apartment was spacious and comfortably decorated in creams and grays.

"This is so nice. Too bad you can't stay here."

"I know. I feel lucky to have gotten it for the month until my new place is ready."

We dropped our bags in the entryway, and I followed Steve into the living area. He yanked the drapes to expose a view above the neighboring rooftops and a glimpse of Lake Michigan.

He cranked open one of the large windows and lit a cigarette. I breathed in the fresh spring air and admired the magic of the city at night.

"Scotch or beer?" he asked, strutting over to the wet bar.

"Back to Scotch, I think for me. A short one please."

Uncertain about what else to do with myself, I continued ogling the incredible view before the advancing darkness turned it into a sea of lights.

Steve handed me my drink and hovered close as he pointed out a few more highlights in the streetscape. "And there, at the end of this block, see that high-rise? That's where I'm moving: 71 East Division."

"Nice. You'll be at the edge of Rush Street but still near Lake Shore Drive."

I noted how close his new apartment would be to where I often met up with friends like Vivian. It was also a quick five-block walk from my McClurg Court studio.

"To your new place," I said, clinking my glass against his.

"Shall we sit?" he asked.

As I took a seat on the curvy cream loveseat—a respectable distance from Steve—doubt and curiosity bubbled inside me. How long should I stay? One drink? Two?

For the next half hour or so, we made light conversation about the store review, next steps with Abe's consultant group, and a few projects Steve had in mind for me. Soon, his face grew serious.

"Because of the work travel and tonight's late arrival, feel free to take tomorrow morning off."

"Thanks. I might. My body is craving exercise. I've missed my morning runs these past few days."

After that, the blasted silence that had hit us in the hallway outside my hotel room returned with a vengeance. My eyes found the ice cubes in my Scotch as Steve set his drink down on the coffee table. He swiveled on the sofa next to me, his eyes probing. He leaned forward, grabbed his Marlboros and a lighter, and moved the ashtray within reach. Taking a long draw, he exhaled, blowing the smoke over his shoulder and away from me.

"I'm sorry Anette had to be the one to tell you about my wife and I splitting up. It was easier to do it that way. You understand?"

I nodded, sipping from the stubby tumbler that was now mostly ice. "It surprised me, though." I looked up at him shyly, my eyes questioning. "I remember running into you at the theater last winter." I let that thought dangle. I didn't say what had been in my mind then. *A little unmatched maybe, but a seemingly happy-enough couple.*

He nodded as if he remembered the encounter with Vivian and me.

Leaning back into the sofa cushions, he took a short hit off the cigarette and eyed the ceiling. "We should never have gotten married. I met her in my last year at West Point. She kept coming in for weekend visits. Dances and other stuff. One thing led to another. The summer after graduation, we eloped to Las Vegas." The pout in his full lower lip eased into a wry half smile. "We got married in one of those wedding chapels on the Strip."

Steve stubbed out the cigarette and looked into my eyes. "Because of my stints in the army and all the moves I made, it's only been the last five or six years that we've actually lived together." He picked up his glass, swirling the ice cubes in the nearly empty tumbler of bourbon. "We're on speaking terms." He smiled at me, adding, "It's amiable." He shook his head as if surprised by the reality. "We're happier apart than we ever were together."

"Still, I'm sure it's a hard thing." I cocked my head at him and uttered the thought I'd been dying to give voice to. "How'd your family take the news?"

"Funny that you should ask that." He paused, studying me. "My dad said he was surprised it lasted as long as it did."

"No kids, right?" I asked.

He leaned forward, resting his forearms on his thighs and peered over at me. "No. She didn't want any." The way he studied his hands, I knew there was more to the story. I suppose it was the Scotch, perhaps it was the honest conversation we'd enjoyed to that point, or his raw and endearing vulnerability, but my next question was out before I considered whether it was inappropriate.

"How about you? Do you want kids?" My voice was soft, sincere.

As his gaze left his hands and considered me, his mouth twitched as if contemplating whether a dismissive gesture, a change in subject, or an honest answer was called for. While I pondered if I'd just crossed some kind of line, he slowly and methodically eased himself into an upright position and rested an elbow on the sofa back. He considered me as if I were a new person in the room.

"You like to go right to the heart of the matter, don't you?" He sighed, and more to himself than to me, he repeated a sentiment he'd voiced the previous evening at Le Meridien. "You really do seem older than your years." Smiling to himself and then at me, he muttered, slowly at first, but as he got out what he wanted to say, his voice picked up momentum. "Yes. I do want kids. A whole slew of them. I'd like a big Irish Catholic family like the one you grew up in, Julie Ryan."

His little speech poked at something within me, stirring it to life. *Yes, I want that, too.*

When I nodded my agreement, he leaned in. His lips brushed mine, ever so slightly, and it left me startled, satisfied, wanting more. I didn't pull away. I sat still waiting, hoping, for a second kiss. A much deeper one.

"I wanted to do that last night." He kissed me lightly again, but this time he didn't draw back to look in my eyes for approval. His lips remained close, parted, barely an inch from mine. "You knew that, right?" he whispered.

I lifted a finger and traced the outline of his mouth. "I suspected," I breathed, looking up into his handsome face. "And I was disappointed when you didn't."

His smile was light, playful, honest. "It didn't feel right. Not on a work trip." He kissed me again, harder this time. His hand brushed my cheek, caressed my neck. "I liked you from the instant we met. That day in Justine's office. I just figured you were way too young." He held my chin, gazing into my hazel eyes. "You are young, Julie Ryan."

My finger swept to his lower lip, shushing him. "In years, yes, but an 'old soul,' remember?"

And then he kissed me again and again, and our bodies slid closer, melded, as our arms encircled each another, exploring. There was no going back. Yet, suddenly he stopped, regarding me with intensity.

"Are you sure about this?"

My lips proclaimed the words, but my heart had decided long before that moment. "Very sure."

That time the silence in the room was welcoming, full of certainty. It was not a *what if?* but a *what next?* and *how soon?* He grasped my hand, helped me to my feet, and led me into the hallway. As we approached the foyer, my eyes flicked toward the corner where I'd dropped my suitcase and briefcase an hour or so before. Like a mean girl shunning the less popular, I dismissed them, glancing away as if they did not exist. They were warning labels, ones I didn't want to read much less acknowledge. The briefcase admonished me about crossing the line and entering a workplace relationship. My suitcase, full of personal articles, rebuked me, too. It was a reminder of where I had come from, the traditional values with which I'd been raised. The ones I was now throwing to the wind.

As we crossed the threshold into the bedroom, I never looked back at those cautionary reminders, my bags. Instead, with both eyes open, I followed my heart and took its lead, striding forward with joy, not glancing backward with worry or doubt.

In the morning, we'd awake on St. Patrick's Day with the startling realization that we were falling in love. Unwittingly, Steve and I would discover that we were charting the same path, our eyes on a meaningful relationship that would result in a union with shared goals: honesty, hard work, strong moral compass, and building a family.

Life was about to get vastly more complicated. For both of us.

33

Heartbreak or Heaven?

Spring 1983

Toothbrush in hand, I poked my head out of Steve's bathroom, muttering, "One good thing about spending the night here after New York . . ."

Steve turned away from the mirrored dresser where he tightened the knot on his necktie and grinned. "I can think of a lot of good things about your spending the night here after New York."

He planted a quick kiss on my lips. I kissed him back, toothpaste and all, still in a daze about the leap we'd made from boss and intern to eager lovers in just twenty-four hours.

Steve shook his head in wonder. "You kissing me like that, Julie Ryan, is one of the reasons this whole thing got rolling." He chuckled to himself. "Sorry, you started to say?"

"Right, about the one thing . . . having my luggage here means I don't have to scrounge for a toothbrush."

He held my chin, kissing me again, harder this time, whispering, "You can borrow my toothbrush anytime."

I guess I don't have to worry about there being a next time.

With a jubilant heart, I zipped my toiletries back into my suitcase. As I dragged the bag toward the entryway, a myriad of thoughts zipped around in my head like lightning bugs. *How does an innocent crush turn into love overnight? And of all days, how does it happen on St. Patrick's Day?* Weightier issues—like how I was going to explain the budding romance to Jenny, Vivian, my current boyfriend, and my parents, as well as how it would affect my role at work—would have to wait until my psyche had more time to digest them.

Steve hovered in the front hall. Immaculately dressed in a light gray pinstriped suit, white shirt, and red paisley tie, he was clean-shaven, and his glossy dark hair was still damp from the shower. He held a coffee mug in one hand. Behind him, the ephemeral trail of cigarette smoke rose from an ashtray on the kitchen counter. One glance at him sent my heart whooshing into a little salsa step.

My hands slipped to my slim hips. In mock jest, I pointed at his chest. "You forgot about wearing green today, didn't you?"

He glanced down and then sheepishly back at me. "I'm not sure I own a green tie." He peeked over at me, a smirk lighting up his face. "You're not wearing green either, Julie Ryan."

"Not yet. I'm headed home. When I see you next—at work—I'll be decked out in some article of green."

He winked, grabbing my suitcase. "I'll walk you down. Help you grab a taxi."

I beamed up at him. *Always the gentleman.*

In the mayhem of hailing the taxi, and its careening down Lake Shore Drive to Ontario Street where I lived, I decided to forego my morning run. I didn't want to disturb or drain the blissful sensation that had infused my entire being after spending the night with Steve. Rather, I wanted to savor the "walking on air" phenomenon for as long as possible. Perhaps, in the back of my mind, I also realized that when I entered the corporate headquarters at 101 N. Wacker, our fresh little love affair would undergo the first test of perseverance. As much as I didn't expect Steve or myself to be consumed by regrets or misgivings, I couldn't know for certain.

So instead of lacing up my running shoes, I putzed around my studio apartment with a smile that rivaled any beauty queen's. I unpacked, showered, and scoured my closet for that special green silk blouse I knew was there. It was St. Patrick's Day. I was an old Rose, and I had woken up happier than I'd ever dreamed I could be. Part of me dreaded going to the office, but the other part couldn't wait to stroll into the ivory tower and put eyes on Steve again.

About an hour later—when I turned away from my credenza at work, a cumbersome stack of reports in hand—there he was, filling the doorframe, the same red paisley tie nudged under the points of his starched dress shirt. *So dang handsome.* I sucked in a breath through parted lips. *It's gonna be hard to work here and hide how I feel.*

"Morning." Steve stepped inside my office but didn't sit. "I thought you were taking the morning off." His forehead creased, then eased. "Nice blouse, by the way."

I smiled. "Thanks. I thought I'd get started on one of those new projects you mentioned. Maybe leave early this afternoon instead. I have class tonight." My eyes traveled from his eyes to his lips, remembering what it felt to be kissed by him and to kiss him back. "Hope that's okay?"

"Of course. Leave as early as you want." He swiveled as if he intended to march back to his office but then thought better of it. "Your work ethic is notable. You needn't be concerned about impressing me. I'm already there, ya know?"

All I could do was grin, grateful that his tall, lanky frame filled most of the doorway, a smokescreen for passersby who might pick up on the obvious chemistry bouncing between us.

Steve hesitated, finding something of interest in the benign wall art over my credenza. "I'm headed into a meeting with the big-wigs. Lunch after. Might not see you before you leave." His gaze dropped down to mine. "How about some racquetball this week-end? I belong to the East Bank Club."

It was a good thing I had left my suit jacket on, covering the sleek green blouse. Our brief exchange had glued its frail fabric to my shoulder blades.

"I'd love to," I breathed.

"Great. Winner can pay for beers."

When he winked and strode off, all I could do was sit and ponder. Would playing racquetball during the daytime—even if it occurred over the weekend—be viewed as inappropriate? Would it set off alarms that the two of us were seeing each other? I sighed, acutely aware of the enormity of what Steve and I were navigating: an eleven-year age gap and a workplace relationship that involved a management trainee and her supervisor, whose divorce was not yet final.

I squeezed my eyes shut. *Where was this headed? Heartbreak or heaven?*

When my eyes refocused and settled on the stack of work atop my desk, I resolved that after class, I would get Jenny on the phone. I knew exactly what I would say.

Remember last weekend? When we were drinking at the Hang-ge-Uppe and you and Viv were teasing me about Steve? Well . . .

I could already hear her response, breathy, and giggly, and not one bit judgmental.

She'd say, *I figured something like that was gonna happen. Eventually. Not necessarily as quickly as it did.* Then she'd pause. *Jules? Don't worry about what Mom and Dad will think. But be careful. There's a lot at stake. Your career. Your reputation. Your heart.* Another moment of silence would pass. *If you're crazy about him, I say, "Go for it."*

My twin sister, always my friend, backing me up and validating the thoughts mirrored inside my own head. *What would I do without her? Who would I even be if she weren't my twin?*

After our racquetball date, and in the weeks that followed, Steve and I continued our love affair much as we had on that magical St.

Patrick's Day. I reported to work every day, flirted carefully with him in the confines of his office or mine, and stopped at his apartment for a drink after my night classes. Often enough I hailed an early-morning taxi from his place back to my studio, went for a jog down the lakefront, and hustled into the office to produce the reports he requested.

On the weekends, if Steve didn't have Army Reserve duty, we played racquetball or took my car —the yellow Mustang he had taken to calling the Easter Egg—out for scenic drives. On Sundays, he whipped up breakfasts of bagels, cream cheese, and scrambled eggs.

"That's all I know how to make," he joked.

If the spring weather was gloomy, we hunkered down at his place, where I might study for class, or together we'd lounge in bed watching car races and golf tournaments on TV. During those early weeks of our romance, we were ultra-careful not to be seen together in a setting that looked as if it might be a date, and we dared not exhibit any amorous looks or behavior when folks lingered in our vicinity. The practice of being careful was unnerving. Between us, the number of the folks "in the know" amounted to a handful: a few friends of mine and his, Steve's sister Christie, and of course, Jenny.

One Friday night in early April, the Windy City was hit with an uncharacteristic spring blizzard. By rush hour, there was hardly a car on the road. Anyone with any sense was hunkered down at home heating up leftovers or a frozen pizza. Such a night felt like permission, a reprieve from a caged-in world. Steve and I trudged the few blocks from his place to a restaurant on State Street to grab a burger.

As thick snowflakes coated our coats and hats, Steve leaned in to kiss me. "I could get used to a life like this," he said.

With a gloved hand, he swiped at snowflakes landing on my nose. "Just chatting away and strolling along with you through the snow. Or kicking leaves with you on a fall day. You're the kinda girl, Julie Ryan, every guy hopes to find."

Julie Ryan McGue

I glanced over at him. To me his words didn't need an explanation. We had spent enough time together that I understood his comment. Now that his divorce was final, I was the kind of woman with whom he envisioned making a future. The idyllic setting and his tender words made me feel as if I was right where I wanted to be.

Much like being jarred awake from a pleasant dream, Steve grabbed my mittened hand with purpose, tugged my arm under his elbow, and marched us up the sidewalk to the restaurant's entrance. *What's going on? Did he see someone we know?*

As he opened the bulky door for me, his ruddy face assumed the stern-all-business-executive-look I knew so well. Behind fogged-up glasses, his eyes flashed.

"We need to talk," he whispered.

My involuntary exhale hit the chilled air, resulting in a column of breath resembling a plume of smoke. *What the heck?*

The rhythm of my heart thumped in double time as we followed the hostess to a cozy leather booth overlooking the snow-obliterated streetscape. I shed my winter belongings, hanging them on the hooks alongside our booth. The display outside the picture window was captivating, like a movie set. It reminded me of the scene in *It's a Wonderful Life* when Jimmy Stewart wanders aimlessly out in a blizzard along the snow-piled streets of his hometown and beholds what the world would have been like if he hadn't been born. Following along with the movie plot, my mind rolled to the forthcoming act when Stewart has his aha moment and rushes home to the dilapidated house he shares with Donna Reed's character. He finds her waiting, worried, and very much in love. Call it sentimentality or an uncanny premonition, but my eyes teared up as I snuggled into my corner of the warm booth.

I turned my attention to Steve.

Across the tabletop, he reached for my hands. They settled into his warm palms as if they were designed to fit there. *Here we go.* I blinked away the brief display of emotion the movie always arouses in me and then summoned the inner courage I was finding I needed to resurrect more and more. All the doubts we both shared about our relationship—the age gap, his divorce, our roles at work—tumbled atop one another in a pile. The effect on me was debilitating.

I lowered my eyes for a second to our clasped hands. "What is it you want to talk about?"

Steve's steady gaze was as crisp as the words he soon delivered. "I want to date you. Out in the open. No more sneaking around. We've been living too close to the edge." He sat back and cocked his head at me. "I've been thinking."

There it was. The patented statement I knew all too well, one that prefaced an extraordinary reflection or idea and that never failed to catch the listener by surprise. This time I was the lucky recipient. I let out an unavoidable sigh.

"Okay . . ." I shifted my gaze to the approaching waitress.

After we ordered cheeseburgers and drafts of the local beer on tap, Steve leaned forward again. He folded his palms around my fists again, rewarding them with a tender pulse, and then that endearing Jack Nicholson–like grin made a winning appearance.

"So here it is. I think now would be the right time for you to end your internship and transfer out of my department. You have, what, two more months left?"

I nodded, trying to quell the sick feeling in my gut. There was no precedent for such a preemptive move in the Hart Scholar program. Proposing the idea would put me under intense scrutiny. *What choice do I have if Steve and I want to take our relationship to the next level?* My eyes squeezed shut as I envisioned the resulting difficult conversations. First with my program director, Rob, and then later with Justine in HR. The stricken look on my face must have telegraphed my incredulity, because Steve swooped in to assuage my doubts.

"Look, this is not out of the question, given your excellent work history—certainly I can vouch for that." Again, that charming smile. "In my book, you're more than ready to assume a position in store management. Which is one of your career goals, right? So, hear me out, please."

I struggled to finish my burger as Steve outlined the plan he'd conjured.

"One of our traditional men's clothing store groups, Capper & Capper, is re-envisioning it's highest volume store per square foot to include women's suiting and accessories. The shop is located off the lobby in the Westin Hotel on Michigan Avenue. Close to your apartment. It would be your chance at management. The opportunity would look like it fell in your lap. What do you think? I can explore it for you if you're interested."

Whether it was the second beer, Steve's persuasive gift, or the spell cast by a snowy evening, I grew more and more excited about the opportunity with Capper & Capper. The true benefit—being able to go out in public with Steve and stop sneaking around—couldn't be ignored. Like Jimmy Stewart's character in *It's a Wonderful Life*, I felt guided by a guardian angel—perhaps one named Susie—and the allure of love in a snowstorm. The decisions we made that night would alter many lives for years to come.

Maybe it was our secluded booth or the insulating blanket of white falling outside, but it felt as if the whole world melted away in that moment of shaping our future together. I looked into Steve's eyes and felt his hands around mine.

"I'm game," I said, matching his big smile.

34

A Few More Steps

Summer 1983

Not soon after that rare snowy dinner out, Steve linked up with Rob, the Hart Scholar coordinator, to discuss shortening my management training schedule so I might apply for the new position at Capper.

Like a morning sunrise, after that there was no stalling the momentum of Steve's well-orchestrated plan. Within weeks of Rob's wholehearted approval and Steve's glowing recommendations, the Capper management team expressed serious interest in my application. The remaining task, one which fell on my shoulders, was to meet with Justine in HR and reveal some of what had transpired behind the scenes.

Over the course of my seven months in the retail stores division, Justine and I had often met to discuss my training program. I'd always found her to be approachable and an inquisitive, intuitive, and concerned mentor. Because there weren't many executive women at the corporate offices, she and I shared a unique, unspoken bond. We were professional women navigating a male-dominated industry, cognizant of a certain reality: being held to different standards than our male counterparts. Intelligence and a strong work ethic didn't always translate into recognition or promotions. One also needed a mentor, a self-promoting voice, and opportunity. I was fortunate to have all that with Rob, Steve, and Justine.

Because I respected Justine and welcomed her steady, reassuring advice, I stewed about how she might interpret the abrupt shift in my plans. I didn't want any suspicion about a deeper motive for my early departure. I knew I had to contain the inner glow that infused my demeanor whenever I spoke, or thought, of Steve McGue. To maintain her respect for me and to honor the debt I owed my female counterparts, my interest in Capper had to be about my career.

Just as I had done on that fateful day when I was introduced to Steve, I waited in one of the chairs outside Justine's inner office. Eyeing the tasteful brass wall clock, I sat rehearsing talking points in my mind until the office door clicked open.

"Hello, Julie. Please come in." Justine welcomed me and ushered me inside, where she settled comfortably into her leather desk chair. "What brings you in today?"

Across the modest-sized mahogany desk, I matched Justine's professional smile.

"I wanted to give you an update." I paused, not just to breathe but to gather confidence. "There's been some discussion between Steve, Rob Myer, and me about shortening my time spent at corporate. An incredible opportunity has presented itself at Capper & Capper."

An interested look crossed Justine's face. "Go on," she said.

After detailing Capper's new men's and women's store concept on Michigan Avenue and the timing of its grand reopening, I unveiled my goals.

"I'm set to interview for the store manager position next week. If all goes well, I could wrap things up here at the end of the month."

Her stricken face and the ensuing quiet did little to quell my insecurities. *Was she baffled because she'd been left out of the loop? Or was she compiling a cluster of observations and side conversations into a realization?* By the time she mustered a reply, I speculated that the anteroom's clock had ticked away a full minute.

Justine rested her forearms on the desktop, clasped her hands, and looked at me through the fringe of her closely cropped black hair. "That does sound like an intriguing option, but . . ." Her eyebrows raised in alarm. "I'd caution you about cutting short your time here. I think your career could benefit by exposure to other areas in the retail division." She paused. "Beyond the planning department."

A reference to Steve. *What did she know?*

I hadn't expected Justine to offer an objection, nor had Steve and I discussed the possibility. My brain scrambled for a counter. I bought thinking time by twisting in my chair and recrossing my legs.

"Thanks, Justine. I appreciate your perspective." I offered her a thin smile. "You're right, my time here has been concentrated in store planning." I took another well-needed breath. "But my year at Jaymar exposed me to other corporate areas. Like data systems, inventory controls, and accounting. Brand marketing and advertising, too."

My hazel eyes widened in sincerity. "To be honest, one of the reasons I'm interested in the store position is to gain experience in managing people. I've spent most of the Hart Scholar program completing special projects and reporting to a single supervisor. I'd really like the chance to build a team and manage Capper's new store." I blinked and then reengaged with her intense stare. "This feels like the right step for me."

Next, it was Justine's turn to twist in her seat, gazing first at me and at the closed door behind us. "Are you sure that's all there is to this?"

Was she referring to Steve?

I tried calming my escalating heart rate. Steve and I had agreed that it was too early to divulge our romance. That announcement should wait, trickle out after a few months had passed, and I was secure in my next role.

Scrunching up my face, I stammered, "I'm not sure what you mean, Justine." But after looking into her eyes and seeing how concerned and worried she seemed to be, it dawned on me what she might be getting at. I looked at her with alarm. "You think that someone has been harassing me here . . . .?"

She tipped her head to one side, her face a big question mark.

"No!" I shook my head vehemently. "My request to transfer out isn't because of anything like that." I sank back into my chair, suddenly beaten up by our exchange. "If that was the case, believe me, you'd have been the first to know." I sighed. "I want to leave because I'm ready for a managerial position."

The tension in her face melted away. She slid back into her chair, and her pleasant smile returned. "Okay, then. If this is the direction you want to take your career, I support it."

We went on to talk about the executive team with whom I was interviewing at Capper. She offered some tips and strategies in talking with them. When she rose and stepped around from the desk, she patted my back gently.

"I wish you all the best, Julie. Let's have lunch in a few weeks. I want to know how things turn out."

After we shook hands outside her office and I thanked her for her time and concern, I strode as fast as was appropriate—and safe, considering the plush carpet and my navy pumps— back to my little office. I couldn't wait to shut the door, sit in silence, and just breathe.

During the walk there, I gave myself a pep talk. *Only a few more steps to go. Nail the interviews with Capper. And soon, very soon, you and Steve can stop sneaking around.*

The other thing that "officially dating" meant was widening the circle and introducing each other to our siblings, parents, and close friends.

In April, I had met Steve's sister Christie when she flew into Chicago for business. The three of us had enjoyed dinner in a quiet bistro near Steve's Division Street apartment. Barely a year younger than him, she resembled Steve but with fairer coloring: blond hair and blue eyes. In conversation, she matched his intellect and humor. I liked her immediately.

When Steve left the checkered-cloth table to smoke a cigarette outside, she gushed, "I can't tell you how glad I am to see my brother so happy."

As relieved as I was about how easily Christie accepted me as Steve's girlfriend, it put the onus on me to make introductions to my family and friends. Since we had started seeing one another in mid-March, I'd grown adept at fielding the question, "When are we going to meet the guy you seem so nuts about?" Depending upon who asked, I might shrug my shoulders and offer a noncommittal smile. Or I might go further and mumble something like, "Soon, I hope. With as busy as I've been with my MBA classes and our different work schedules, it hasn't worked out."

Although my parents never voiced it aloud, I had the sense they thought I'd forgotten all the values they'd instilled in me. Perhaps they thought I'd lost my mind, too. Older man. Divorced. Working in the corporate world together. Practically living together. Maybe they were confused about how to deal with me since I'd stepped out of the conservative zone in which they lived.

My parents had married soon after my mom graduated from Rosary (now Dominican University), a local all-women's college. Before she married Dad, she had never lived anywhere else besides her family's rambling seven-bedroom home in Oak Park. In contrast, I lived on my own, worked in downtown Chicago, traveled frequently with my job, and had a key to Steve's apartment. Mom had been a third-grade teacher in a small Catholic school and oversaw a classroom of thirty-some kids. I had my own office in corporate headquarters, and if all went according to plan, I'd soon manage a high-profile, high-volume clothing store on the Mag Mile. As young women, our worlds couldn't have been more different.

If I talked to my folks by phone or met up with them at the Oak Brook house for Sunday dinner, they'd ask, "How's work? How are your classes?" While they weren't disinterested in my dating Steve, they didn't probe. I counteracted this by mentioning things he and I did on the weekends—like catching the latest blockbuster film, *Return of the Jedi*, at Water Tower—and dropped in tidbits of how smart and honest he was, his military history, his Irish heritage, and that he'd been raised a Catholic. Bonus points I thought would carry weight with them.

Jenny's boyfriend, Grant, was also Catholic and of Irish descent, but unlike Steve, he had never been married. He'd graduated from IU two years before us and worked in a completely different industry than Jen—law enforcement. My folks had yet to meet Steve, but Jenny and Grant had driven up from Indy on the big summer holiday weekends, Memorial Day and Fourth of July, and spent time at our family's new lakefront cottage in Palisades Park. I had found Grant to have a magnetic personality. He had an easy laugh that made his blue eyes twinkle. He could get the whole room chuckling at his stories and jokes, and as Grandma Mimi said, "He's very easy on the eyes."

Much like we had done ever since we were girls, Jenny and I chattered on the phone most evenings. We discussed the blips and bumps in our careers, our goals and dreams, our family, and the guys we loved—what we liked, what bothered us about them, and if we thought they were really "the one." In those conversations, Jenny revealed how serious her relationship with Grant had gotten. When I shared my innermost thoughts about my relationship with Steve, Jen's advice boosted me.

"Mom and Dad have met Grant, now, several times. They've never met Steve. Once they do, Jules, they'll fall in love with him, too. Give 'em time."

While my folks never overtly grumbled about my dating Steve, I felt their judgment, the comparison between Jenny's choice and mine, and it stung. I chose to bide time, ignoring the underlying current of doubt and disappointment. I knew what I wanted, and Steve was all of it and more.

After I landed the job at Capper—and once the business of getting the store staffed and stocked was all sorted out and the grand reopening planned and executed—Steve surprised me after class one night with a grandiose idea.

"I think we should plan a road trip. Celebrate summer. All your hard work. And us, too." His arms had encircled me, pulling me in close. "What about taking a drive over to Michigan?"

I leaned back to study his face, my eyes bright. "Sounds wonderful."

Two weeks later, on a Saturday after I'd closed the store, Steve vroomed up under the broad awning at my McClurg Court apartment building in a rented, current-model red Corvette. While he had mentioned he was renting a car, I hadn't dreamed it would be a sports car. So flashy, so fun, and so Steve.

The doorman whistled and hustled over to open the passenger door for me.

"You're looking good in that, Mr. Steve," he said, winking first at him and then at me.

After I loaded my overnight bag next to Steve's in the tiny trunk, he revved the engine a few times, and we took off. Grinning and laughing, we soared down Lake Shore Drive. Our first stop was to my parents' summer house in Palisades Park, where we planned to spend the night—in separate bedrooms, of course.

When I had called my mom about visiting, she'd been firm. "I don't need to know how you live your life while in the city, but in my house, those are my rules."

I'd rolled my eyes and snickered much like I had done as a teenager when confronted with her old-fashioned ways and corny ideas, like cutting off her apron strings.

"Okay, Mom," I'd said, and left it at that.

"Since your sister and Grant plan to be here that weekend, too, you and Jen can sleep in the upstairs guest room. I'll put the guys together in the lower level."

"I'm sure the guys will hit it off just fine."

With all that out of the way, I filled Mom in on the rest of our plans, half expecting more pushback, but it didn't come. Steve and I intended to stay at Palisades for one night and then drive up the shoreline to stay in a bed-and-breakfast near Saugatuck. On Monday, my regular day off from the store, we envisioned meandering back to the city via country roads, maybe lunching at a local diner, and stopping at a few art galleries or wineries along the way.

Mom's comment before ending our call had warmed my heart. "I look forward to getting to know Steve. I'm sure he's just as wonderful as you've portrayed him to be."

So as Steve shifted and maneuvered the flamboyant red car through downtown traffic and onto the jam-packed expressway toward Michigan, I hummed along with Neil Diamond as he sang "September Morn" on the radio. The lyrics about lovers uniting and acting out scenes in some romantic drama summarized my vision for our weekend getaway. I sighed peacefully as I melted into the luxurious leather seat. When Steve's hand wasn't on the gear shift, it clutched mine. Above us, the humid summer breezes swirled through the open top, sending loose strands of my long, fine hair swirling around to tickle my exuberant face. Life was so good, perfect even. I was twenty-four, I had completed the bulk of my graduate coursework, my career was set on a nice trajectory, and I had met the man I wanted to marry.

Two hours later, as the sun descended, filling the sky with glorious striations of orange and pink, we coasted off the highway and down a secluded road to the Palisades Park entrance. As I climbed out of the fancy car to unlock the gate, Steve lit up a Marlboro, inhaling several long draws. Clambering back in, I squeezed in tight to him, slipped my arm behind his shoulders, and brushed his neck and hairline lightly with my fingers.

Over the roar of the 'vette's powerful motor, I quizzed him. "Are you ready for this?"

He stubbed out the cigarette in the car's ashtray, nodding.

"I am. Ready to meet Jeanne and Jack Ryan. Have a bite to eat on that gorgeous deck you've raved about and then tip back a Scotch or two with you, your dad, and whoever else."

I offered him a broad smile, hoping it disguised the odd mix of nerves and excitement swirling in my chest.

"All right then." I pointed ahead at the shadowed opening below centuries-old entangled oak and pine trees. "You'll have to take it slow with this car. The roads are rutted and narrow. Barely enough room for two cars to pass."

Steve maneuvered the sleek red Corvette onto the unpaved road carved into a steep wooded ridge. I closed my eyes, absorbing the familiar smells and sounds engulfing the car: the dank earth, the thick mustiness of decaying leaves, and the distant pounding of waves hitting a pebbled shore. All things I had experienced each summer since childhood. I felt myself relaxing. *Oh, how I love Palisades. How good it is to bring Steve here.* As we threaded around the many forks in the road, banking high and zooming low, past the dozens of summer cottages handed down through generations of families like mine, I educated Steve more about the allure of Palisades.

"Okay, now I'm adding sunsets, bonfires, and moonlit nights to the list of favorite things to do with Julie Ryan. They're right up there under leaf kicking and trudging through snowstorms."

I giggled, kissing him on the cheek. "The parking area is up ahead. Pull in there next to my dad's white Ford." As I said that, I wondered what my folks would think about the flashy car.

We slung our overnight bags across our shoulders, taking care not to slip on the sandy boardwalk that led to my folks' cream-colored clapboard cottage. Halfway down the trail, we paused to ogle the remnants of what had been an exquisite sunset.

I cuddled into Steve's shoulder, my heart thumping in my chest. "Ready?"

His lips were soft, the kiss tender. "Ready as I'll ever be," he whispered. "C'mon. Let's go meet your parents."

When I pulled the porch's screen door open, my parents, Jenny, and Grant were elbow to elbow over a card game in the sitting area.

"Hello, everybody. We're finally here," I yelled. Giggling like a teenager, I made introductions.

Without hesitation, Steve reached for my father's hand first, and then my mother's, saying, "Nice to meet you both. I've heard a lot about you—the whole Ryan family, too—from this gorgeous daughter of yours." He showcased his winning smile, swung an arm around my shoulders, and beamed down at me.

The only ones not sizing each other up were Jenny and me. She gave me a little gesture I knew all too well: a brief nod and quick smirk. The combo implied, *I told you so. This'll be okay.* I figured the wink following her secret signal meant, *He's just as charming as you described.*

I winked back.

While Dad fussed over drinks for Steve and me, and Mom fixed us plates of sliced ham and potato salad, Grant and Jenny pulled us onto the screened porch where we settled into the white wicker furniture. As much angst as had ruffled through our hearts and minds, neither Steve nor I should have worried. Drinks and stories and joking and laughter carried on long after midnight. Over Mom's infamous Sunday brunch of eggs, bacon, and French toast the next morning, cheerful, easy conversation continued. Following that, Dad, Steve, and I waged ruthless games of Scrabble on the deck. It thrilled me to observe a camaraderie building between them as they exchanged statistics about their beloved White Sox and Bears.

Once Dad went inside to read the latest Tom Clancy novel, Grant and Steve wandered down to the beach in front of the cottage where they lowered into brightly colored folding chairs and popped open beers. From our perch above them on the deck, Jenny and I caught snippets of their dialogue. Our eyes flickered with pleasure as we heard them land on common ground. Steve touched on his career in the army, and Grant shared a few of his escapades as a Texas highway patrolman.

Craning her neck around to check our parents' whereabouts, Jen wagged a finger for me to huddle up. "Well, it looks like it's gonna happen. This afternoon—probably after you guys leave—Grant is going to get Dad alone on the beach, take a walk with him"—she paused, her face glowing— "and ask Dad's permission to marry me."

I tried not to squeal as I squeezed her hard, my hug warm and genuine. "You thought he was going to wait until Labor Day weekend. I'm so excited for you guys. Mom will flip out."

As we whispered more about the engagement and spring 1984 wedding plans she and Grant hoped to arrange, my mind wandered, tickling with the possibility that the next time Steve and I came to Palisades, it would be him asking my father to take a walk on the beach.

A few hours later, when Steve whipped the Corvette back on the main road toward Saugatuck, my smile was as wide as the beach we had enjoyed all morning. I threaded my arm between Steve's neck and the seat, cupping his shoulder.

"My family really liked you."

He touched my cheek. "I liked them a lot, too."

As we sailed down the road with the Corvette's top down, our voices in sync to another Neil Diamond hit, a light feeling filled my core. Like a puzzle, all the tough life pieces I'd been anxious about had clicked into their proper place: my exit from the corporate offices, the Capper store launch, the introductions between my family and Steve. I mused about how aligned our lives had always been—Jenny's and mine—and how we always seemed to hit the same benchmarks within a few months of one another.

I closed my eyes, content with the assumption my engagement to Steve would happen in the not-too-distant future. I had no reason to expect any different.

35

A Walk on the Beach

Fall 1983

Given all the obstacles we'd surmounted over the previous year—the finalization of Steve's divorce, our dating on the sly, the chess game of career moves that landed me at Capper, the contrived meetings with my parents and then later in the summer with his folks, too—none of those benchmarks suggested what would soon transpire on a late September morning. It was a day when the barometric pressure shifted, upending the previously warm Indian summer temperatures and plunging Chicago's lake-front into dense fog.

On the night before the weather front moved in, I locked up my Michigan Avenue store after another record-breaking Saturday sales day and walked the few blocks to Steve's place. With the key he had given me, I let myself in and called out for him. Spying his seated profile out on the balcony, I freed my swollen feet from the prison of my work shoes, tossed my navy suit jacket over the sofa, and slipped through the sliding glass door.

Next to him on the end table rested a full ashtray—his favorite, a wide-mouthed ceramic frog with an outstretched tongue on which lay a burning cigarette—an ice bucket, a bottle of Jack Daniel's, and a half-empty tumbler of amber liquid. All things that sometimes made it to his side when celebrating a personal milestone or deliberating about an idea while waiting for me to join up with him.

I leaned down and planted a light smooch on his mouth, noting the unpleasant taste of too many cigarettes. I hid my scowl—I had been dropping heavy hints about cutting back on the Marlboros—and plopped down into the only other chair on the small balcony.

He glanced at me and picked up the smoldering cigarette. "How was your day?"

"Another record Saturday," I said, puzzled by his nonplussed reaction.

He seemed uncharacteristically distant, distracted. Knowing the rigors of his job, I attributed his reserve to pending strategy decisions and performance reviews. It turned out that I was right, but I was also very wrong.

When he muttered, "I've been thinking about things," I felt the blood leave my face.

His subsequent sideswiping glance, the downturned lips, and melancholy spirit telegraphed what Steve had been considering while in the sole company of Marlboro Reds and Jack Daniel's. His Saturday-afternoon strategy session had little to do with retail stores and everything to do with me, us, the future I thought was stamped in ink.

I scooted to the edge of the unforgiving outdoor chair, shielding my eyes from the intense western sun as Steve mumbled words that caused my brain and lungs to seize.

"I'm sorry . . . but I don't think this"—he wagged his finger, pointing first at me and then at this own chest— "is going to work out."

I sat rigid, frozen, staring at him in shocked disbelief. It was as if he'd announced he'd been diagnosed with an incurable disease. My brain couldn't compute how doubt and misgivings about our future had somehow taken root while I was busy selling crisp shirts and tailored clothing to young professionals on the Mag Mile. Above us, the afternoon's summer sun continued its unrelenting blaze. Sweat seeped through my pantyhose and dampened the back of my navy skirt. Grimacing, I leaned toward him and forced my mouth to work.

"Last night you asked me to marry you."

My words were crisp, accusing, full of hurt. Like a prosecutor, I let my opening statement settle before supporting it with further evidence.

"I've been sleeping in your apartment almost exclusively, running back and forth between your place and mine for months, so how can you say you don't think you can marry me? What happened between last night and now?"

He countered with maddening bravado. "Well, I'm just not ready. I don't know how else to say it. I have enough doubts that I think we should take a break. Maybe stop seeing each other for a bit."

"Huh?" I felt an army of tears advancing. "What about all the time we've spent here, hanging out, laughing, and loving one another? All the drives in the 'Easter Egg,' the Corvette trip to Michigan?" My voice dripped with anger and frustration. "Our late-night talks about having a family, a whole brood of Colleens and Danny boys? And you romanticizing about leaf kicking, scuffing along in snowstorms, and catching the green glow after sunsets with me?" I punctuated my blast of truths with a nasty staredown. "What happened to the whispered *I love yous* and all the *I think I've been waiting for you my whole life* statements?"

I left the balcony to blow my nose and splash cold water on my face. I returned with a wad of toilet paper. Yet, over the next few hours, along with more booze, cigarettes, and a hastily reheated frozen Gino's deep-dish pizza, our argument circled like a bird of prey. No matter what I said, or how he answered, the argument continued heading south like the weather.

Once darkness filled in the landscape, Steve stood. "I can't talk anymore. I'm headed to bed."

I watched as he slipped through the slider and took off down the hallway. For a moment, I debated about whether to follow him or go back to my studio, but I was beat, too worn out to make the effort. While he brushed his teeth, I slumped against the pillows on my side of the bed, silently seething. With a glance I couldn't read, he climbed beneath the covers and turned his back to me, saying nothing. We slept next to one another all night long, but there was no spooning, just pillow punching, angry cover swiping, and silent sobbing from me that left wicked mascara smears on the white bedding.

The next morning, he was the first one up. The smell of coffee pushed me out of bed. At the small kitchen table, I poured myself a cup and glowered at him, daring him to be the first to speak, to apologize, to admit our argument had all been a ridiculous mistake. But he didn't say any of those things. I was so tired and frazzled I didn't know whether to argue some more, move all my things out, or climb back into bed.

After a few minutes of pathetic silence, Steve broke the impasse. "I need to clear my head. Let's take a walk on the beach."

While I processed his odd request, my mind peeled back to the moment at the cottage when Jenny confided how Grant planned to ask Dad for a walk on the beach so a marriage proposal could be made. What Steve was suggesting wasn't the walk I had imagined for myself back then. My stomach churned. *Where was my life going?*

"All right," I said, draining my second cup of coffee. "Let's go sit on the beach and talk."

In the brief time it took for us to throw on jeans and sweatshirts and wander through the thickening fog to a bench on Oak Street beach, my brain rambled through a multitude of strong thoughts and feelings. My reflections ranged from *We've come all this way.*

I've jeopardized my reputation, made a career leap to continue seeing you, introduced you to my family—who were, by the way, very disappointed in my judgement at first, to *Now, they've fallen in love with you, and I with your parents. Why are you doing this to everybody?* Too tired to fan the smoldering fire of the previous evening, I kept those thoughts to myself.

As we sat on that cold green bench staring through fog at the lakefront we could only hear, I uttered different thoughts. To my own ears, my voice sounded pitiful, like a daytime soap opera diva.

"You're really going to break up with me because I'm so much younger than you?" I bore in on him with the enormity of his idiocy. "That was always the case, ya know. But it didn't seem to bother you on the eve of St. Patty's Day or in the months since. Why is it bugging you now? What has changed?"

Steve dropped his head into his hands, lifted it, and rubbed his eyes with the gray sleeve of his army sweatshirt.

I whispered. "Is it your divorce? Are you having cold feet because you don't want to get married so quickly after that?"

He turned to me with surprise, smiling weakly. "I think that's the gist of it really. It's only been six months."

I blinked at him. "So, instead of breaking up, why don't we just postpone the marriage discussion for a while?"

As soon as I made that painful concession, out of the lakefront's silence, out of the gray that enveloped us, a yawing sound—much like an old man moaning—grew louder and louder.

Steve sat upright, his forehead creasing. "What's that? Do you hear it?"

I squinted at the fog. "I do. It's a low-pitched wail. Maybe a hurt animal?"

"Dunno." Steve scanned the fuzzy horizon.

We left the bench, my sneakers sinking into tufts of soft sand, as we blindly scoured the southern shoreline in the direction of the painful lament.

I leaned into him, whispering, "It sounds more like a bagpipe than a sick animal." I grabbed his warm hand, entwining my fingers with his. I looked into his warm brown eyes pleading with him for answers on so many levels. "But on a Sunday morning? On Oak Street Beach? In the middle of the fog?"

We stood together like that hunched close, straining our eyes, spellbound as the bellowing, mournful chords heightened in volume and intensity.

And suddenly, there he was.

A legitimate bagpiper bedecked in a navy and green, pleated plaid kilt, white knee socks with decorative tassels, and black leather lace-up slippers. As if in a trance, he processed toward us along the water's edge. He held the accordion-like instrument slung over one shoulder, and in the other hand he clutched the hookah-like pipe that pressed against his lips, poised and at the ready as he gathered enough breath to produce sound. Steve marveled at me and I back at him as we watched the musician sip and suck and blow and belt a melody of pain and heartache.

My eyes teared up, more for how it aligned with the misery shredding my insides than for the pleasant Irish-related memories the sound normally evoked. As I watched the bagpiper approach— no one with him and no reason for him to be there—I became immersed in the melody. It seeped into my core. As it settled, I felt heard and validated. Suddenly, courageous.

I jabbed my finger at the bagpiper. "See that? Hear it? Do you really think you should be breaking up with the girl you fell in love with on St. Patrick's Day?"

Steve shuffled his feet and shook his head in disbelief. "I'm stunned. Of course you didn't orchestrate that, so who could? Why is he here?"

In response, I lifted my palms toward the heavens.

The grin I loved made a glorious but brief comeback. "You think it's a sign?"

I raised my eyebrows. "What do you think, Steve?"

"Not sure." His eyes left mine, crinkling as he studied the bagpiper, absorbed the spellbinding music, and contemplated the meaning of the apparition.

Just as quickly as the bagpiper had surfaced, he retreated, all the while blowing and bellowing a fresh lilting tune. Enthralled, we watched until we could no longer see the musician or hear his tunes.

Steve reached for my hand. "Let's go," he said, squeezing it. "Back to my place."

I searched his face for a sign of where his thoughts had landed, but all I glimpsed was fatigue.

"Okay," I said gently, harboring a secret wish that the ethereal fog and its Irish specter had somehow cast a magical spell over our troubled relationship.

With my hand firmly tucked into Steve's, we retraced our steps along the beach and back up to the road. As we navigated the way back to his apartment in reverential silence, my mind rewound through my family's personal history, showcasing the many struggles my parents faced in their long marriage together: infertility, miscarriages, a stillborn, financial woes, Susie's disability, and her sudden death. It hit me how much they had dealt with as a couple, how their love and trust in each other boosted them through the rock-bottom lows, and how they rejoiced as one in life's high notes.

As beautiful as love makes us feel, I wondered, why was it so difficult to attain? To sustain?

"Love is patient. Love is kind" (1 Corinthians 13), a Bible verse I'd memorized during my Catholic upbringing came to mind, too. My parents' almost-thirty-year marriage epitomized those values and served as a guidepost to me at that moment. The reflection calmed me, diffused my hurt, and dissipated some of my anger.

Steve must have sensed a softening, for he turned to me and threw his arm around my shoulders. Pulling me in, he kissed the top of my head and whispered in my ear.

"Hang in there with me, Julie Ryan. I love you. I'll get there."

I hugged him hard, breathing in his hope-filled words and inscribing them in my heart.

"I'm not going anywhere, anytime soon."

36

For Better, For Worse

Fall 1983

I nside the building's elevator, Steve jammed the button for the eighteenth floor and then rubbed his hands over his forehead. He slumped hard against the elevator wall—the usual ruddiness gone from his cheeks—and tossed me an endearing look.

"As much as I'd like to talk about what just happened with the bagpiper, and where that puts us, I need a nap first."

Relieved, I gave him a soft look. "I'm worn out, too."

Back in the apartment, we let exhaustion take our hands and lead us into the bedroom where we both succumbed to a few hours of badly needed sleep. While we dozed, the warm September sun burned off the fog. Yet the lingering tones of the bagpiper playing his soulful music along the water's edge refused to fade. I was sure the incident and its peculiar timing was a heaven-sent hint, a message. Maybe even a shove toward reckoning.

Following the delicious nap, Steve and I returned to the balcony, as was our habit on sunny weekend afternoons. He lit a cigarette, and as I set down our favorite snack—melted Brie cheese, sliced apples, and two ice-cold Cokes—he turned to me with a cautious smile.

"I'm sorry I put you through all that last night." His tender brown eyes begged me to listen. "As I've said before, I was miserable in my first marriage. It took me years to undo something I should never have gotten into. The thought of that happening again . . ." He turned his attention to the smoke rising from the tip of his cigarette and disappearing over the balcony's metal railing. "I think that was at the root of our argument last night." He lowered his eyes. "Plus, I had too much to drink."

He twisted in his chair, scrutinizing my face. "So, if you're really okay with waiting to discuss marriage—you said as much on the beach this morning—I think we're okay."

Stubbing out his cigarette, he gave me a chagrined look.

Steve's apologetic speech was what I needed to hear, but I wasn't about to let him off the hook so easy. The previous twenty-four hours wracked me as if I'd been in a car accident. Steve's meltdown had come out of nowhere, blindsided me, hurt me in places I didn't know pain could settle. I was still reeling from it.

I cocked my head to one side, peering at him from under my dark lashes. In the second it took for me to answer, I let him see hurt, forgiveness, and reluctance in my face. He read my look, swung his chair around, and wrapped both of his hands around mine.

"Again, I'm sorry. I love you. This is going to work out."

"I hope so. I want it to." I let a light smile tease my lips. "Did the bagpiper showing up have anything to do with you getting your head on straight?"

He shrugged, chuckling. "Maybe. I wouldn't rule it out." His eyes explored my face, and he lifted my chin with his hand. "I guess I'm on warning now. Don't mess with an Irish princess." And then he kissed me with such tenderness it was as if the previous twenty-four hours had never happened.

That evening over dinner at Geja's, our favorite fondue restaurant in Old Town, Steve and I did our best to steer clear of the issues that had led to our argument. But once our bellies were full, we managed to tread squarely upon another hot topic.

We were plunging forks full of pineapple chunks, strawberries, and pound cake into a pot of warm chocolate when Steve squinted over the table at me.

"You know, my lease is up next month. I'm going to have to renew it or find another place." I opened my mouth to say something, but he held up both hands like a traffic cop. "Hear me out. We've talked about your moving in with me before."

I swallowed hard, fretting that we were headed toward another quarrel. Slumping against the stiff cushioning of our secluded leather booth, I folded my arms across my chest. Having already renewed my own lease, and without a ring on my finger, I was hesitant about sharing an apartment. I knew what my parents would think about it, too. They'd never set foot inside the front door.

Steve's jawline sharpened. "You, moving in with me—our living together—would go a long way toward making me comfortable about getting remarried."

The breath building up in my chest refused to let words form on my tongue, but the longer I stared into his handsome face—which gleamed with the hope and promise I had yearned to see the night before—the less important my reservations became.

This is your life. Lead it your way.

"What do you say? Let's start looking for a place."

All at once, a thousand yeses filled my head. If moving in with Steve was the first step in getting him comfortable with marriage, I was all in. I wanted him to be my husband—for better, for worse—and for us to start a family and build a future together.

I reached for his hand. "I'll look into getting out of my lease."

When I revealed the news, my folks reacted much as I had anticipated. First, my mom gave Dad a sharp look. He responded with a sheepish shrug which meant, *What do you want me to do?* and then she snorted her exasperation with him, me, and the situation she wished she could control.

Now, as I think about how I handled that moment, I'm proud of the courageous, confident, and strong-willed young woman I had become. At twenty-four, I was no longer the insecure girl who feared being less than the perfect daughter or who dreaded her mother's often explosive temper.

Through downcast eyes, Mom muttered, "I hope you know what you're doing."

I patted her hand. "Don't worry, Mom. Steve and I are going to get married. Just not right away."

To my mother's credit, she didn't barrage me with useless Catholic guilt, nor were there any ultimatums. Instead, her brown eyes filled with concern, and she mumbled words I had heard often during my upbringing. "Your father and I love you. We only want what's best for you."

Somehow, I managed to get out of my lease, and by Thanksgiving, Steve and I settled into an airy two-bedroom apartment on Ohio Street just around the corner from my old studio. Combining our hodgepodge of furniture and different decorating styles proved tricky, so Steve invited the VP of Retail Store Design to offer suggestions. In the end, that outreach served two purposes. Our apartment became a place where we were eager to host friends and family, and it tore the lid off our previously hush-hush work romance.

True to expectations, my parents did not drop by our new place or send a housewarming gift. Nor did my mother offer to help with the movers as she had done when I relocated to Michigan City. As much as I convinced myself that my folks were too busy readying the Oak Brook house for Christmas or that they were immersed in the plans for Jenny and Grant's April wedding, I knew the real reason. They were upset about my decision to live with Steve before we married.

Even though my parents lived about thirty minutes from the chic, high-rise apartment Steve and I had rented, they were not the first guests we entertained. Around noon on the day after Christmas, Steve told the doorman of our building to buzz his parents up from the lobby.

When he swung open the apartment door, Mary Lou and Louie burst into a cheery round of "Happy Birthday to you . . ."

Steve leaned down to kiss his petite mother. "Thanks, Mom. Can you believe your son is thirty-six?"

Louie clapped him hard on the back. "Are you kidding, son? There were so many times I thought you'd never make it past sixteen."

At first glance, Steve's parents appeared mismatched. At six foot four, Steve's lanky and athletic father towered over us all. Louie had played basketball at Bowling Green before serving in the navy in World War II. Even in her stylish heeled boots, Mary Lou was at least a foot shorter than her husband. While Steve favored his mother in looks with her dark hair, glasses, and brown eyes, his quick wit and temperament resembled Louie's. One never needed to guess what side of an issue either of them landed. As a teenager, Steve had often quarreled with his dad, but now as adults they shared a mutual respect.

Louie drew me into a bear hug. "How's our girl doing?"

His smile—although partially hidden below a thick, almost-handlebar mustache—was friendly and genuine. Pointing at Steve, he gave me a teasing look. "Is he treating you right? 'Cause if he's not, let me know. I'll set him straight."

Steve chuckled. "Are we gonna stand out here in the hallway, or will you bring your suitcases in and join us for lunch?"

I had met Mary Lou and Louie several times over the previous summer and fall. On our first visit, Steve and I had driven the "Easter Egg" to their townhouse in rural Michigan, a place where they had retired once their farm sold. While Steve and his dad played golf, Mary Lou and I had gone morel mushroom hunting after dropping off large print books to her homebound library patrons. It had been a simple but formative weekend. We grilled burgers, sat outside, shared stories over iced tea and beers, and then divided into teams for ruthless rounds of Trivial Pursuit.

When our yawning started, Mary Lou plodded to the hall closet, filled her arms with pillows, sheets, and blankets, and helped Steve and me make up the den's pull-out sofa. There was no judgment in her eyes about our sleeping in the same room. I found Steve's folks to be much as he had described them: welcoming, unpretentious, and incredibly well-informed about everything from politics to agriculture. While it wasn't a secret that they kept in touch with Steve's ex-wife, they conveyed how much they wanted to know me better.

Steve reached down for his mother's bag. "Here, Mom, let me get that," he said, and motioned for them to follow him down the newly painted mauve hallway.

"You and Dad can settle into the guest room while Julie and I fix sandwiches."

My insides tickled as I envisioned Mary Lou and Louie sleeping in the full-sized antique bed Grandma Mimi had given me when I was a teenager. Because of his height, I wondered if Louie was used to his long legs dangling over the edge of inadequate bedframes.

After lunch, cupcakes, and another rendition of "Happy Birthday," Steve and his dad hunkered down around the eat-in kitchen table. Mary Lou and I wandered into the open living area where I pointed out highlights in Chicago's skyline. While she dug in her purse for a pack of Virginia Slims, I drew her attention to a tall, white, pinstriped-looking building.

"That's where we're going to dinner tonight for Steve's birthday. The Mid-America Club, where he's a member."

She and I settled into the beige faux-suede sofa I'd inherited from my folks and chattered about city life, Louie's continued health issues following a bypass, my challenges in retail store management, and the few courses I needed to finish up for my MBA.

Mary Lou adjusted one of the hairpins in the tight bun she always wore at the base of her skull. "Do you mind, if I slip off and take a nap before dinner, dear? It was an early morning for me."

With the guys hanging out in the kitchen and Mary Lou off in the guest room, I retreated to the dining room table with a yellow marker and my brand management textbook. Because that area was adjacent to the kitchen, snippets of the dialogue between Steve and his dad funneled around the open doorway. It was easy to tune out their discussion about the stock market, but I perked up when I heard my name.

"So, what are your plans, son?"

"What do you mean, Dad?"

"Are you and Julie going to set a wedding date soon? She's a gem. It's obvious how crazy you are about her and vice versa." He cleared his throat. "You're not getting any younger. Neither am I."

Low-pitched murmuring followed, and it centered on Louie's cardiac issues, the new man in Christie's life, and how unlikely it was that either she or Steve's younger brother and his wife would have children.

I blushed when Louie got straight to the point.

"Do you want a family?"

Steve's astonished laugh filtered into the dining room. "Jeez, Dad. The ink on my divorce papers has barely dried."

I frowned. *There it was again.*

"Son . . ."

"Okay, Dad. I'll spell it out. We're going ring shopping in a month or so, around her birthday. I'll propose later this spring. We think maybe a fall wedding. Something small. Nothing like the three-hundred-person deal her twin sister, Jenny, is doing."

My heart did a little gallop. Steve and I had discussed those details but hearing him voice them to his father gave them authenticity. I closed my eyes. *Love is patient. Love is kind.*

Steve chuckled, saying, "And yes . . . we plan on having kids." My whole body sighed, "That's really what you wanted to hear, right? Our making you and Mom grandparents?"

Louie's delight mingled with Steve's. "Sooner rather than later. God willing," he said.

I returned to my textbook, flipping the page to a fresh chapter. The words ran together as I considered Louie's final statement: *God willing.* I had no worries about that. I was young, healthy, and at the perfect childbearing age. Puffing myself up with ignorant pride, I discounted my mom's infertility issues. My birth mother had delivered healthy twin daughters. Hearing Steve's pronouncement to his dad gave me the confidence I needed in our relationship. Now, just as my parents had done more than two decades before, I could look forward to creating my own perfect American family.

37

Wedding Snow

1984

Steve's arm rested in the warm space between my shoulders and the beige sectional sofa we had placed below the room's massive wall of windows.

He set down his *New Yorker*. "You and I have somewhat of an anniversary coming up." His face brightened. "March 16, the eve of St. Patrick's Day. The night I fell in love with you."

I dropped my class notes into my lap. Snuggling into his chest, I smiled up at him. "What would you like to do?"

He laid his head atop mine, whispering, "How 'bout I get a reservation at the Cape Cod Room in the Drake Hotel?"

"Sounds perfect. I love their Bookbinder's Soup."

We sat cuddling like that for a moment, mesmerized by the scene playing out several stories below our window. In the dusk, a serpentine line of cars twisted around the *S* curve on Lake Shore Drive, their red taillights flickering like a digital clock in need of a reset. Next to me, Steve fidgeted, his forehead creasing into three soft lines—a trait he shared with his mother.

He disentangled himself from me and strolled off, mumbling, "I'll call. See if we can get in."

As I listened to him pick up the kitchen's wall phone and dial

411 for directory assistance, my mind skimmed along, relishing in the sequence of events that had occurred almost twelve months before. The shared cab ride from O'Hare. Steve's invitation to come up for a drink at the place on Astor. The magic of our first kiss and night together.

Our waiter, a thick, curly-haired guy with red cheeks—a man who looked more like he should be home pressing a kilt in preparation for the city's forthcoming parade—ambled over with a pitcher of water.

"Welcome to the Cape Cod Room. Are you folks celebrating anything special with us on this chilly Friday night?"

Over the tops of our menus, we both smiled.

Steve answered him. "Yes, an anniversary of sorts."

"Wonderful. Then I bet you'd be interested in the Cape Cod Room's rich history. The tale of two famous newlyweds who celebrated here. It's detailed on the back of the menu."

When he stepped away to fill our drink order, I flipped over my menu, revisiting the story I had read before. During their honeymoon, Marilyn Monroe and Joe DiMaggio had dinner at the Cape Cod Room. Joe had carved their initials (*JD* and *MM*) into the wooden bar top.

Sometime after our courses of oysters Rockefeller, Bookbinder's Soup, and shrimp DeJonghe, I slipped away to the ladies' restroom. When I returned, our waiter appeared with two snifters of cognac.

Steve and I clinked glasses. "Happy 'sort of' anniversary," he joked.

I blew him a kiss. As he fumbled in the pocket of his suit jacket, a mischievous look passed across his features. I assumed he was searching for his cigarettes, but instead, he slid a small black velvet box across the white linen tablecloth toward me. A stupefied but glorious grin spread across my face.

Steve's voice was thick, deep, as he mumbled, "Open it."

Inside lay the gold filigreed band we had selected weeks earlier at a shop on Jewelers Row. Set in its gleaming center was a magnificent pear-shaped diamond. Radiant and lustrous, the engagement ring exemplified the glow in my heart. Body pulsing, I stared at the ring I had expected to receive sometime after Jenny's April wedding.

Steve reached for my hand, whispering, "Julie Ryan, will you please marry me?"

I stared into Steve's brown eyes, a place where I saw joy, love, hope, and the promise of a long life together.

I swiped at a sudden tear. "Yes, Steve McGue. I'll marry you."

"Slip it on," he coaxed.

My eyes danced as I plucked the band from the snug slit hidden within the velvet box.

"It's a perfect fit. I love it," I cooed. "I love you, too."

I leaned across the table and his lips met mine. Sitting back, I twisted my hand, enthralled with the ring and with Steve for surprising me that night with the proposal.

Before the restaurant's infamous baked Alaska arrived, I peppered Steve with questions. *Do your parents know? Did you ask my dad? When did you manage it without my knowing?*

Steve tipped his head back and laughed. "Yes, everyone's in the know. Including your sister. I had to consult with her on a few things." He winked at me. "To answer your last question, your dad and I slipped off for a moment the night we celebrated your twenty-fifth birthday with Jenny and Grant."

No matter where I was—waiting on a customer at my store on Michigan Avenue, sitting in a night-school business class, or sharing a meal with Steve—my eyes gravitated to the glittery ring on my left hand. Falling in love with Steve had been a storybook romance, a whirlwind, but also fraught with obstacles that were overcome only through honest conversation, love, and—yes—patience.

He and I were in sync about the wedding we wanted: small, only close friends and family; downtown, in one of Chicago's elite clubs or restaurants; and soon, before the year ended and we turned a year older. But when it came to solidifying a wedding venue and date, my parents were adamant.

"Please, let us get through Jenny's wedding first."

With only three weeks to go, my mother agreed I should start looking at possible reception spots and fold her in later.

"Okay, but I have a request." I watched anxiety build up in Mom's face again. Knowing what I was about to ask, I giggled like the schoolgirl I had become inside. "I'd like to wear your wedding dress. Would that be all right?"

"Oh my goodness." Her hands smacked together with glee. "Of course. But after all the dresses we looked at with Jenny, wasn't there one that caught your eye?"

"No, Mom." I shook my head. "I have always loved your dress—the intricate lace overlay, the back and sleeves lined with satin buttons, the fluffy petticoats underneath. The times you let Jenny and I try it on when we were young girls . . . well, I always felt like a princess."

Mom dug into her purse for a tissue. "I'm touched. Your dad will be thrilled."

Less than a month after Steve proposed to me on our "sort of" anniversary, I proceeded down the long center aisle at Holy Name Cathedral as Jenny's maid of honor, my arm linked with one of Grant's brothers. Even though Jenny and Grant lived and worked in Indianapolis, being married in the Chicago area and saying their wedding vows at the cathedral were important to her. It mattered to me, too. Besides being an architectural jewel in the crown of the

Archdiocese of Chicago, Holy Name had played an integral role in our personal history, one that began before our parents adopted us through Catholic Charities—but a tale that tied us to them, nonetheless.

Mom loved rehashing the family legends that were signs proving Jenny and I were meant to be our parents' daughters. Our baptism at Holy Name. On her birthday. Our birthday coinciding with the feast of Our Lady of Lourdes, where my parents had prayed for a family.

While it may have been a hardship for our parents to raise twin daughters—financially, emotionally, and energetically—they made it seem as if parenting the two of us was a treasured task too long in coming. Adopting Jenny and me had given them an instant family—twice the family they anticipated—and for them "two were not too many," but rather just the right number of blessings.

My face gleamed as I took my place alongside Jenny's other bridesmaids at the edge of Holy Name's altar. As we turned to face the congregation in expectation of the bride's entrance, I viewed my mother's face. It shone with unabashed pride and joy. Mine did, too. In six months' time, my mother would sit in the identical pew, listen to equivalent musicians strike up the same chords for an identical processional while my father escorted me down Holy Name's magnificent center aisle.

It struck me how closely aligned my sister and I were and had been since before our births. Our lives were locked in a familiar, well-established—maybe irrevocable—pattern where one of us lagged briefly behind the other as the other surged ahead. When reaching a juncture, the one in the lead paused, waited for the other, so that as a pair the two of us might walk in lockstep toward the next destination. As Dad often joked, we were "womb mates," but Jen and I were so much more. We were halves to an incredible whole, a sisterhood only other twins could fathom.

With joy in my heart, I watched my beautiful sister stroll along-side my father down the aisle toward Grant and our cousin, Father Bob. Daylight streamed through the church's enormous, arching stained-glass windows, illuminating the stone in my ring. After I adjusted the train of Jenny's white gown, I searched for Steve in the crowd. We shared a special look, which meant *Soon, it will be our turn.*

Once Jenny and Grant flew off on their honeymoon, Steve and I stepped into the limelight of my parents' attention. We booked Holy Name for the Friday after Thanksgiving, secured the private dining space on the ninety-fifth floor of the John Hancock build-ing, and set about altering Mom's dress to fit my taller, more athletic physique.

Once those weighty decisions were tackled, another one remained. Addressing it felt like déjà vu. As Steve's future wife and a professional woman looking to progress up the corporate ladder, we faced the inevitable. If I stayed at Hartmarx (the new corporate entity), at some point I would report to him again. In addition, my bosses—the CEO of Capper and the regional group VP—were uneasy about how our marriage would affect their reporting rela-tionship to Steve.

In May, when the group VP invited me for coffee, I knew where the conversation was headed.

"It would be best for you to look for a different job. Outside the company."

As crushed as I was to leave the people and the position I loved at Capper, again my future with Steve took precedence. In June, after three years of night-school classes, I received my diploma from Northwestern's Kellogg School, and a month later I joined ITT as a marketing rep selling their new line of personal computers in a three-state area. Two months later, one of my favorite clients,

ComputerLand of Chicago, hired me away to manage their new store on Ohio Street, a few blocks from our apartment. Thrilled to be back in retail store operations and managing a sales team close to home, I focused on finalizing the details of our wedding.

Everything I had hoped for, dreamed about—a partner I loved and respected, and a career that fulfilled and challenged me—lay at my fingertips. I felt as if I were floating on air, but as the date of our wedding grew closer, Mom blindsided me.

"Your father and I think it's best for you to move back home. Here to Oak Brook. The week before your wedding." Her voice crackled with righteousness, like bacon crisping in a frying pan. "It's just not proper for a bride to live with her fiancé on the days leading up to their nuptials."

Because I lived within walking distance of work, I protested, pointing out how inconvenient her idea was. "Staying in the suburbs will add two hours of commuting time to my workday. And"—I huffed—"the plan you're suggesting means I won't get to see Steve."

"Julie, a few days' separation is a good thing." My mother's dark eyebrows arched, emphasizing her unyielding position. "It creates mystery. Anticipation." The thin line of her lips separated, suggesting the hint of a smile. "Trust me. There are a few things I know about managing a man. And a marriage."

Later that evening, I whined to Steve about my mom's entreaty. "Can you believe the absurdity of this?"

Chuckling, he reached for his pack of Marlboros on the coffee table. "As ridiculous as we both find her request, I think you have to honor it." His brief smile became sardonic. "Especially since they're paying for the wedding."

Because Mom had long ago turned my old bedroom into an art studio, when I moved back in with my folks, I had to sleep in Jenny's old bedroom. Sharing a bathroom with my sixteen-year-old sister

Lizzie was not half as bad as negotiating with Patrick and her over the use of the "kid's" upstairs telephone line.

The chaos of those few days—between the work commute, the rigors of my job, and helping Mom with last-minute wedding details—consumed me. Steve had to keep reminding me, "It's only for another day or two."

And then all of a sudden, it was Friday. Wedding day!

Instead of being overcome with crying jags or jitters or frayed nerves, I couldn't stop grinning. I was ecstatic. Marrying the man I loved was one of the moments I had been waiting for, planning for, and dreaming about since I was a young girl playing dress-up and watching old Hollywood movies with my sister. I wasn't about to let anyone, or anything, spoil the day for me.

Once Jenny, Lizzie, Christie, and I returned from the hair salon, I went to Jenny's walk-in closet and retrieved Mom's dress. Freshly pressed and altered to fit me, the dress was now all mine. As if caring for a precious jewel, I spread the full-length gown out across Jen's large canopy bed. Reverentially, I smoothed out its ivory lace bodice with the empire waist and fanned out its voluminous skirts.

Opening the bedroom door, I yelled into the hallway, "I need help getting into my dress."

Jenny and Mom rushed in and helped me climb into the dress, zip up the back, and fasten the dozens of satin-covered buttons edging the sleeves.

Mom's eyes were full of the pride I'd witnessed in the church at Jenny's wedding. "You look gorgeous, honey." She kissed my cheek. "I hope you'll be as happy as your father and I have been."

Dad hollered up the two-story staircase. "Traffic report is terrible. We're going to be late. I'll phone the church and have them alert Father Bob and Steve. We need to load into the limo. Soon."

Am I going to be late for my own wedding? What will Steve think?

The rest of the afternoon was a magical blur. It was as if a fairy godmother waved her wand and set everything in motion. With not a minute to spare, our limo pulled up to the steps of Holy Name. As we hustled inside and out of the chilly November air, the ushers seated the nearly 125 guests. Lizzie, Jenny, Christie, and I adjourned to the bride's room where we waited until Mom poked her head inside.

"C'mon, girls. Time to line up."

While the bridesmaids paired up with Patrick, Skeeter, and Steve's brother, Mike, I waited in the only heated corner of the cold vestibule. When my rosy-cheeked father took my arm and led me to the back of church, an excited buzz filled my body. Once we heard the piercing, resonant sounds of violins playing Pachelbel's Canon, we entered the church. My smile widened as my eyes scanned past the crowd to the altar.

And there he was—my Steve—tall, dark-haired, and handsome in his tuxedo, white ruffled-front shirt, and shiny black shoes— that Jack Nicholson–like smile radiating love in my direction. In my Cinderella-esque wedding dress, I drifted toward him down the aisle. All eyes were on me—IU sorority sisters, colleagues from Hartmarx and ComputerLand, cousins, high school classmates, aunts, uncles, and my parents' friends—but my focus was on Steve.

One of the readings I selected for the Mass was 1 Corinthians 13: "Love is patient. Love is kind." In keeping with Catholic traditions, during the "Ave Maria" I walked alone to leave a long-stemmed rose by the statue of Our Lady, the Virgin Mary. My connection to Our Lady, to Holy Name Cathedral, and to Steve filled me with peaceful belonging. Holding Steve's hand during our vows is etched in my mind forever. The announcement Father Bob made at the end of Mass, "Ladies and gentlemen, I present to you Mr. and Mrs. Stephen McGue," brought thrilling applause.

Once we emerged from the cathedral and our guests sprinkled us with rice, Mom wrapped me in Grandma Mimi's mink stole, the one she'd inherited when Grandma passed away months before due to old age. Steve helped me climb into a horse-drawn carriage. As we kissed, the coachman pulled away from Holy Name, and then as if on cue like a movie set, it started snowing. The light, full flakes fluttering about cast a storybook spell. I truly felt like Cinderella with her prince, coachman, and pumpkin-turned-into-a-white buggy as we trotted off the few blocks down Michigan Avenue to our wedding reception.

Along the way, passersby shrieked, "Look, it's a bride!"

When Steve pointed at me, saying, "That's you," I giggled like a silly schoolgirl.

My face aglow, an inner voice repeated, *At last. Steve is your husband. You are his wife.*

Smiles smeared our faces as we bumped along in the horse and buggy. My body and mind coursed with a plethora of strong emotions: relief, bliss, hope, love, but also an overwhelming sense of gratitude for my life and the opportunities I had been given.

All told from start to finish—the place on Astor where we first kissed, Oak Street beach where the bagpiper played, the retail stores I managed, Kellogg graduate school, our various apartments, and our wedding and reception venues—everything took place within the same walkable quadrant of the city. My married life with Steve was just beginning and so were the joys and challenges we'd face together in the months and years ahead.

38

The Mom I Want to Be

Winters 1985 & 1986

When Steve and I returned from our honeymoon in Maui, we shopped around for a place to buy and settled on a roomy but very vertical townhouse on a gated street in Old Town. On a dreary and very cold January morning, a month after Steve turned thirty-seven, we closed on our first house.

In February, after Jenny and I celebrated our twenty-sixth birthday, Steve reached for the phone in our new family room, settling it onto his lap. As he dialed his parents' number, I scooched in close to him on the beige sofa to listen to both sides of the conversation.

"Hey, Dad. Is Mom around?" Steve winked at me. "Tell her to get on the line. I've news to share." Covering the receiver, Steve whispered, "He's yelling for her to pick up in the bedroom."

As my palms went to rest on my abdomen, we shared sunny smiles.

"You both there?" He gave me a thumbs-up. "Remember a year ago when you cornered me in the kitchen, Dad?" He paused, adding deliberate tension. "You said 'I'm not getting any younger.'"

I heard Mary Lou snicker. "That sounds like Louie."

Louie huffed. "Hush, Mary Lou, let Steve finish."

Steve smirked. "You also asked if we planned on having family."

Into the static on the phone line, he blurted, "Congratulations! You're going to be grandparents!"

Over their hoots and "oh, wows," Steve added, "Julie's only ten weeks along, but we couldn't wait to tell you."

An hour or so later, Steve's mom called back.

"Your dad's resting," she said in a quiet voice. "It's the most astounding thing, honey. Your dad's cardiologist—and me, too—have been after him for years to quit smoking." She lowered her voice to a whisper. "Louie's so taken with the idea of a grandchild . . ." Her voice caught. "After your call, he looked me square in the eyes. 'Mary Lou, I can't breathe these smoke-filled lungs onto my new grandbaby. I'm done smoking.' Incredible, right? What a gift this baby is. Will be."

After we disconnected, I stared at Steve. "Maybe it's time you quit, too."

He raised his eyebrows—not because he was upset with me, but because the idea had significant merit.

The day after we talked with Steve's parents, we drove to Oak Brook to meet my folks for Sunday supper at Dad's favorite steak place, the Flame. Once the waiter brought our drinks, Steve raised his glass.

"To family." We clinked glasses and then with a devilish smile, Steve considered my folks. "And yours is about to be a whole lot bigger. In September, you're going to be grandparents."

Telling our second set of parents doubled our joy. By the end of the meal, Mom and I had discussed nursery furniture and ideas for a baby shower, and she even offered to help stencil the nursery's border with teddy bears.

Three weeks after Steve and I revealed the news to our immediate families, I woke up feeling off, as if I'd eaten something bad. I went into ComputerLand anyway. By lunchtime, I shut the door to my office and phoned my obstetrician, Dr. Roche, to report some abdominal cramping. He suggested bedrest and told me to call if anything changed. Over the weekend, I started bleeding. Shocked and frightened, we went to the ER near Northwestern's Prentice Women's Hospital, and at Monday's follow-up appointment, Dr. Roche confirmed our fears. I was miscarrying.

Morose, I went straight home and climbed into bed. I cried, thinking about the cute teddy bear stencil I'd found and the baby shower Aunt Ginger had offered to host. When I'd gained some composure, my first calls were to Jenny and my mom. My sister listened with concern and sympathy, but it was when Mom said, "I'm so sorry you're going through this, dear," that I couldn't hold back the brokenhearted sobs.

She didn't have to say, *I know how you feel.* My miscarriage was an unspoken understanding between us, a loss neither of us wanted to have in common.

Through my tears, I mumbled, "I can't believe you went through this six times before adopting Jen and me."

The magnitude of what my mother had sustained time and time again struck me. How did she bear it? The roller-coaster ride of opposing emotions. One minute delirious with the joys associated with motherhood, only to have her hopes dashed. While I had understood on a basic level how infertility had led to our adoption, it wasn't until my own miscarriage that I grasped its meaning on a visceral level. It had taken a toll physically and emotionally on my mother, and now it did the same with me.

My mom breathed a deep sigh into our connection. "Disappointments are part of life, honey, but"—a smile seeped into her voice—"some things are worth waiting for." And then the positivity I remembered from when I was a growing girl surfaced. "You and Steve will get through this. Together. I'm certain, you'll be a mother in no time."

Her words, uttered so long ago, "Life is a fragile gift," surfaced, resonating once again.

As I lay in bed hugging a heating pad to my aching belly, Steve wrapped his arms around me.

"I'm sorry," I mumbled, my voice stuffy from too much crying. "I know you're disappointed about the baby." I gripped his hand. "We've talked about having a lot of kids, but what if *this* is not just 'something that happens sometimes,' like the doctor said? I know my mom's miscarriages don't relate to me . . ." My chest shuddered from too much spent emotion. "What if my 'other mother' had a history of them, too? It stinks I can't know anything about her."

Steve's heavy breath ruffled the loose brown hair at the nape of my neck.

"Now is not the time to worry about stuff you can't know. Or change." He swept my hair aside and kissed my neck. "Like I told my mom and dad. In a few months, we can try again." His gentle hold on me tightened. "I love you."

Steve's love and support was vital to my healing, but I couldn't shake off the feeling that somehow I had let him down, or that I had done something wrong that had affected my pregnancy. And while I didn't voice it to Steve, I wondered if I had the wherewithal to withstand multiple miscarriages, as my parents had. If we got to that point, was adoption something Steve and I might consider?

My mother's optimism was spot-on. Several months later, after we celebrated Mother's Day weekend with both her and Mary Lou, I missed my period. At Sunday Mass at Holy Name, I folded my hands together and gazed at the side altar where six months before I had left the long-stemmed rose. Closing my eyes, I prayed to Our Lady, much like my parents had done at the shrine in Lourdes. *Please help us build our family. Let this baby be okay.*

Once my pregnancy hit the fourteen-week mark, Steve and I cautiously filled in our families and colleagues. As ecstatic as we were about becoming parents, we waited until closer to my February 8 due date before assembling the nursery. The miscarriage had been a reality check. Not only was I anxious about my body's ability to carry to full term, but I also worried about the myriad of other things that could go wrong—like the freak outcomes my mom experienced during her pregnancies with Mark and Susie—and those nagging what-ifs plagued me into the wee hours of the night.

I was not the only one being careful. When Jenny became pregnant, she and Grant waited until she had passed the twelve-week mark before announcing they were expecting. She was due in August, which meant our babies would be six months apart in age. True to our history, we were locked into parallel paths on a similar timeline.

The week before my February due date, my dad called Steve with a proposition.

"I found a twenty-four-hour junket that can get us to and from New Orleans for the Super Bowl. What do you think? Who knows the next time our Chicago Bears will ever get this far. I hate to miss it."

When Steve brought the idea to me, I stared incredulously at him. "That's the weekend before our baby is due."

"I'll only be gone twenty-four hours," he muttered, hope written all over his face.

I still can't believe I relented. Even though I didn't go into labor—and Steve returned home crowing about the Bears' victory and what a great time he had with my dad—I remained irritated with him. That annoyance escalated when I reminded him about our upcoming ballet tickets.

He frowned. "I really don't like ballet. Why don't you take Vivian?"

I huffed. "We bought them for my birthday, remember?"

He looked at me sheepishly. "How 'bout I just take you to dinner beforehand?"

On a cold and windy February evening—four days before my twenty-seventh birthday—Steve dropped me off after dinner and I met up with Vivian. We hustled into the warm lobby of the Auditorium Theatre. When I removed the voluminous wool coat—a garment I was looking forward to shoving into the back of my closet—Vivian giggled, pointing at my huge belly.

"I can't believe you're *that* pregnant," her slender hand moved to touch my stomach, "and out at the ballet." Her face scrunched up with laughter. "Thanks for inviting me. Seeing Baryshnikov dance—especially since this is one of his last performances as a professional dancer—is a real treat for me." She hugged me, adding, "On top of spending time with you."

The outing turned out to be more memorable than simply witnessing a legend. Before the intermission, the mild contractions I'd been aware of since lunchtime intensified. Without letting on to Viv, I began timing them. When they became regular and spaced out to seven and eight minutes, I whispered to her what was happening.

"I'm going to call Steve," I said. *He should be here with me.* "I'll have him pick me up out front. My hospital bag is packed. We can go straight to the hospital from here." I offered her a sheepish smile. "Sorry about this." I pointed at the stage. "At least we got to see Mikhail dance."

Vivian and I slipped out of our prime balcony seats. In the lobby, she shook her head in awe as we waited for Steve to pull up. "This is a night I'm sure I'll never forget."

Despite my discomfort, I grinned. "Me either."

Holding my elbow, she walked me out to the car. "Good luck, you guys. Let me know."

When the car door slammed, I reassured Steve that I was okay. "I'm not mad at you anymore." Wincing with a contraction, I added, "Mostly because we're about to have this baby. You don't need to run red lights or anything, but we should head to the hospital."

He grabbed my hand. "Sorry. I should have gone to the ballet with you." And then a big fat smile spread across his face. "Let's go meet our little person."

Once we got to Prentice, we checked into a labor and delivery suite, and a nurse handed Steve a set of blue scrubs. Beneath them, he wore his favorite army sweatshirt—the one he threw on most Sundays while we watched football or took walks, and the same one he wore the morning a bagpiper appeared out of the fog.

Before daybreak, fatigued and anxious, Steve's hand gripped mine through the final stages of crippling contractions. Dr. Roche—who was an uncanny older version of my Irish-looking father—coached me in that same gentle, nonplussed voice he'd used when informing us I was miscarrying.

"Breathe . . . push . . . breathe. One more time. Almost there."

I gripped Steve's hand even harder, focusing on my Lamaze breathing.

All at once, Dr. Roche's kind, compelling laugh filled the delivery room. "*Aha*, wonderful. Here she is. Congratulations. You have a baby girl."

Steve gripped my shoulder, his face a thousand sunsets and sunrises. When he planted a kiss on my sweaty cheek, I forced a smile and quickly turned back to the doctor and his team working on our daughter.

"Is she—" I began, but Dr. Roche interrupted me.

"Healthy and perfect in every way."

I squeezed my eyes shut. Tears leaked out the sides. So many prayers answered, dreams fulfilled. None of the pain or lack of sleep mattered. Everything was at it should be. All of us healthy and relieved to be in that moment.

The head nurse quizzed us. "What're you going to call your daughter?"

"Mary Colleen," Steve boasted. "It means 'little girl' in Gaelic. The 'Mary' part," he paused, squeezing my hand, "is after some special ladies, one of whom is my mother. We're going to call her Colleen."

The flurry of activity that followed—the camera that Steve unearthed from my bag, his perpetual grin and butterfly kisses, a nurse snatching our first family photo, the little pink skull cap, Colleen's swaddle and mewing cries in my arms, her dark hair and round face like Steve's, her fascinating turns and stretches that mimicked the moves my belly had made just hours before, the cart that appeared with a bulky phone and Steve's subsequent phone calls to our parents and Jenny—I wished I could have slowed down the momentum. Everything happened so fast, and it would be hours and days before I processed the magnitude of what Colleen's birth meant and signified for me.

Minutes after the nurses had settled Colleen and me into our hospital room, Steve answered a quiet knock at my door.

His grin was magnanimous. "Come in and meet your granddaughter."

Louie and Mary Lou had driven the 140 miles from Michigan to Chicago in two hours, a record time. After hugs and murmurs of "We're so glad she's finally here," there was much throat clearing and sniffling when our tight pink bundle was placed in the crook of Louie's arms. When it was Mary Lou's turn, Steve handed his dad a foil-wrapped pink cigar.

He grinned. "Don't worry, Dad. You can enjoy that one. It's chocolate."

For the next few hours, the phone next to my bed never stopped ringing. We heard from Jenny and Grant, my siblings and Steve's, close friends like Vivian, and some co-workers. As I fielded those congratulatory calls, I radiated happiness, marveling at my perfect daughter asleep beside me in her clear plastic bassinet.

Steve had already left to settle his folks into our townhouse and to squeeze in a nap when my parents showed up.

Snuggling Colleen, Mom scrutinized her. "She has your nose, but I think she takes after Steve." My mom adjusted the baby's blanket and peered at me with a loving, knowing look. "She was worth waiting for, wasn't she?"

It wasn't until visitor hours ended and I had my daughter to myself that I began sifting and sorting through the significant layers surrounding Colleen's birth. Sharing the much anticipated and breathtaking moment with Steve. The creation of our family, one of the foundational steps in building the future we envisioned. The exhilarating yet humbling privilege of stepping into motherhood after suffering a miscarriage. The awe-inspiring blessing of beholding a healthy, normal child.

When Colleen whimpered in her tiny bassinet, I plucked her up. Soothing her and pulling her into my chest, my eyes closed. Heart to heart, the two of us dozed, peaceful and content. In that half-sleep state, realizations engulfed me. My twin sister and I had been my parents' firstborn, and now my daughter had slipped into that identical slot for Steve and me. A tangential thought surfaced and evaporated. Had Jenny and I fulfilled that same title role for our first mother, a woman I hoped someday to locate and get to know?

At twenty-six, I had become a mother at the same age as my mom, Jeanne. While I didn't know it at the time, my first mother had also been twenty-six when Jenny and I were born, and both of our birth names contained the same name Steve and I had given our daughter: Mary.

Now, I also understand how much Colleen's birth contrasted with my own. My birth mother had labored alone, unwed, besieged with shame, and judged harshly by those who cared for her. My first mother's parents, my birth father, and his parents were ignorant about and absent during the entire experience. There were no celebratory phone calls, baby showers, or pink cigars. Unlike my daughter, Jenny and I did not sleep in bassinets by our first mother's bed. She did not see or hold us. Instead, we were whisked off to the nursery until the transfer to St. Vincent's orphanage. When our first mother left the hospital, she returned to a woman's shelter where a friend welcomed her with a mournful look and consoling hug.

Three days after Colleen's birth—on my twenty-seventh birthday and the feast day of Our Lady of Lourdes—Steve pulled into the pick-up zone at Prentice. A nurse helped him load all the flowers and baby gifts in the trunk, buckle our daughter into her infant seat, and settle me into the front beside him. When we entered our quaint brick-lined street, I spied a pink banner swaying in the stiff February wind across the front door of our townhouse.

It's a girl! it proclaimed.

Steve grinned at my pleased reaction. "Your mom made that for us."

Once Colleen was asleep in the nursery that Mom and I had painted yellow and adorned with a stenciled border of pastel teddy bears, I lingered in the rocker. I watched her little chest heave with life-giving breath. My flesh and blood. Steve's, too. Such a miracle. My firstborn daughter's birth meant a cycle had been broken. I would know and nurture my biological kin and guide her through her life, as my adoptive mom had done for Jenny and me.

In that quiet room, I rocked softly, reflecting upon the mom I wanted to be. Firm, with respect to morals and values, but kind when enforcing them. Unyielding, when it came to affection and attention. Permissive, if it meant exposing Colleen to safe adventures and opportunities in which she showed curiosity. I also vowed not to force her to do or to be anything that didn't feel right to her or me. I longed for her to have confidence, to be patient with herself, and to know and love herself.

As I stilled the rocker, I promised her my unflinching love and support to achieve that end. Unlike me, she would know her identity from the beginning, and we would always belong to each other as mother and daughter.

Acknowledgments

This book was long in the making. Not because it took years to determine how and what I wanted to write, and not because additional time was required to massage the pieces in place, but for the simple reason that a lifetime needed to elapse before I possessed the courage, patience, and wisdom to evaluate my family's truths. *Twice the Family* is a reckoning. My reckoning with my past and with the people and events that formed me and influenced my unique perspective.

While this book is in part my story, one that includes my twin sister—without whom I would not be who I am—it is about the making of the family in which I grew up. An American family assembled through love and adoption, and who sustained unimaginable heartache. We survived, and thrived, thanks in part to faith, love, and shared goals and values. To my parents, brothers, and sisters, I respect and love you all.

Twice the Family could not have come together without the collaboration of my mother, Suzanne Ryan, and my sister Jennifer Hogberg. At times, it took all three of us to dig into, poke at, and weave together the painful threads of stubborn memories. Some truths emerged that had not previously been known to all of us and that determined and enriched the telling of this tale.

I am profoundly grateful to the individuals who influenced how this book came together. Talented people like Deb Engle from Story Summit. We met in Santa Fe at the Her Spirit Writers' Conference, and I knew immediately I needed her mentorship on this project.

Without Deb's talent, diligence, and commitment to storytelling, this manuscript might be misshapen or come up lacking.

Much gratitude to my other writing coaches like Laura Davis, Laurie Scheer, and Linda Joy Myers. And of course, kudos to Brooke Warner and the staff at She Writes Press for your patience, gentle guidance, and unrelenting support. Thanks to my publicity team led by Marissa DeCuir at BooksForward for getting this story out to my readers in all the right places.

Praise and credit also go to the women in my writing groups who helped form this story in one way or another: Rikki West, Kim Fairley, Evelyn La Torre, and Lynda Smith Hogan. Without fail, each of you brought something to our online sessions for me to consider. Our bimonthly meetings were something I looked forward to, not just for your help with craft, but because of your friendship. I also want to recognize my She Writes Press memoir cohort, also called the "Dori Zoom" group. What fun I've had connecting with you ladies and sharing our writing and publishing journeys.

To my immediate family, I thank you for your love, support, and understanding when I disappeared from life to crank out another chapter, failing to answer and return your calls simply because I was in "the zone." Love and gratitude to my late husband, Steve, for unknowingly launching my late-in-life writing career when he demanded I investigate my adoption story. Thanks for loving me, believing in me, and propping me up with the mantra, "Words are your superpower."

I would be remiss if I did not mention and offer thanks to a group of women with unique skills, who informed this tale through channeling those on "the other side." Because of their gifts, I learned that there were more questions I needed to ask. As a result, secrets were tapped into.

Shout out to Marsha Craig, the website guru who handles my online presence. You are a goddess. And I am indebted to Andrew

Tallackson at *The Beacher Newspapers* for taking me on as a columnist so many years ago. Your encouragement and support has meant the world.

Thanks also goes to my "touched by adoption" world: Linda Fiore, Lisa Holmes-Francis, and my tribe in the Catholic Charities Post-Adoption support group. Sharing and validating our adoption stories greatly influenced how this book unfolded, too. And to the members of the "Memory Circle" led by Barri Leiner Grant for your careful listening and unflinching support when I struggled with grief during the pivotal chapters concerning my husband, Steve. Writing while grieving was an effective tool for helping me take grief to a place of love.

I offer deep appreciation to Catholic Charities for maintaining an adoption policy that kept twin girls together in 1959. I can't imagine how different my life would have been without my twin sister by my side. Without your conscientious bent toward keeping a child's best interest in mind, *Twice the Family* would be a different story entirely.

Hugs to the members of my inner circle—you know who you are. Thank you for being part of my life, helping me to become, and bolstering me with courage to do what I do—just write from the heart.

Finally, I extend thanks to the friends, neighbors, and readers who follow my work. Your avid support and continual feedback fuel me with purpose each and every day. I owe you. I promise to show up and continue to provide material. For in each day, in each moment, a story exists.

About the Author

Photo credit to Mary Lou Johnson of Sarasota

Julie Ryan McGue is an American writer, a domestic adoptee, and an identical twin. Her first memoir, *Twice a Daughter: A Search for Identity, Family, and Belonging,* released in May 2021, won multiple awards. Her work has appeared in the *Story Circle Network Journal, Brevity Nonfiction Blog, Imprint News, Adoption.com, Lifetime Adoption Adoptive Families Blog, Adoption & Beyond,* and *Severance Magazine.* Her personal essays have appeared in several anthologies, including *Real Women Write: Seeing Through Her Eyes* (Story Circle Network) and *Art in the Time of Unbearable Crisis* (She Writes Press). Her collection of essays, *Belonging Matters: Conversations on Adoption, Family, and Kinship* (Muse Literary), released in November 2023. She writes a biweekly blog and monthly column (*The Beacher Newspapers*), in which she explores the topics of finding out who you are, where you belong, and making sense of it. Julie splits her time between Northwest Indiana and Sarasota, Florida. *Twice the Family: A Memoir of Love, Loss, and Sisterhood* is her third book.

Author Website and Social Media Handles:
Author website: www.juliemcgueauthor.com
Facebook: www.facebook.com/juliemcguewrites
Twitter: www.twitter.com/juliermcgue | @juliermcgue
Instagram: www.instagram.com/julieryanmcgue | @julieryanmcgue
GoodReads: www.goodreads.com/julieryanmcgue
LinkedIn: www.linkedin.com/in/julie-mcgue-a246b841

Reader Discussion Questions

1. How well does the quote in the front matter of *Twice the Family* exemplify the themes of the book?

   We do not choose to be born. We do not choose our parents. We do not choose our historical epoch, the country of our birth, or the immediate circumstances of our upbringing . . . But within this realm of choicelessness, we do choose how we live.
   —Joseph Epstein

2. From what section of the book does the title, *Twice the Family*, originate? Was it significant to you? If not, why?

3. The story in *Twice the Family* touches on family building, special-needs children, grief, loss, faith, belonging, and the unique bonds between siblings. Which of these subject matters resonated with you?

4. Did you or anyone you know consider adoption? Do you know any adoptees, birth parents, or adoptive parents? How did these relationships affect how you viewed *Twice the Family*?

5. How have society's view towards family building, i.e. adoption, infertility, and abortion, changed since the Baby Scoop Era (1920s to 1980s) in which *Twice the Family* takes place? What does it mean to build a family?

6. Like all of us, our lives are shaped by the times. What aspects of society remain unchanged since the days when Julie and Jenny

were young girls? Could this story have happened as it did in present day?

7. What role did faith play in Jeanne and Jack's relationship, and in addressing the difficulties they faced in achieving their dream of a big American family? How did faith and their parents' traditional values affect Julie and Jenny's attitudes as they matured?

8. At the time in which Julie and Jenny were raised, it was often the custom to place special-needs children in asylums. Why didn't Jeanne and Jack choose that option for Susie? How did Susie's life and death change the Ryan family?

9. Do you believe in the rule of threes, i.e. that bad news comes in groups of threes?

10. Of all the situations and setbacks that the Ryan family faces in *Twice the Family*, which one warmed your heart, angered you most, frustrated you, inspired you, shocked you, or caused you to analyze your own life?

11. What impressed you most about Julie and Jenny's relationship? Their ability to intuit each other's thoughts and feelings, to support one another seemingly unconditionally, or something else?

12. Because Julie and Jenny were adopted, what role did nature versus nurture play in the twins' development, if at all?

13. The author depicts traumatic events occurring in her community: a plane crash, an encounter with male predators, and a murder. How did these incidents influence or prime your reactions to the traumatic family events that followed?

14. As Julie and Jenny chart their own paths through college, careers, and in relationships, they make choices that differ from

the traditional values their parents imparted. Did any of these turning points surprise or disappoint you? Did they mirror your own path to maturity?

15. After reading *Twice the Family*, did your attitude shift in any of these areas: infertility, adoption, abortion, sibling relationships, family values, faith, and the role of hardship in forming character?

16. The main theme in *Twice the Family* is the concept of belonging. How did the close-knit family in which Julie and Jenny were raised affect their sense of belonging? In what ways did it stifle them? How can we belong yet chart our own paths?

17. What did you learn about the feeling of belonging? Is it innate, learned, biological, situational, or environmental? How do things like place, setting, objects, animals, and emotions contribute to belonging?

18. Was there something you felt the author should have left out or expanded upon? What aspect of the story interested you most, inspired reflection, or caused a shift in perspective?

19. Of all the characters, who reminded you of someone you know, love, or despise? Which character reminded you of yourself? Which character did you want to get to know better?

20. Would you recommend *Twice the Family* to others? Having read this book, how likely are you to pick up the author's other books, *Twice a Daughter: A Search for Identity, Family and Belonging* (She Writes Press) or *Belonging Matters: Conversations on Identity, Family, and Kinship* (Muse Literary)? What would you like to see the author tackle for her next book?

Looking for your next great read?

We can help!

Visit www.shewritespress.com/next-read
or scan the QR code below for a list
of our recommended titles.

She Writes Press is an award-winning
independent publishing company founded to
serve women writers everywhere.